C000300057

GUNNERS
AND
GOONERS

10.1.22

Dear Jarr,
Happy Birthday.
Not all the Arsenal
memories are full of joy,
but most are.
Love, Heidi, DB & Daniel
x x x

GUNNERS
AND
GOONERS

EDDIE SYMES

Copyright © 2021 by Edwin Symes

All rights reserved. No part of this book may be reproduced or used in any manner without written permission of the copyright owner except for the use of quotations in a book review.

FIRST EDITION

Book design curated by PublishingPush.com

CONTENTS

FOREWORD

I first met Eddie on the North Bank in 1965 when Joe Baker and George Eastham were our heroes.

I'm even in the photo with his North Bank banner at Bristol in 1967, when I missed a reserve game after claiming to have the flu.

I was fortunate to live the dream, playing for and winning trophies with "The Arsenal', our beloved football club, in front of many of my mates.

Undoubtedly, if I hadn't become a professional footballer, I imagine my life would probably have been similar to Eddie's.

Hopefully, this book will either bring back some happy, funny memories or give an insight into the life of an Arsenal fan of our generation.

Charlie George

WITH CHARLIE GEORGE

INTRODUCTION

My brother George first took me to the Arsenal Stadium at Highbury on a regular basis in Season 1957-58, when I was 8 years old.

In July 2020, I was 71, therefore I thought this would be a good time to share some of my stories, photos and memories of my life following "The Arsenal", including:

- My Early Years at Highbury.

- The Original North Bank Boys.

- How the North Bank got its Name.

- Where the North Bank Banner came from.

- Terrace Battles.

- Funny Moments.

- Great Characters.

- European Trips.

- All the Triumphs and Tragedies.

Apart from where relevant to the story, I won't be going into match details as they are available elsewhere in books, blogs etc.

I was born in 1949 in Westminster Hospital, which was only a hefty goal kick away from Westminster Abbey, and many people have often asked me how I became an Arsenal fan, coming from that area.

During the 1930s, my mum's father, my grandad, had three sons as well as another daughter and, along with his eldest son, Albert, was an avid Chelsea fan. When his other two sons, Jimmy and Billy became teenagers, they nagged him to be taken to a match at Stamford Bridge as well.

So, one Saturday, he decided to take them to see Chelsea play the Champions, Arsenal. All was going to plan until the teams ran out onto the pitch and Jimmy and Billy declared that they preferred the red shirts of Arsenal and afterwards started going to Highbury on a regular basis.

I think that's termed an "Own Goal".

Naturally, when my brother was old enough, they took him to Highbury with them, where he witnessed Arsenal win the League in 1953 after he'd seen them lose the 1952 FA Cup final at Wembley against Newcastle United.

He then introduced me to the "Glory Game" when he thought I was ready, but not until after he'd trained our pet budgerigar to say, "Up the Gunners".

Now, please enjoy the story of my life as a fan of "The Arsenal" during these ensuing years.

1

THE GEORGE SWINDIN YEARS

MY JOURNEY BEGINS

Although I had been to Highbury a couple of times during the previous season, 1956-57, when Jack Crayston was still the manager, I was too young to remember much about it, so I will start with my memories of George Swindin as manager.

One memory I do have from Jack's season is that my brother, George, took his brand new 88mm movie camera to the match where Arsenal beat the Team from the Lane 3-1 in October 1956, and as he stood in the middle of the North Bank filming, the bloke next to him kept nudging my brother's elbow and spoiling the film. Maybe he thought George was spying on the team?

Also, I remember that when we watched the film at home, after the ball entered the net when Cliff Holton scored for Arsenal, all we could see was the roof of the North Bank as my brother had lifted his arms in celebration, completely forgetting that he had the camera in his hand.

NORTH BANK HIGHBURY

Another story regarding my brother that season was when, in April 1957, he decided to go on his Triumph motorbike, with our uncle, Billy Ward, on the pillion seat, to see Arsenal play at Sunderland.

Obviously, there were no motorways in those days and I think they underestimated how long the journey would take, because they didn't arrive until half time and missed the only goal of the game.

On the journey home, in the early hours the next morning, Billy fell asleep leaning on my brother's back and when they stopped at some traffic lights in the suburbs of North London, the bike toppled over, trapping my brother by his leg underneath it.

Billy, calmly got up, walked over to a nearby bench and promptly lay down and went back to sleep.

COUSIN JOHNNY LEACH –
MY BROTHER GEORGE – ME

Thankfully, a passing milkman lifted the bike off my brother before anybody drove into him.

At the beginning of Season 1957-58, I was taken to Highbury regularly by my brother and we were often part of a family group including my uncles, Jimmy and Billy, my older cousins, Albie Ward and Johnny Leach and occasionally my dad who unfortunately worked shifts.

The first game that I can remember was a midweek match against West Bromwich Albion in August 1957. By a strange twist of fate, they would also be the opposition when I took my grandson to his first game on a midweek evening in August 2002.

I would stand with Johnny at the very front of the North Bank, or North Terrace/Laundry End as it was then known, while the others would be just a few steps behind us.

My eyes would be level with the players' feet and the Clock End goal looked so far away it could have been at Highbury Corner.

Other memories of that particular era for me included having a woollen red and white striped scarf and bobble hat, an Arsenal rosette, and my brothers' wooden rattle, which he'd painted red and white and onto which he'd also nailed some "star-shaped" plastic badges which had photos of the players' faces inserted.

MY RATTLE

I still have that rattle amongst my Arsenal memorabilia.

As there was no club shop, various blokes would be in the streets outside the ground selling these and other items from small mobile stands.

No replica shirts in those days!

You could only buy a full set of ten football shirts, plus the goalkeeper's one, from the "London Federation of Boys' Clubs" shop in Blackfriars Road.

STAR BADGES OF PLAYERS

Also, I recall the two black boards stretching around one of the corners at either end of the pitch which contained large white letters of the alphabet, with each letter representing a league match that was being played elsewhere. Remember, all games started at 3 pm on Saturdays in those days. These letters could then be matched up with the ones on the back of the matchday programme to notify the fans of the half time scores at those games. No electronic scoreboards in those days. And let's not forget the England vs Young England games on the night before the FA Cup Final.

More memories from the time include the police band marching up and down the pitch at half time with a Drum Major leading the way twirling a mace, which he would toss in the air and catch again, despite the jeers of the crowd trying to put him off. I only saw him drop it once in all those years.

I also remember the "Percy Dalton's" peanut seller, who used to walk up and down the terraces, plastic cups of Bovril, "Murray Mints" and hot meat pies with real gravy.

Also, almost everyone over the age of fifteen, plus some younger ones, were smoking cigarettes and wearing a jacket and tie, with either a dark mac or overcoat in the winter.

I can recall two funny incidents from those days; once, my 10-year-old cousin, Johnny, needed to go to the toilet at half time during a match and our Uncle Jimmy took him to the ones behind the terraces. Johnny went in while Jimmy waited outside. Typically, Johnny came out of a different exit and promptly got lost! Luckily, a policeman spotted him wandering around and took him to the main office. By now, Jimmy was panicking and, after checking the toilets, he came back to tell us that he'd lost

Johnny. Meanwhile, Johnny had been asked who he'd come to the game with. As he didn't know Jimmy's surname, he replied "Uncle Jim".

A few minutes later, an announcement was made over the tannoy; "Would Uncle Jim please come to the main office and collect little Johnny".

Almost 60,000 fans in the stadium were in hysterics, including my family.

The second funny story, was when, before a midweek night game, while the players were on the pitch doing their pre-match warm-up, which mainly consisted of taking shots at the Arsenal goalkeeper, Jack Kelsey, I decided to climb over the railings to get his autograph.

As I was about halfway over, one of the players hit a shot that went wide and hit me on the head causing me to fall into the area between the railings and the pitch perimeter.

Jack Kelsey walked over, picked me up and placed me back down on the terrace behind the railings, much to the amusement of my family.

I eventually got Jack's autograph when he signed his book, "Over the Bar", which my brother bought for me sometime later.

In January 1958, Arsenal were, surprisingly, knocked out of the FA Cup in the 3rd Round at Northampton, therefore, on 4th Round day, they played a friendly match against the German team, Eintracht Frankfurt, at Highbury; this was the first foreign team that I saw.

On February 1st 1958, Arsenal were beaten 5-4 at Highbury by a Manchester United team who, tragically, were playing their last game in England before the Munich Air Disaster.

So, I was fortunate enough to see the famous "Busby Babes", including Duncan Edwards, who would probably have become the greatest English player of all time.

A few years ago, I was in Dudley and visited his grave, which is still impeccably maintained by United fans.

I also recall, that the day after the crash, I went to school and almost every boy had suddenly become a Man Utd fan and that's the main reason United, initially, gained so much support outside of Manchester.

In October 1958, my brother took me to see the first game that Arsenal played at Old Trafford after the Munich tragedy. Man Utd had just bought Albert Quixall from Sheffield Wednesday for a club-record fee of £45,000 and shortly after kick-off, the Arsenal midfielder, Tommy Docherty, nearly broke Albert's leg with a crunching tackle that upset the locals and, obviously, Albert.

Injuries like these usually meant that the trainer would run onto the pitch with a bucket of water and a "Magic Sponge"; after a few minutes rub-down, the injured player would be up and running again, unlike the prolonged treatment they receive nowadays.

In November 1958, I saw Arsenal play in a friendly at Highbury against Juventus, who had the Welsh legend, John Charles, in their team.

Two of my favourite Arsenal players at the time, Jack Kelsey and Danny Clapton, came on at half time after playing for their respective countries in the England vs Wales International match at Villa Park earlier in the day.

Because of watching friendly matches such as this and going to see Glasgow Rangers beat Sparta of Rotterdam 3-2 in a quarter-final play-off match at Highbury in March 1960, and later, on our black and white television, watching Real Madrid beat Eintracht Frankfurt 7-3 in the final in May, my love of the European Cup, now known as the Champions League, was born.

In April 1959, I remember all the publicity when a Birmingham player, Jeff Hall, died after contracting polio and this resulted in all us school kids being inoculated against this disease.

As X-Boxes and PlayStations were still many years away, I used to sit in the back of an ex-army lorry that belonged to the greengrocer dad of my mate, John Butler, playing the board game "Wembley" with some other kids, Reggie Stepney, Stephen Brain, John Berry, Robert Hall, Alan Hefron and my cousins, Richard Shilling and Johnny Leach.

During the next few seasons, my brother, ever the optimist, used to take me to FA Cup away games, always telling me that, "this is our year".

Hence, I visited exotic locations such as Bury, Colchester, Sheffield United, where Jack Kelsey broke his arm, Rotherham, Sunderland, Man Utd, where the fog postponed the game and West Bromwich Albion, watching many games, often played on incredibly muddy or snowbound pitches.

The Arsenal League positions during my early years:

12th in 1957-58 behind Champions Wolves.

3rd in 1958-59 behind Champions Wolves.

13th in 1959-60 behind Champions Burnley.

11th in 1960-61 behind Champions from the Lane – a sentence that I've never had to write again!

10th in 1961-62 behind Champions Ipswich.

The Arsenal FA Cup Exits:

1957-58   3rd Round, 3-1 away at Northampton.

1958-59   5th Round, replay, 3-0 away at Sheffield United.

1959-60   3rd Round, 2nd replay at Hillsborough, 2-0 against Rotherham.

1960-61   3rd Round, 2-1 away at Sunderland.

1961-62   4th Round 1-0 away at Man Utd.

You definitely can't call my generation of Arsenal fans "Glory Hunters".

European Cup Winners:

1955-56	Real Madrid beat Rheims 4-3.
1956-57	Real Madrid beat Fiorentina 2-0.
1957-58	Real Madrid beat Milan 3-2.
1958-59	Real Madrid beat Rheims 2-0.
1959-60	Real Madrid beat Eintracht Frankfurt 7-3.
1960-61	Benfica beat Barcelona 3-2.
1961-62	Benfica beat Real Madrid 5-3.

In Season 1960-61, my family, except my uncles, Jimmy and Billy, who had remained halfway up the terrace behind the goal, decided to move from our spot near the front of the North Terrace to right at the back, just under the roof at the Avenell Road side of the stadium.

As there was only the corrugated iron wall behind me, I could stand on a fold-up stool and lean on my brothers' shoulders to have an uninterrupted view of the game.

Many other kids also had stools and boxes to stand on, and, if there was a big crowd, some others would even be passed over the heads of fans and allowed to sit around the perimeter of the pitch.

About this time, I recall my brother taking my schoolmate, John Berry, and myself to the "Boys and Girls" exhibition at Olympia.

After a while, we came across the stand for the Subbuteo table football game.

I already had this game but we noticed that they had just introduced the moulded form of players that are still made to this day, whereas before these they were made of very thin plastic.

The three of us asked if we could try out this new type of players on the green baize pitch that had been laid out for demonstrations.

We eventually played for a couple of hours and we drew such a large audience, many of whom purchased the game, that the salesman gave John Berry and me two sets of teams each.

During the school holidays, my cousin Johnny and I used to go to the Aubert Court flats behind the Clock End and from the balcony, we'd watch the Arsenal players training on the outdoor cinder pitch.

After they'd finished, we'd join the other kids and get the players' autographs as they came out of the Marble Hall via the main entrance.

Nobody could ever get the signature of the Scottish International, Tommy Docherty, but one day, someone said that he'd used the maintenance tunnel under the pitch to leave the stadium through the exit adjacent to the West Stand on Highbury Hill.

Johnny and I ran around to that exit and Tommy was still standing outside.

I politely asked him to autograph my book and he replied, "Later, Sonny". When I told him that I wouldn't be there later, he just said, "Well, fucking hard luck then".

As you can imagine, I was shocked that an Arsenal player would say that to a 10-year-old kid.

Needless to say, I've never forgotten or forgiven him, even after 61 years.

On the pitch, one of my first heroes was David Herd, who later went to Man Utd as part of their team-rebuilding after Munich.

During my early seasons, when I attended most Arsenal home games, I was fortunate to witness some of the legendary players of that era playing for the opposition teams. These included:

Tom Finney [Preston], Nat Lofthouse [Bolton], Stanley Matthews [Blackpool], Jimmy Greaves [Chelsea], Billy Wright [Wolves], Jimmy McIlroy [Burnley], Johnny Haynes [Fulham], Gerry Hitchens [Aston Villa], Ronnie Clayton, Bryan Douglas [Blackburn], Ivor Allchurch [Newcastle], the Busby Babes and Danny Blanchflower, Dave Mackay and Cliff Jones [The Team from the Lane].

Unfortunately, I also witnessed some of the least talented players in the history of Arsenal:

Jim Fotheringham, Mike Tiddy, Gordon Nutt, Johnny Petts, Bill Dodgin, Peter Goy, Ian McKechnie, Alfie Biggs and Ray Swallow.

This list also includes Mel Charles, the younger brother of the famous John Charles, who played for Wales, Leeds and Juventus.

Although Mel wasn't as bad a player as the others, he must be included because of the record Arsenal transfer fee of £45,000 involved at the time and especially, as 37,000 fans, including Johnny and myself, turned out to watch his Arsenal debut in a reserve game against Charlton at Highbury.

Johnny even got his photo in the "Charlie Buchan's Football Monthly" magazine, when getting Mel's autograph after running onto the pitch before kick-off. I didn't bother though!

I recall Chelsea, with Jimmy Greaves in their team, winning at Highbury 4-1 in 1959-60, then winning 4-1 at Highbury again in 1960-61.

Then yet again, without Jimmy Greaves and even just before getting relegated, they won 3-0 in 1961-62.

Then again, they won 4-2 at Highbury on their return to the top flight in 1963-64.

Yet again, they won 3-1 at Highbury in 1964-65.

Lastly, they won 3-1 at Highbury in 1965-66.

Arsenal finally beat them 2-1 in February 1967, for their first victory at Highbury since beating them 5-4 in March 1958, when David Herd scored a hat trick.

Imagine the stick I got from the Chelsea fans in the flats where I lived in those days!

SEASON 1961-62

In the League, the Arsenal defence managed to concede five goals on three occasions and four goals on four occasions which contributed to a total of seventy-two for the season, which, believe it or not, was the least conceded in the decade from 1956-57 up to 1966-67.

The only highlight that I can remember is David Herd scoring, with a diving header after his initial shot had rebounded from the crossbar at the Clock End, against the legendary Man City goalkeeper Bert Trautmann, in Arsenal's 3-0 victory at Highbury.

All of the Arsenal fans in my family went on the "Football Special" train to the 4th Round FA Cup tie against Man Utd at Old Trafford in Season 1961-62, as we were fairly optimistic about a decent cup run because Arsenal had recently signed George Eastham and Johnny McLeod.

We were all standing with the other Arsenal fans near the halfway line, when, about thirty minutes before kick-off, a thick fog came rolling in over the top of the stand.

Within minutes, you couldn't see across the pitch, nor could you see either of the goals. The referee came out and immediately postponed the match.

What a waste of time, as none of us could afford the time or money to go again when the game was eventually rearranged for an evening in midweek, which Arsenal lost 1-0.

In February 1962, one of my brother's future in-laws decided to take me to see the Team from the Lane play at home against Dukla Prague in the European Cup.

I think he was trying to convert me but it backfired because, although Dukla lost 4-2, obviously, I was supporting them, especially as they wore red shirts with yellow sleeves and looked just like Arsenal. I can also remember their two most famous players though, Masopust and Jelinek.

In October 1963, I bunked off school to see Masopust again, along with some other legendary players such as Yashin [Russia], Schnellinger [Germany], Baxter, Law [Scotland], Kopa [France], Puskas [Hungary], Eusebio [Portugal], Di Stefano and Gento [Spain], this time playing for the Rest of the World team which lost 2-1 against England at Wembley as part of the FA Centenary celebrations.

In April 1963, I even went to the England games at Wembley for the "Under-18's International Youth Tournament", which was also part of the FA Centenary celebrations, where, after beating Scotland 1-0 in the semi-final, England beat Northern Ireland 4-0 in the final with the goals coming from an own goal from Napier, one from Johnny Sissons [West Ham] and one each from Jon Sammels and Ray Whittaker [both Arsenal]. The future hard men, Tommy Smith [Liverpool] and Ron Harris [Chelsea] were also playing for England along with David Sadler [Man Utd] and one of the squad players was a certain David Pleat [Forest]. I wonder what would become of him?

George Hammond and I were now spending most of our spare time play-ing four-a-side football in the "Cages" of the flats where we lived, with the mainly Chelsea-supporting kids, Tony Coombes, Dave Stevens, Peter York, Eddie Ranford, Dennis Taylor, Johnny Jones, Terry Harris, Peter McDermott, Derek McDougall, Brian Dobson, Gordon Haswell, Keith McPherson and one Stuart Thompson, who eventually ended up on the Chelsea Board of Directors with Ken Bates.

The best season George Swindin had as manager of Arsenal was when they finished 3rd and reached the 5th Round of the FA Cup in 1958-59, with a team consisting of many Internationals such as Danny Clapton [England], Tommy Docherty, Jackie Henderson, David Herd [Scotland] and Jack Kelsey and Mel Charles [Wales].

DAVID STACEY

2

THE BILLY WRIGHT YEARS

In the summer of 1962, Billy Wright, the ex-England and Wolves captain and the first Englishman to win 100 caps, was brought in to replace George Swindin as manager.

Billy Wright immediately bought my all-time favourite Arsenal player, Joe Baker, from Torino for a club-record fee of £70,000 and expectations amongst the fans were running high as the new team was taking shape around a decent forward line consisting of Johnny McLeod, Geoff Strong, Joe Baker, George Eastham and George Armstrong.

The problem was, although they were capable of scoring three goals, the defence was even more capable of conceding four.

Jack Kelsey had retired in 1962 after an injury sustained playing for Wales against Brazil and Jack McClelland was his replacement, with Ian McKechnie as the reserve goalkeeper.

Neither was capable of replacing an Arsenal legend.

Since 1951, when Arsenal had invited Glasgow Rangers to inaugurate the new floodlights at Highbury, the two teams had met in a friendly match every season, alternating between their respective stadiums, and these games gave Arsenal fans the opportunity to watch many Scottish football legends such as Jim Baxter, Eric Caldow, Willie Henderson, Davie Wilson and Ralph Brand.

In 1962, Jack Kelsey was given the Glasgow Rangers game at Highbury as his Testimonial match.

In the winter of 1962, most football matches in Britain were postponed for many weeks due to the heavy snow and frost, even in London.

The only game that Arsenal played during that time, which my school-mate George Hammond and I attended, was an away friendly against the Team from the Lane.

When the thaw eventually came, Arsenal progressed to the 5th Round of the FA Cup and were drawn at home against Liverpool.

This match was the first time that many Arsenal fans witnessed the fans of an away team congregating together and singing and chanting in unison.

Thousands of fans of Liverpool, who had only been promoted the previous season, had amassed in the middle of the North Bank and their main chant was, "Ee aye addio, we're gonna win the cup".

We'd never seen the Kop or even heard, "You'll Never Walk Alone", as that song came later.

I was in my usual spot, on my stool leaning on my brother at the back of the terraces, when my Uncle Billy arrived just before kick-off and was moving through the crowd to get to his favourite spot halfway up the terrace behind the goal.

Uncle Jimmy spotted him and told Billy to join us because the middle area was full of Scousers but Billy insisted on going to his usual place. Apparently, when he got to it, a Liverpool fan who was much bigger than him was already standing there.

Billy asked him to move and the fella refused, so, after a bit of pushing and shoving, Billy thumped him. We could see the commotion and then the police diving into the crowd and pulling two blokes out and as they were being led around the pitch, we all saw that Billy was one of them.

So, my Uncle Billy Ward, became the first Arsenal fan that I personally knew to be thrown out of Highbury, but he wouldn't be the last.

He later got fined in court and his wife, my Aunt Doreen, banned him from ever going to football again and he upheld the ban right up to his death in 1999.

The sight of all those Liverpool fans singing and chanting together had awakened something in many of the thirteen to sixteen-year-olds at Highbury that day. Although those teenagers didn't know it at the time, they would start to be drawn together during the following seasons.

Arsenal finished 7th in the League behind Champions Everton.

Man Utd won the FA Cup after beating Leicester City 3-1.

Milan won the European Cup after beating Benfica 2-1.

SEASON 1963-64

By virtue of finishing 7th in the League the previous season, Arsenal qualified for European competition for the first time, in the Inter-Cities Fairs Cup.

After beating Staevnet in the first round, Arsenal were eliminated by FC Liege in the 2nd.

The thought of Arsenal competing against the top European teams and winning the European Cup was one of the things I dreamt of, along with winning the League title and winning the FA Cup, as up to now, this had only happened on my Subbuteo pitch.

Like many of my generation, I had watched the great Real Madrid, Barcelona, Benfica, Milan and Inter Milan teams on the television but only in black and white, and, although I'd seen Arsenal play Eintracht Frankfurt, Juventus, Real Madrid and Glasgow Rangers in friendly matches, it just wasn't the same as proper competitive football.

I was now aged 14 and going to some away games on my own, by coach, with the Arsenal Supporters Club and the required reading at the time was now "Charles Buchan's Football Monthly" as I'd outgrown "Roy of the Rovers".

Later in the season, my classmate from school, George Hammond, would join me on these trips where the coaches would leave Highbury Crescent opposite Highbury & Islington tube station at 7.30 am for games in the Midlands and 10.30 pm the previous night for the Northern teams.

There used to be a café in Highbury Fields where we could get breakfast before departing on the early trips. By a strange coincidence, in 2014, when I was recovering from a heart attack in hospital, I noticed one of the nurses drinking from a coffee mug with the Arsenal badge on it.

During our subsequent conversation, it transpired that her parents used to own that café during the sixties. Small world or what?

Nothing much had changed on the pitch; the forwards were still scoring plenty of goals, especially Joe Baker, but alas, the defence were still leaking almost as many and the statistics can confirm this. Arsenal scored 90 goals and conceded 82 in the League, despite signing goalkeeper Jim "Fingers" Furnell from Liverpool and the Scottish International centre-back, Ian Ure from Dundee.

On the opening day of the season, I travelled back to London by train from my parents' caravan near Herne Bay in Kent, where we were on holiday, to watch Ian Ure make his debut against Wolves. Arsenal lost 3-1, so the omens for the coming season weren't looking too good, especially when, as there were no substitutes allowed in those days, Joe Baker had to go in goal away at Leicester after Jack McClelland was injured and Arsenal lost 7-2.

The usual inconsistencies were highlighted during October 1963, in one of the greatest derby games against The Team from the Lane, ever seen at Highbury.

They had probably their best ever team, containing star players, Jimmy Greaves, Dave Mackay, Cliff Jones, Danny Blanchflower, John White and Bobby Smith and were winning 4-2 with only five minutes left, when Joe Baker scored at the North Bank end, and, with seconds remaining, Geoff Strong equalised.

Most of the 68,000-strong crowd went crazy! Just remember, there was no segregation of fans in those days, but amazingly, there was no trouble either.

Different times indeed!

In the FA Cup of Season 1963-64, after beating Wolves at Highbury in the 3rd Round, I went, with some of my family, to the 4th Round game away at West Bromwich Albion.

On arriving in the stadium, I had never seen so many Arsenal fans at an away game before, as they had occupied most of the terraces on one side of the stadium.

As usual, David Stacey was parading around the side of the pitch, dressed in his red and white suit and top hat, carrying a board with the words "Arsenal fans say, may the best team win" written on it.

I don't think many of us agreed with him though, and from the abuse he was getting, I don't think many Albion fans agreed with him either.

This fantastic support was rewarded with a 3-3 draw and it seemed that many Arsenal fans had reached the same conclusion that my brother always had – "this was our year in the FA Cup".

Arsenal won the replay at Highbury to reach the 5th Round again, playing against Liverpool at Highbury again, sadly, losing again, with all their fans singing in the North Bank again. Déjà vu!

However, during this match, there was one incident that has passed into folklore for my generation, when my hero, and that of many other young fans, Joe Baker, finally got fed up with Ron Yeats, the Liverpool captain, kicking him up in the air from behind every time Joe received the ball.

Incredibly, 5' 8" Joe turned and punched 6' 4" Ron and felled him, giving him a few more digs on the way down for good measure. Obviously, they were both sent off and I think that hurt us more than them, but an Arsenal legend had been created.

In October 1992, my mate Alan [Spook] Ing and I were privileged to meet Joe and many Scottish football legends at Joe's Testimonial dinner in Edinburgh.

When I gave him a framed print of the incident with Ron Yeats, Joe was thrilled to bits, saying that he "now had the proof he needed to show his golfing pals". More about this night in a later chapter.

Arsenal finished 8th in the League behind Champions Liverpool.

West Ham won the FA Cup after beating Preston North End 3-2.

Inter Milan won the European Cup after beating Real Madrid 3-1.

So, my dreams were now gone for another season, although there were promising signs for the future with some fine young players, namely John Radford, Jon Sammels, David Court and Terry Anderson, coming through from the Youth team to join the other already established youngsters, George Armstrong, Terry Neill and Alan Skirton.

During the summer of 1964, the ex-England International full-back, Don Howe, was signed from West Bromwich Albion, to give some experience to these emerging young players.

The significance of Don's arrival would reap massive rewards for Arsenal and their fans in years to come; the only problem was, nobody on the Highbury terraces could see that far into the future.

The only glimpse of success that I saw at that time was when I went to a few games with my mates from the council flats where I lived and saw Chelsea win promotion against Portsmouth in 1963 and jealously watched some European games against Roma, Milan, Munich 1860, Benfica and Barcelona during the next few seasons.

This was a period when Chelsea were challenging for many trophies with a young team managed by my old mate, Tommy Docherty. I was still getting stick in the "Cages" from the Chelsea boys and it was just my luck that, after I moved from those flats, Arsenal won the Double in 1971 and I couldn't give them some of it back.

1964-65

On 22nd August 1964, the opening day of the season, I went by coach to the away game at Liverpool.

This was my first visit to Anfield and Liverpool paraded the League title trophy in front of a baying, singing, swaying crowd in the Spion Kop, before beating Arsenal 3-2.

I'd never seen supporters doing that in a stadium before and have never forgotten the sight of it.

This was also the first game that the BBC showed, containing an hour of highlights, in black and white, on their new "Match of the Day" television programme.

Joe Baker, naturally, scored the first goal of the game, and the defence, naturally, conceded more than Arsenal scored.

In September 1964, I travelled to Leicester away and saw Arsenal win 3-2, before just a few weeks later, Billy Wright would sign the Leicester captain, Frank "Tick Tock" McLintock for a record Arsenal transfer fee of £80,000. Frank was, in my opinion, one of the greatest signings Arsenal have ever made, being a proper captain in every sense of the word and I don't think Arsenal ever saw another like him until Tony Adams emerged in 1987.

In the same month, I also went to a midweek night game at Stamford Bridge, to see Chelsea versus Man Utd and their new 17-year-old "Wonder Boy", George Best. Well, he certainly lived up to his name, scoring after 20 minutes and eventually becoming "The Best" British footballer I've ever seen.

Because bands like the Beatles and Rolling Stones were still in their early days, there weren't too many pop songs around, therefore, many fans used to sing traditional songs, such as Birmingham's "Keep Right On", West Ham's "Bubbles", Newcastle's "Blaydon Races", the Team from the Lane's "Glory, Glory", Portsmouth's "Play Up Pompey" and Liverpool's "You'll Never Walk Alone", or failing that, rhythmic clapping and chanting.

"Clap, clap; Clap, clap, clap; Clap, clap, clap, clap, ARSENAL", was a popular one, although many of us would chant, "Joe, Joe, Joe Baker". Twenty-five years later, this would have evolved into, "Ooh to, Ooh to be, Ooh to be a Gooner". Another was, "2, 4, 6, 8, who do we appreciate? Arsenal".

Very prehistoric, compared to the anthems that came later.

DARLINGTON. JANUARY 1965

In January 1965, George Hammond and I, took one of the Arsenal Supporters Club coaches to the FA Cup 3rd Round match at Darlington. After arriving, many fans decided to go to the local pubs but as we were too young to go in pubs, George and I went to the railway station to meet the other Arsenal fans who were coming on the "Football Special" train from London. Once the passengers had disembarked, we joined all the other fans marching down the road to the stadium, where, on entering the ground, we stood under the roof of the covered end behind the goal that Arsenal fans had been allocated.

Two elderly Arsenal supporters, who travelled to most away games by coach and always stood at the front of the North Bank, were "Old Flo" and "Soapy". For an obvious reason, Soapy always had a spare seat next to him on the coach and he would always wear a red and white halved football shirt, white shorts and red and white hooped socks. At most away games, about half an hour before kick-off, Soapy would climb onto the pitch, where he would take a corner kick, hitting an old brown leather football into the penalty area, then running in and smashing the ball into an empty net to the delight of

SOAPY

the Arsenal fans. He'd then calmly pick the ball up before returning to the terraces. The police never arrested him as they could see it was just a bit of harmless fun, especially if Soapy fell over in the mud. Sadly, this innocent ritual was lost forever at Darlington.

After Soapy had taken his customary corner and smashed the ball into the net in front of us, some local fans invaded the pitch from the side terraces and tried to nick his ball. This action resulted in initially three Arsenal fans, then many more, coming to Soapy's rescue and fighting them off. George and I couldn't believe it, as we'd not seen a mass brawl, especially in the penalty area, involving Arsenal fans at a football match before. Those first three Arsenal fans on the pitch gave me my first glimpse of my future mates, Hoyboy, Tringy and Alfie Job.

After the game, which Arsenal won 2-0, most of our fans departed on the "Football Special" train back to London, leaving those who'd arrived by coach to sample the delights of Darlington, before eventually leaving at 11 pm. As we were still schoolboys, George and I weren't allowed in the pubs where the Arsenal fans had gone for the evening, and so, after having something to eat in a café, we then wandered the streets until, sometime later, we were confronted by a large group of local teenagers who made it quite clear that they were going to beat us up. Well, licensing laws or not, we weren't going to get a good hiding, so we ran for our lives until we reached the pub where the coach stewards, Barry Baker and Peter Maynard, were drinking with the other Arsenal fans and we crashed through the doors to safety, gasping for breath. After that lucky escape, we both decided, there and then, that we wouldn't be so naive ever again.

PETERBOROUGH. JANUARY 1965

In the 4th Round, George, my cousin Johnny, my brother and myself all went to Peterborough, where Arsenal would suffer one of the most infamous defeats in their history, losing 2-1 to a team that had not long ago been promoted from Non-League football.

This day was memorable for four reasons;

1 – The Result.
2 – The funeral of Sir Winston Churchill.
3 – Johnny remembering me threatening to hit some bloke, with my rattle, after he kept chanting, "Peterborough, Peterborough, Ooh, Ooh, Ooh," in my face.
4 – The last Arsenal away game that I ever went to in England with my brother.

Arsenal finished 13th in the League behind Champions Man Utd.

Liverpool won the FA Cup after beating Leeds United 2-1.

Inter Milan won the European Cup after beating Benfica 1-0.

SEASON 1965-66

Arsenal fans were fairly optimistic about the coming season, due to the team at last now having five experienced quality players, Joe Baker, George Eastham, Frank McLintock, Don Howe and George Armstrong, ably supported by the youngsters with plenty of potential, such as, Peter Storey, Peter Simpson, Jon Sammels, Sammy Nelson, Mickey Boot, Tommy Baldwin and John Radford, who'd scored a hat trick on his Highbury debut the previous season.

George Hammond and I were still regulars on the Arsenal Supporters Club coaches to many away games and here are some samples of the prices at the time;

Blackpool – Newcastle – Sunderland = 22/6d. 2020 Equivalent Rate = £20.00 approx.

Other Lancashire and Yorkshire clubs = 18/-. 2020 Equivalent Rate = £17.00 approx.

Midlands Clubs = 11/-. 2020 Equivalent Rate = £10 approx.

That's mainly why schoolboys, and teenagers such as us, travelled by coach to away games.

BLACKPOOL. OCTOBER 1965

On the morning of the game at Blackpool, George and I joined a few other young Arsenal fans in a busy amusement arcade on the seafront. After playing on the penny slot machines for a while, we noticed some older local blokes trying to hit a punch ball hard enough to ring the bell and win a prize. We had been watching a few of them fail to hit the ball hard enough, when one of the teenage Arsenal fans stepped forward to try his luck. He promptly head-butted the punch ball and the dial went up and rang the bell to win his prize, a beach ball. All the older blokes then retreated as the young Arsenal fan looked at his mate and they both started laughing. That's how I first met Johnny "Laney" Lane, the head-butter, and my old mate Mickey [Putney] Childs. All of us young Arsenal fans, who also became mates that day, namely, Rod Moore, Johnny [Mullers] Mullard, Graham Wrench, Johnny Nash, Kenny Hall, Kevin Fenlon and Big Alex, then went to the beach to have a game of football with "Laney's" prize, before going to the match and seeing Arsenal score three goals but as usual, concede five. Rod Moore can even remember talking to David Court and George Eastham on the promenade in the morning as they were taking a pre-match walk. In the evening, the coaches stopped off in Manchester and we all went to the Speedway at Belle Vue stadium until it was time to get on the coach back to London. These coaches were often freezing cold, because the driver was worried that he'd fall asleep if the heater was on for too long, and so, with this in mind, many of us took blankets with us and left them on the coach while we went to the game. A few teenage girls sometimes went on these coach trips and Graham and Nashy eventually married two of them.

Over the coming weeks and months, many other teenage Arsenal fans would meet us on these coach trips and friendships were formed that have lasted to this day, through our common love of "The Arsenal".

WRONG END AT LEICESTER

In October 1965, for some strange reason, our new mate, Putney, George and myself decided to go into the "Home End" away at Leicester. We were soon spotted, though, and escorted out by the police. Just as well, because we had red and white scarves on.

BOWLING IN SUNDERLAND

I can also recall going to Sunderland with George and Putney, on a freezing coach, with our blankets, of course, arriving at the stadium in the morning, where we discovered that the game had been postponed due to heavy snow. All the Arsenal fans on the coach offered to help sweep the pitch but the offer was declined.

As the coach driver had to wait until at least 6 pm before driving back to London, we spent the afternoon ten pin bowling, in the "Black Cat Club", home of the Sunderland supporters. To be fair, they made us most welcome, but it was a hell of a long way just to go bowling. Just for fun, when we stopped at the services on the way home, George decided to lie down in the middle of the M1! Luckily, it was about midnight so there was no traffic about.

XMAS DRINK IN SHEFFIELD

Another wonderful(?) day out was on the 27th of December 1965, when George and I went to the Arsenal match away against Sheffield Wednesday at Hillsborough.

Before the game, we were having a drink in the bar under the stand, even though we were still only sixteen, when, just after I had put my beer on the counter, a couple of plainclothes coppers appeared and grabbed George, who was still holding his beer in his hand. One of the coppers asked me, "Is that your beer on the counter?" Obviously, I said no as I'd left my naivety in Darlington the previous season. The copper smiled and promptly nicked poor George for under-age drinking. To cap a bad day, Arsenal lost 4-0 but they did win the return at Highbury 5-2 the following day.

It wasn't rocket science to realise that Arsenal weren't going to win the League that season, so most of us went to Blackburn for the 3rd Round FA Cup tie, hoping for a good cup run.

No chance – Blackburn Rovers, soon to be relegated, won 3-0.

Previously, at the Fulham League game, Putney and Laney had marched around the terraces holding a large red and white flag between them.

On it was written "Baker & Eastham, England's only hope in 1966", referring to the forthcoming World Cup Tournament.

They had brought this flag with them to Blackburn, standing waving it behind one of the goals, with the Arsenal fans, including George and myself, gathered all around them.

Obviously, the Blackburn fans were not happy about this situation and made repeated attempts to snatch the flag. Unsurprisingly, a mass brawl broke out and I recall seeing Peter Maynard, the Head Steward from the coaches, getting particularly upset and clumping many of the local fans.

LETTER FROM BILLY WRIGHT

They never got the flag, but another season of dreams had ended in January.

Matters got even worse when George Eastham and my hero, Joe Baker, were transfer-listed.

I even wrote to Billy Wright regarding Joe, and he replied that, "he had no intention of selling him".

A few months later, after scoring 100 goals in 156 games, Joe Baker signed for Nottingham Forest.

Many years later, Peter Maynard told me how glad he was when our generation turned up for away games, as the coaches had almost always been full of elderly men and women in the past.

THE DEMISE OF BILLY WRIGHT

By now, the Arsenal fans were in open revolt against Billy Wright, and, after demonstrations which included a bonfire on the North Bank, "Highbury Hates Wright" stickers and after one home game against Blackpool, an ambulance carrying the injured Don Howe to hospital was attacked outside the Main Entrance in Avenell Road, because of a rumour that Billy Wright was being smuggled out of the stadium inside it, the fans then decided to boycott home games, resulting in a record low attendance of 4,554 in a 3-0 defeat against Leeds on the 5th of May 1966. Putney, Tringy and Charlie George are the only three that I personally know who were in the crowd that night.

Inevitably, Billy Wright was sacked and I admit to being one of the protesters in 1966, although, in hindsight, he did introduce many of the players from the Youth team who would form the basis of the successful Arsenal Squad a few seasons later.

> Arsenal finished 14th in the League behind Champions Liverpool.
>
> Everton won the FA Cup after beating Sheffield Wednesday 3-2.
>
> Real Madrid won the European Cup after beating Partizan Belgrade 2-1.

Also, in the summer of 1966, the long-serving left-back, Billy "Flint" McCullough, who had played more than 250 games for Arsenal, joined Millwall, thereby ending the "famous" McClelland/Magill/McCullough triumvirate of Northern Irish names that formed the first three names of the team that my generation had learnt off by heart from the matchday programmes.

ARSENAL'S FIRST WORLD CUP WINNER

George Eastham was the only Arsenal player in the triumphant England squad in 1966.

Surprisingly, as far as I know, there is no official recognition of this achievement at Arsenal, not even a banner on one of the walkways over the railway from Drayton Park, yet without players like George Eastham, Joe Baker, Frank McLintock, David Herd and Jack Kelsey, Arsenal would probably have been relegated at some time during the decade between 1955 and 1965.

In the summer of 1965, I had left school, but luckily for me, I had a former schoolmate, Steve Constanti, whose father had bought two World Cup season tickets for every game at Wembley for his two sons.

After the first game, England vs Uruguay, Steve's brother had to go on a pre-arranged holiday and his dad offered me the spare tickets, including one for the only game at the White City stadium, France vs Uruguay, which, at 0-0, was one of the most boring games of the whole tournament. However, future events more than compensated for this wet night.

1966 WORLD CUP TICKETS

As we were going through our Mod phase at the time, we drove to Wembley on Steve's Lambretta scooter, which enabled us to park easily near the stadium. So, standing together, we witnessed both the ugly side of football, with Argentina's Rattin, and the beautiful side with Portugal's

Eusebio, along with a resilient Mexico, which only the genius of Bobby Charlton finally wore down.

If everyone who's ever said they were at this World Cup final actually got in, then Wembley stadium would have had to have been ten times the size it was on that momentous day.

I know that Steve and myself were there, also my mate, Granty, whose dad got him a ticket from the Knightsbridge hotel where he worked as a doorman. Granty's dad also got me the autographs of the Portuguese team who were staying there.

My old pal, Tringy, was also there and even spent a month watching the World Cup in Mexico in 1970. A month? In Mexico? In 1970? I could just about afford two weeks in a caravan at Herne Bay!

1966 WORLD CUP WILLIE

3

THE BERTIE MEE YEARS

We're the North Bank Highbury

SEASON 1966-67

In a move that shocked most Arsenal fans, before the season started, the club physiotherapist, Bertie Mee, was appointed as manager to replace Billy Wright.

Within a few weeks, he had recruited Dave Sexton as his assistant and bought Bob McNab from Huddersfield Town, Colin Addison from Sheffield United and used Tommy Baldwin as part of the deal for George Graham from Chelsea, while also promoting Pat Rice to the first-team squad.

Changes were definitely beginning to take shape on the field with, allegedly, Frank McLintock deciding it might be a good idea to ditch the famous white collar and sleeves on the shirts.

Off the field, things were changing amongst the younger fans also.

As organised hooliganism at football grounds began in about 1965 and rapidly spread across the country, it became necessary for away fans to congregate together in the stadiums, railway stations and pubs etc., for self-protection.

Naturally, this became the norm at home games as well.

The group of teenage friends, including myself, who'd initially met on the coach trips to away games, were now also meeting behind the North Terrace goal for home games at Highbury where we were soon joined by other young Arsenal fans, who joined in the singing and chanting about the team and individual players.

I've listened to many so-called experts and analysts over the years saying that hooligans were not football fans.

Maybe a few people latched onto a club for a chance of a fight but, in my experience, most of the Arsenal fans that I grew up with were spending all of their spare time and money following Arsenal up and down the country, long before the hooligan era appeared.

Many of these teenagers, now old men, still go to matches nowadays with their kids, and even grandkids, without causing any trouble, of course.

Like I said previously, fans initially got together for self-protection, especially at away games, although at a later stage, many succumbed to the misguided belief that they were actually fighting for the club.

I remember two early examples of how behaviour soon changed.

Before one game at a northern town, after getting off the coaches, we noticed an elderly man walking along the local High Street carrying his shopping bag.

Someone had the cunning plan, whereby about twenty-five of us silently lined up behind the old boy in single file and, whenever he paused to look in a shop window, we did as well.

People who were also out shopping were now laughing at our antics, especially when he crossed the road and we all followed, holding up the traffic as we did so.

He was totally oblivious to our presence and we only had to stop when he entered a small supermarket and the staff called the police because they thought we were going to rob the place.

Childish, silly, innocent fun.

The second example was a few weeks later, in November 1966, away at Everton.

During a 0-0 draw, Peter Storey, who was now a regular in the first team, decided to tackle Alex Young, or "the Golden Vision", as most Everton fans called their hero, causing him to slide across the cinders that surrounded the pitch and crash into the hoarding.

The Scousers were not happy and when we returned to our coaches after the game, many of the windows had been smashed. Not innocent fun!

Good job we had our trusty blankets for the journey home. It was still freezing cold, though!

NORTH BANK NAMED

There had always been a large banked terrace at the Northern End of Highbury Stadium since it was built in 1913.

Much of the earth that was used came from the overspill from when the nearby Piccadilly Line underground station was built in 1906.

Like many football grounds at that time with a similar high terrace, usually behind one goal, such as Liverpool and the two Sheffield clubs, it was called the "Spion Kop", after a famous battlefield hill in South Africa during the Boer War.

Over the years, it also had a few other names, such as, "Gillespie Road End", "Laundry End", "North Terrace", and, before the roof was erected in 1935, the "Clock End".

At many grounds, teenage fans were also congregating together, usually behind one goal on a covered terrace and these areas became their "Ends" and were named "Stretford End", "The Kop", "The Shed", "Gladwys Road End", "Scratching Shed", "Leazes End", "Boothen End", "Trent End", "Holte End" etc.

Man City actually had a side terrace named the "Kippax".

At Arsenal, it was very hard to sing songs about the "Laundry End" or "North Terrace", so, one day, after a few beers, we decided to call it the "North Bank", the same as West Ham and Wolves had called their Northern Ends.

During Season 1966-67, the North Bank's reputation for noise and aggression was gaining momentum.

In December 1966, I decided to make a banner with the North Bank name on it, because the Arsenal hierarchy still insisted on calling it the North Terrace in the matchday programme.

My dad actually did the lettering layout, as he thought my original attempt was a complete mess.

After a few hours of ironing on the sticky tape-backed letters and stitching the sides to hold the poles in, the banner was ready to take to the 3rd Round FA Cup game at Bristol Rovers in January 1967.

I have a copy of the original photo taken that day, of the banner being displayed among Arsenal fans on their way to the stadium from Bristol's "Temple Meads" railway station.

Although you can't see us, I'm holding one pole and my cousin, Johnny, is holding the other.

When I gave a copy to Charlie George a few years ago, he was gutted that he hadn't received it earlier, because he's in the middle of the photo with his mates, including Hoyboy, and he'd mentioned this game in his autobiography, as he'd told the Arsenal reserves' trainer, Tom Whalley, that he had the flu and couldn't play that weekend.

My mate, Gary Davies, always recalls that it started raining on the way to the stadium and he, along with Lenny Togwell, Dodger, Edwin and many others, dashed into a Dunn's hat store and all of them emerged wearing "borrowed" trilby hats.

As I went through the stadium turnstiles, I saw my old schoolmate, George Hammond, queuing to enter the ground.

By an odd coincidence, as I reached the top of the terraces, the crowd surged forwards and for some reason, known only to himself, a copper grabbed me and frog-marched me down to the exit gate, just as George was coming in.

When he saw me being escorted out, George fell about laughing, saying "you've only been in there two minutes". As the game wasn't all-

ME & GEORGE HAMMOND

ticket, I just paid to get back in at the same turnstile, getting a strange look from the operator, who must have thought I had a twin brother.

Luckily, my cousin Johnny was still holding the banner.

Arsenal won 3-0 and had reverted back to their famous red and white shirts for FA Cup games.

BOLTON – FA CUP FEBRUARY 1967

In the 4th Round, we went by coach to a game with Bolton Wanderers away. On arrival at the ground, we were put behind the goal where Bolton's noisiest fans stood; when were the police going to wise up?

Within a few minutes, fighting broke out and I saw a big bloke hit a little Arsenal fan, who'd only been jumping up and down while chanting.

So, I hit the big fella and said, "Pick on someone your own size". It turned out he was a plainclothes copper and he clumped me back and tried to drag me out of the terrace towards the exit.

Other coppers soon arrived, including a sergeant, and all my mates gathered around me and I became the centre point of a tug-of-war competition.

Johnny told me to pretend that the copper had broken my jaw and I needed urgent treatment.

When I mentioned this to the sergeant, he said, "Alright then, we'll take you to the Infirmary".

I replied, "No thanks, I want to go to hospital".

The coppers let me go because they were laughing so much, I think?

As usual, when attending away games up north, we went back to Manchester for a few beers.

As the Bolton game had ended in a 0-0 draw, at the replay on the 22nd of February 1967, the North Bank banner was unfurled for the first time at Highbury, announcing to the wider world who we were.

Eventually, the police would advise clubs to ban flags and banners because the supporting poles, usually broom handles, were being used as weapons.

Many fans then suddenly developed limps, giving them an excuse to carry a walking stick.

Not before the 5th Round FA Cup game, away at Birmingham, though!

BIRMINGHAM CITY – FA CUP MARCH 1967

On the way to St Andrew's, Birmingham's stadium, Arsenal fans, marching from the railway station and coach park, were pelted with bottles and billiard balls from the upstairs window of a pub.

Needless to say, the pub was stormed and severely damaged, including a piano pushed from an upstairs window.

Inside the ground, Arsenal fans were allocated a section behind the goal, opposite the end where the noisiest Birmingham fans stood.

As there were no fences separating the terraces, we all decided to march along one side, proudly carrying the North Bank banner, and change ends.

The "Brummies" weren't too happy about this situation, to say the least, especially as, despite some fierce fighting, we wouldn't budge.

This fighting spilled over into the streets outside the ground after the game, which Arsenal lost 1-0.

JOCK

The North Bank was now becoming well known across the country and before home games, about twenty of us would usually meet up in the "Gunners" pub at midday, leaving at about two-thirty, or earlier for the bigger games, to make the short walk to the North Bank, where Hoyboy and some others would usually be waiting for us.

"Jock", the copper, would normally be there as well, and we'd ask him, "How many fans have they brought today?"

Jock would reply, "A few hundred" or maybe, "A couple of thousand", depending on the opposition.

Next question; "How long, Jock?" His reply; "You can have three or four minutes". Thanks Jock.

Then we'd all charge in and scatter the away fans, until Jock or one of his colleagues tapped you on the shoulder with his truncheon, saying, "That's it, stop fighting or you're nicked".

Many years later, some of us were walking to the ground when we saw Arsenal and Man Utd fans fighting in Avenell Road. Jock was on traffic duty and shouted at the fans to stop fighting. We all stopped and asked if he needed any help? He replied, "Just stay right where you are, laddies".
We just stood there laughing.

AROUND THE COACHES

Drayton Park became the scene of many pitched battles after games at Highbury, as it was where the away fans' coaches were usually parked.
The chant of "around the coaches" would often ring out on the North Bank, near the end of a game.
This was the cue for hundreds of Arsenal fans to make their way to Drayton Park and confront other fans, usually smashing a few coach windows for good measure.
I can still remember seeing North Bank boys actually inside the coaches fighting with people.

LEAGUE CUP

Arsenal had entered into the League Cup for the first time in 1966-67, and after taking three games to overcome Gillingham, were knocked out in the 3rd Round by West Ham 3-1 at Highbury.

On Friday, March 3rd 1967, history was made when Arsenal played Man Utd at Highbury in the first football match to be broadcast live, either on Pay TV or back to Old Trafford, or possibly both.

When we arrived at the stadium, there were hundreds of United fans already on the North Bank.

The police had formed a line to stop Arsenal fans from getting at them, but I will always remember Yarney arriving with a long wooden pole – I still don't know how he'd got it into the ground – reaching over the police line and hitting United fans with it.

A few other United fans had taken the liberty of sitting on the terraces, until Putney went berserk, dragging them to their feet, before clumping or head-butting them.

Hoyboy tells me that one of the funniest things he remembers about this night was seeing Putney pulling individual United fans through the police cordon, one by one, and bashing them.

We finally got to the middle of the North Bank as the police and United fans were gradually pushed across towards the Gillespie Road exit.

Jon Sammels scored for Arsenal with a long-range effort and the game finished 1-1.

In April, we went to see Fulham and Arsenal draw 0-0.

We stood on the fairly new "Hammersmith End" and as Fulham have always been and still are, a family club, there wasn't much trouble.

However, for some reason, a fight broke out at the front of the terrace and Granty went charging down to join in, shoving three large "Paddies", still in their overalls and steel toe-capped boots, out of the way as he did so.

Big mistake, as one of them turned and punched Granty in the face, breaking his nose.

Granty was carted off to hospital and was waiting for us at Earl's Court station after the game.

He got a bit upset when we all started laughing at the bandages and plasters on his face.

He gets even more upset when we remind him that he's the only fan to get beaten up at Fulham.

Yet again, another season ended without any glory on the pitch but the team was slowly improving.

Arsenal finished 7th in the League behind Champions Man Utd.

The Team from the Lane won the FA Cup after beating Chelsea 2-1.

QPR won the League Cup after beating West Bromwich Albion 3-2.

Glasgow Celtic won the European Cup after beating Inter Milan 2-1

Arsenal won Quiz Ball thanks to Ian Ure, Terry Neill, Bertie Mee, Jimmy Young and Cardrew "The Cad" Robinson.

BANNOCKBURN REVISITED 1967

In August 1967, Glasgow Rangers, with a certain striker named Alex Ferguson, came to Highbury for their traditional bi-annual friendly.

Sadly, we wouldn't see them at Highbury again until the Testimonial match for Nigel Winterburn in 1997.

These games were usually played in midweek but this fixture was changed to a Saturday.

In 1973, I met two Glaswegian fellas, Alan and Tommo, when we were all working in the bars and nightclubs in Spain. They became great mates and, although they still live there, we keep in touch. Tommo recalls seeing Arsenal at Ibrox in a friendly when he was a kid.

On the day of the Rangers game, most of the pubs around Highbury had been packed with Scottish fans since opening time.

However, a few of us did manage to squeeze into the "Gunners".

Many older Scots were in there and we enjoyed some friendly conversations with them about football.

One bloke even gave me his Rangers lapel badge.

We decided to get into the ground early, at about two o'clock and discovered the North Bank was almost totally occupied by Rangers fans.

These were not the usual teenagers that normally came with English clubs, but mainly steaming drunk, middle-aged men.

They were actually standing around crates of bottled beer.

We had to stand at the very back of the North Bank, for those that remember, the other side of the gangway that ran across from the Avenell Road entrance to the Gillespie Road entrance.

There were a few fights before kick-off and fans from both clubs were being ejected by the police.

What made us laugh was seeing that one of the first Rangers fans to be led around the pitch was "Big Hughie", a Scottish Chelsea fan whom we recognised.

Sometime during the second half, a few bottles were lobbed in our direction, because some Arsenal fans around us had been singing and chanting.

Bonnie and Eddie Harnetty both managed to catch a bottle each, throwing them straight back.

Due to the sloping terrace, they hit the roof girders above the Rangers fans, shattering all over them, causing many to have cuts to their heads and faces.

As you can imagine, the Rangers fans were not happy, to say the least.

What you can't imagine unless you were there was the barrage of empty and even full bottles that landed all around us, causing us to scatter in all directions to avoid the glass shards that were bouncing off the floor of the concrete terraces.

A broken shard from one of these flying bottles hit Buster Wrench in the mouth and he still has the scar on his lip as a reminder.

A massive gap opened up in the North Bank and for the first time ever at Highbury, I saw the police, including "Jock", with their truncheons drawn, charge the Rangers fans on the North Bank as the rioting continued.

Apart from the police fighting with Rangers fans in the centre, some of us were fighting with them also, mainly on the fringes though, as we were vastly outnumbered by the Scots.

After the game, which Arsenal won 3-0, the Rangers fans smashed up most of the pubs and some shops in the Highbury area and we had to lick our wounds and beat an honourable (I think) retreat.

GLASGOW RANGERS MOSAIC

For those who don't know, the Battle of Bannockburn was a famous Scottish victory against the English in 1314.

SEASON 1967-68

The Arsenal team was now looking good, especially as they had abandoned the all-red shirts, allowing the fans to be fairly optimistic about winning a trophy at long last.

Off the pitch it was getting hectic as well, as the North Bank reputation had spread far and wide, tempting more fans from other clubs to come to Highbury in greater numbers.

During the previous Season, 1966-67, Chelsea, Man Utd, Everton and Man City supporters had already been involved in fighting on the North Bank.

To their credit, Chelsea always turned up in large numbers, never actually managing to take it over, until a midweek League Cup match in 1976.

The same goes for West Ham, who would occupy much of the North Bank in April 1970.

On August 19th, the opening day of Season 1967-68, Stoke City were the visitors and many Arsenal fans were out for revenge after being attacked at Stoke a few months before.

After a few running battles on the North Bank, where some Arsenal fans had used coshes and razors, about forty Stoke fans had gathered in Avenell Road after the game, looking for the culprits.

NORTH BANK BANNER AT BRISTOL –
CHARLIE GEORGE IS UNDER THE N OF NORTH

What they hadn't realised was that hundreds of Arsenal fans were waiting for them in Drayton Park, having already smashed many of the windows of their coaches.

Eventually, these Stoke fans walked down Gillespie Road, followed by scores of Arsenal fans, and near Arsenal tube station, were caught in a classic pincer manoeuvre, that General Patton would have been proud of.

They got absolutely battered and one of their leaders was chased as far as Holloway Road, by an Arsenal fan carrying a shotgun.

This incident even made the front page of the evening newspapers.

Next up were Liverpool and, as usual, they brought good support with them. That didn't matter though, as by now, away fans entered the North Bank at their peril.

In September 1967, the Arsenal striker, George Graham, got married in the morning before the game against the Team from the Lane, with Terry Venables as his best man.

George celebrated with a 4-0 victory and in hindsight, this was when Arsenal started their almost complete domination of North London football for the next 50 years.

In the next game at Highbury, Man City, who would eventually become champions, arrived with a strong team on and off the pitch, resulting in a 1-0 win for Arsenal and fierce fighting on the North Bank, throughout the game.

The fighting continued after the game in Avenell Road and even some of the "Big Highbury" boys, who normally stood on the "Clock End" got involved.

It was only October and we'd already taken on Glasgow Rangers, Stoke, Liverpool and Man City.

Although the fans of the Team from the Lane became notorious in later years, they never turned up on the North Bank until the 1980s.

Also, in October, only a few of us went to Old Trafford to see Arsenal lose 1-0 against the future European Cup winners because due to their success as Champions, most United home games had capacity crowds and tickets for away fans were hard to get.

ARSENAL RUN OUT AT OLD TRAFFORD IN BLUE KIT

The game was memorable for Ian Ure and Denis Law getting sent off for fighting and Arsenal wearing their new away strip of "Scotland-style" dark blue shirts and white shorts.

In November, against West Ham, I was dragged out of the North Bank by the police and thrown out of the stadium. Like at Bristol previously, I just paid to get back in again.

WINTER 1967

I mentioned earlier the "Big Highbury"; these were older fellas who usually never got involved with minor issues such as fighting at football matches.

The "Little Highbury", mostly teenagers, were definitely involved on the North Bank though, along with others from Islington, Holloway, Holborn, Bethnal Green, Hackney, Boreham Wood, Finchley, Hoxton, Camden, Streatham, Essex, Stevenage and other places in Hertfordshire and Kent, and included my few close mates and myself from Westminster.

Talking of Westminster, in November 1967, Arsenal were playing away at Burnley in the 5th Round of the League Cup.

This match was only available on television, via Pay TV, in two areas of London. Luckily, my mum's council flat in Westminster was in one of them.

So, about a dozen of us crammed in to see Arsenal force a 3-3 draw and a week later, we would be at Highbury to see Arsenal win the replay 2-1.

In between these two cup games, Arsenal also lost 1-0 away at Burnley in the League, where Pat Rice made his debut, coming on as a substitute.

Dave Sexton had walked out on Arsenal to manage Chelsea and Don Howe had replaced him. Don's influence was noticeable, with the team appearing to definitely toughen up.

With Pat Rice now at right-back, Peter Storey was moved into midfield, with Frank McLintock moving to centre-back to replace Ian Ure.

BOXING DAY 1967

We went to Chelsea on a Boxing Day.
Left them all dead now, after the fight.

Bow Street on a Monday,
That's all right.

Ooh, we are the North Bank,
Yes, Yes, Yes,
We're the mighty North Bank.

[Adapted from *Autumn Almanac* by the Kinks.]

Coming out of Fulham Broadway station, we could hear the Arsenal fans who'd entered the "Shed End" early, singing the Beatles song, "Hello, Goodbye", although the words had been altered to, "You say Hello, but we say Fuck Off.

Fuck Off, Fuck Off, we don't know why you say Hello, we say Fuck Off".

When we entered the ground, there was a police cordon consisting of two lines, with one line holding back the Arsenal fans and the other holding back Chelsea fans.

All sorts of small objects were being thrown back and forth over the heads of the police, with only occasional fistfights breaking out, despite some desperate surges from both sets of supporters.

Arsenal lost 2-1. Despite the score being the same, next season would be very different though.

This was the winter when the game at Highbury against Sheffield Wednesday had a low attendance of 27,000 due to the police restricting the crowd for safety reasons, as the Clock End and other exposed terraces were frozen, although the pitch was playable thanks to the undersoil heating.

The match was eventually abandoned when further heavy snow fell.

Arsenal wore red shorts that day, for the first time that I know of.

WEMBLEY AT LAST – MARCH 2ND 1968

Although inconsistent in the League, Arsenal had progressed to the semi-final of the League Cup and were drawn against Huddersfield Town with the 1st Leg at Highbury. Arsenal won 3-2.

The next cup match was away at Shrewsbury in the FA Cup 3rd Round.

As we'd never heard about any trouble at their home games before, it came as a complete surprise when we were bombarded with stones, bricks and lumps of concrete by their fans who were on the roof of the covered terrace behind the goal where we were standing.

Some Arsenal fans climbed up the drainpipes to fight them off and I was amazed that the flimsy corrugated iron roof never collapsed.

From where we were standing, we noticed one very aggressive bloke running around grabbing Arsenal supporters, and, when he came our way, Rod Moore clumped him.

It turned out that this bloke was a plainclothes police officer from London, who'd been sent on the "Football Special" train to assist the local police.

A few other coppers helped him drag Rod out and load him into a police van before they carted him off to the nick.

On arriving there, they couldn't put Rod in the cells because they were already full with Arsenal fans, including Bonnie and his mates.

The Duty Sergeant asked where the arresting officer was and another copper told him that he'd returned to the stadium.

Happily, Rod was released without charge after the game, which finished 1-1.

Luckily, a Shrewsbury fan who'd also been released, showed Rod the way back to our waiting coach.

Arsenal won the replay 2-0.

WEMBLEY VIA HUDDERSFIELD

Now we had the match we'd all been waiting for, the League Cup semi-final, 2nd Leg away at Huddersfield.

This game was also transmitted live on Pay TV to my mum's flat in Westminster and about twenty of us now crammed even tighter into her front room to watch it.

Arsenal won 3-1, with Terry Martindale, he's never forgotten, winning our sweepstake, when Frank McLintock scored the first goal.

Hoyboy remembers coming out of Huddersfield's ground, not believing he was finally going to see "The Arsenal" play at Wembley.

Twenty teenagers in my mum's flat were feeling exactly the same way.

Like most of my generation, we were so excited to be going to Wembley to play Leeds United in the League Cup Final that it didn't matter to us if it wasn't the FA Cup Final.

Apart from England Internationals, I'd only been to Wembley for two Amateur Cup Finals, one in 1959, Barnet vs Crook Town, with my uncle Billy and the other in 1963, Sutton vs Wimbledon, with my mates from the council flats in Westminster.

After waiting eleven years since I first started going to Arsenal in 1957, I, along with most of my generation, finally saw the famous red and white shirts walk out at Wembley for a Cup Final on March 2nd 1968, but not before a mass brawl in the Wembley car park where, at one stage, Arsenal fans were scrambling over car bonnets to get to the fans disembarking from the Leeds coaches.

Imagine the disappointment when Arsenal lost the match 1-0, due to a hotly disputed goal from Terry Cooper, after Jack Charlton had impeded Jim "Fingers" Furnell.

So, it was back to the FA Cup for another chance of glory, as, after we'd seen Swansea beaten 1-0 away in the 4th Round, where there was some serious fighting in the streets beforehand and some nutcase had, inexplicably, tried to saw the goalposts in half the previous night, Arsenal had reached the 5th Round.

BIRMINGHAM FA CUP 1967-1968

In a repeat of the previous season, Arsenal were drawn against our "old mates" Birmingham in the FA Cup 5th Round, only this time it was at Highbury.

The "Brummies" had obviously been planning their revenge for this match, as they had got into the stadium early, almost filling the central section of the North Bank, thereby reversing what we'd done the year before at St Andrew's.

Despite repeated attempts, we couldn't force them out and had to endure seemingly endless renditions of "Keep right on to the end of the road".

Eventually, it turned out to be the end of the road in the FA Cup for Arsenal as well, as a mistake by the goalkeeper, Jim "Fingers" Furnell, led to a late equaliser for Birmingham.

Not many Arsenal fans went to the replay, where two goals from Barry Bridges gave Birmingham a 2-1 victory, although "Bootsie" Miller and myself did.

Bob Wilson came into the team that night, eventually establishing himself as Arsenal's number one goalie. "Fingers" was transferred to Rotherham at the end of another trophy-less season.

ARSENAL SUPPORTERS CLUB FOOTBALL TEAM

Many of us, who travelled on the coaches to away games, had now started playing for the two Arsenal Supporters Club football teams on Sunday mornings over at Hackney Marshes.

ARSENAL SUPPORTERS CLUB
FOOTBALL TEAM 1968

These teams included Putney, Spook, Kenny Hall, Graham and Buster Wrench, Colin Short, Charlie MacCready, Johnny Nash, Johnny Round, Fred Lawman, my cousin Johnny Leach and myself. Others, who never travelled on the coaches but played, included Dave and Vic Pooley, Hoyboy, Keith Pioli, Eddie Coight and a West Indian fella named Harvey Thomas.

Our team was managed by Tony Wrench, the father of Buster and Graham and big Bobby Stanley was the "Magic Sponge" man. Incidentally, Bob was a West Ham fan who worked with Putney and became a good mate of ours, often going to Arsenal games with us if West Ham weren't playing. He eventually got a tug from the ICF and explained that he never stood with us when Arsenal played the Hammers. Out of respect, everyone sang "Bubbles" at his funeral in 2014.

Talking of Fred Lawman, he was introduced to us when Charlie once brought him along for a trial game. Les Cardy, who, as the Secretary, was in overall charge of the teams, was almost blind and wore glasses with thick bottoms, similar to milk bottles. As Charlie was injured that day, he stood close to Les, giving a running commentary of the game and throughout the first half, Charlie would shout, "Well played, Fred, great pass, Fred, great tackle, Fred, great header, Fred, great shot Fred" and so on. Much to everyone's amusement at halftime, Les turned to Charlie and said, "Your mate Fred is having a good game, ain't he? We'd better sign him up".

The first season we played in the Supporters Club League, along with Charlton, Chelsea, Fulham, Gravesend, Millwall, Orient, Romford, the Team from the Lane plus London-based Man Utd, Glasgow Rangers, and Newcastle Supporters Clubs.

I also arranged a friendly with some of my old Chelsea-supporting mates from Pimlico, memorable for when, in the dressing room before the game, one of them said he was having trouble with a knot in his boot laces and immediately, a flick knife thudded into the wooden bench next to him and a voice said, "Try this". As you can imagine, these games against the fans from other clubs were a bit lively, to say the least, with some games even getting abandoned, so the Arsenal Supporters Club Committee decided to join the North Middlesex League the following season.

Despite the games still being at least as competitive, if not more so, due to Turkish and West Indian clubs and possibly the hardest team I ever played against, the predominately Irish Manor Celtic being involved, both of our teams won their respective Leagues and also a cup.

Sadly, at the end of the season, Les Cardy, after only ever having players receive three cautions in the previous four seasons, decided to expel Spook and Dave Pooley, as they were the worst culprits when the teams received many more cautions, plus a few send-offs during that season.

The two teams would eventually break up when many of us walked out in protest at the expulsions and the Arsenal Supporters Club wouldn't win anything again for many years.

Arsenal finished 9th in the League behind Champions Man City.

WBA won the FA Cup after beating Everton 1-0.

Man Utd won the European Cup after beating Benfica 4-1.

HIGH HO, HIGH HO!

NICKED

Below is a list of all the blokes that I'd met during the previous years, such as the players from the Supporters Club football teams that I mentioned previously, plus those who never played, despite being regulars on the coach trips; Rod Moore, Lenny Togwell, Johnny Mullard, Bonnie, Alan [Tringy] Carter, Alfie Job, Bootsie Miller, Johnny Lane, Big Alex, Terry Kelly, Mick Peppiatt, Adrian [Young Radford] Moruzzi, Pat Kelly, Eddie Minnick, Kevin Fenlon and Bobby Marshall.

Their friends who were introduced to us, were Whitty, Bob Stanley, Eddie Harnetty, Yarney, Gary Davies, Eddie Prenderville, Vic Connell, Jimmy Hutchings, Johnny [Hayesey] Hayes, Herbie Austin, Greek George, Bob Jones, Dave May, Danna Ward, Dixie, Alfie Scully, John Sanger,

Malcolm Froy, John Crosby, Kenny Banham, Dave Lovejoy, Jimmy Gray, John Buckland, Barry Crouch, Fred Hill, Charlie and Kevin Douglas, Roger [Dodger] Wicks, Edwin Childs, Teddy Taylor, Peter Landers, Brian Kent, Greek Dennis, Mickey Pearce, Bobby King, Kevin Moran, Peter [Schulzy] Shervill and Vic Wright.

Not forgetting the mates that I already knew from Westminster; George Hammond, Danny Sutherland, Ray [Granty] Grant and my cousin Johnny Leach. Amazingly, out of all of these, only Colin Short, Dave Lovejoy and, to nobody's surprise, Hoyboy, were actually arrested and convicted for offences at Arsenal games, although at least seven of them had been, or were still, in prison for crimes not related to football.

Ironically, Granty and myself were first nicked on holiday at Butlins in 1967, when we went into the nearby town for a drink and ended up fighting with two local blokes.

As we were returning to the holiday camp, a van load of police arrived and took us to the nick.

We were sitting in the charge room, protesting our innocence, when another two coppers arrived with the blokes that we'd left on the pavement.

On seeing us, one of the blokes pointed at me and said, "That's the one who hit me".

I immediately jumped up and shouted, "I've never punched anyone in my life", hitting him so hard that he fell over the desk.

Unsurprisingly, the coppers then dragged me and Granty off to the cells.

Early the next morning, a copper was sent round to our homes. My mum was away on holiday, whereas Granty's dad was still asleep in bed in the top floor flat of the big house he lived in.

When the copper rang the bell, waking him up, he leant out of the window and the copper said, "We've got your son and his mate locked up in the cells, as they've been nicked for fighting".

Granty's dad replied, "Well, fucking keep them there then", slammed the window down and went back to bed.

No chance of us getting bail then?

SEASON 1968-69

High Ho, High Ho,
To Tottenham we will go,
With a bottle and brick,
And a walking stick,
High, Ho.

On August 10th 1968, somehow, without mobile phones, social media or even a previous home game, word had spread that the North Bank boys were going to meet at midday at Manor House, and march to the Lane for the opening game of the season.

At least five hundred Arsenal fans gathered on the pavement outside the pub, spilling into the road.

Remember, these were the days before police escorts, CCTV or video cameras.

This was one of the only times that I can remember, when all the different gangs that made up the North Bank met up together outside of a stadium.

1968

It was a formidable little army, which was swelled with others jumping off buses and coming from side streets and council estates along the route.

Putney had appeared at the head of the march, with a large plastic cockerel that he'd painted red.

He claimed to have got it from a workshop near his house in Highbury that made them for the Courage brewery.

On reaching the junction at Seven Sisters Road, after Dave Mackay's tie shop had been left with no windows, a lone copper roared up on his motorbike, skidded and fell off.

The fans descended on him like locusts. Eventually, he managed to break free and ran to the nearby police station.

The police piled out and Putney was arrested for assaulting and swearing at a police officer.

He was charged, bailed and met up with us in the stadium later.

On the Monday in Court, he got off the assault charge but was fined £10.00 for swearing.

Meanwhile, Prenders had jumped on a bus going to the ground.

He later recalled going into the "Corner Pin" pub, where the boys from the Lane usually drank and found "Parish", one of their leaders.

Prenders was recognised and someone asked him, "What are you doing in here?", when he replied, "They're coming to get you", Parish hit him saying, "Well, they ain't here yet".

When we arrived about twenty minutes later, Prenders was still wiping the blood from his nose; naturally, we were in hysterics when he related the story.

Even more naturally, the pub was empty.

We filled the Park Lane End, as their fans had wisely moved to the Paxton Road End.

Phil Beal scored an own goal as Arsenal won 2-1, and we all went home happy.

Little did we realise that we would be back again later that season.

We attempted to march again in the following seasons but the police had stopped us forever.

In Season 1969-70, their fans had moved to "The Shelf" and in 1970-71, not many to them got in the ground at all.

AUGUST 1968 VS IPSWICH AWAY

On a hot summer's day, Arsenal fans descended on Ipswich in their hundreds, with two of them, allegedly, robbing the till of a department store, containing about two months of the average man's wages, before seeing their favourites win 2-1.

SEPTEMBER 1968 VS LEEDS AWAY

Many of us went to this game by coach, and after parking, we made our way to the "Peacock" pub opposite the ground for a beer.

Suddenly, there were many Leeds fans outside, desperate to get revenge for the hiding they'd got in the Wembley car park at the previous League Cup Final.

We had no choice but to go outside and fight our way through them, which, armed with wooden bar stools, we did, despite a couple of us getting a few cuts and bruises.

We managed to get into the stadium intact and Arsenal lost 2-0.

A few days later, some of us went to Scunthorpe for a League Cup match that Arsenal won 6-1, with David Jenkins scoring a hat trick.

In those days, there was a lot of animosity between Arsenal and Leeds fans, as the two teams were competing with each other for most of the trophies.

I recall one incident when going to a game in the north. We were on a train that was waiting in a Midlands station, when another train pulled in alongside ours.

This other train was full of Leeds fans going south to London for a match. Immediately, fans from both trains were trying to get at each other through the small exit doors and the trains were rocking like galleons at sea in the days of Horatio Nelson and Francis Drake.

SOMETHING FISHY

Next, it was off to Old Trafford in October, to see Arsenal draw 0-0 with Man Utd, where I remember the referee threatening to abandon the game, as Arsenal's star player that day, Bob Wilson, was getting pelted with missiles from the Stretford End.

After the game, we had a few beers and then were quietly eating our fish and chips outside the shop before getting on the coach to go back to London.

Suddenly, Mullers shouted out that my mates, George Hammond and Barry Baker, were being attacked by four local blokes inside the shop.

Someone ran in and clumped three of them, causing nasty facial and head injuries, before the fourth one put his hands up, pleading not to be hit.

They hadn't realised that the Arsenal fan had a knuckle duster on his fist.

When the police arrived, they searched everyone looking for it, but it had already been hidden on the coach.

LEAGUE CUP SEMI-FINALS 1968-69

After beating Sunderland, Scunthorpe, Liverpool and Blackpool, Arsenal were drawn against the Team from the Lane in the League Cup Semi-final.

Arsenal won the 1st Leg 1-0 at a packed Highbury Stadium in November.

On the night of December the 4th, 1968, about ten of us were walking up the High Road, on our way to the 2nd Leg game, singing this song, adapted from The Scaffold's "Lily the Pink".

"We'll drink, a drink, a drink,
To Radford The King, The King, The King,
the saviour of, The Ar-se-nal,

"Cos we invented, professional football,
and now,
we're gonna, win the Cup.

Just as we reached the "Corner Pin" pub, a large group of fans of the Team from the Lane were gathered outside and, as we finished the song, one would-be hero shouted, "I knew you'd stop singing when you saw us."

I think Big Bob nearly took his head off with a punch, before they scattered all over the road as we charged at them.

Inside the ground, another fan of theirs was stabbed during fighting on the terraces.

Arsenal fans filled the Park Lane End, as usual, causing sheer bedlam when, with only a few minutes left, Raddy scored the equaliser, putting Arsenal on their way to Wembley again.

Many of us were now wearing sheepskin coats to games and due to this, had become well known.

The boxing promoter, Frank Warren, has allegedly recalled in the book "The End", that "Hoyboy, Putney and the Postman" were the three main culprits on the North Bank in those days. Apparently, I was nicknamed the Postman as I used to be a telegram boy when I first left school and once turned up to a midweek night game in my uniform.

FA CUP 1968-69

In January '69, most of us went by train to the 3rd Round FA Cup match against Cardiff.

This was only memorable for Lenny getting slightly injured after stabbing himself in the leg with a bayonet that he had in his raincoat pocket, as he was climbing over some railings.

We were all in hysterics; Lenny was not amused.

The match was a 0-0 draw, with Arsenal winning the replay 2-0, then beating Charlton at home 2-0 in the 4th Round, to set up an away game at West Bromwich in the 5th Round.

FEBRUARY 1969 VS WBA AWAY FA CUP

Arsenal travelled to West Brom, accompanied by thousands of their fans, for the 5th Round FA Cup match that was, for some reason that I don't recall, played on a midweek evening.

We also went by train to this game, as I remember lying in the luggage rack above the seats because our compartment was crammed full.

After a while, two coppers appeared at the door and started lecturing everyone that any unruly behaviour would result in us all being evicted from the train at the next station.

The others could hardly contain their laughter, as the coppers hadn't noticed me lying up near the roof.

On the way to the ground, Putney saw a small shop and ran ahead to get a bar of chocolate.

While he was standing at the till with his hand outstretched waiting to pay, the Arsenal hordes descended and stripped most of the shop bare around him.

It all happened so quickly that the owner could only grab the till and cower beneath the counter. When he finally stood up, Putney was still standing there, holding out the money for the chocolate.

Arsenal lost 1-0 and some West Brom fans were waiting outside for us on a bridge after the game.

One idiot ran along the parapet of the bridge wall to try to get at us, but an Arsenal fan shoved him and he toppled over the edge.

We waited for the splash but it never came, so somebody looked over the wall, before exclaiming, "It's not a canal, it's a railway bridge!"

A fight ensued and I somehow ended up with a denim jacket with a large "Albion" badge sewn on the back.

I checked the pockets and all I found was a sweaty corned beef sandwich in a paper bag.

Coming back on the train, Granty, who was playing cards, said, "I'm starving; has anyone got anything to eat?"

I pulled out the sandwich and gave it to him and he scoffed it down without a murmur as he was too busy concentrating on his cards.

About twenty minutes later, Kenny Hall asked me, "Was there anything in that denim jacket?"

When I replied, "Only a sweaty corned beef sandwich", Granty nearly dropped his cards.

More hysterical laughter.

LEAGUE CUP FINAL VS SWINDON. MARCH 15TH 1969

Another of my most embarrassing days following Arsenal up to that time, alongside defeats to Northampton, Rotherham and Peterborough, was when Arsenal, as one of the hottest ever favourites in a Wembley final, managed to lose 3-1 to a "Don Rogers" inspired, third division Swindon Town.

1960'S & 70'S MATCH TICKETS

No words or excuses about flu, injuries, tiredness or a muddy pitch due to the "Horse of the Year Show" a few days earlier, can describe the disappointment that I and all Arsenal fans, especially those of us in the 98,000 crowd, felt on this day.

This disastrous day was the beginning of the end for some of the Arsenal players.

Other players later reflected that the criticism they received spurred them on to achieve greater things in the next few seasons.

Thousands of Arsenal fans, including myself, wish we could have seen into the future that day though, as another season would end without a trophy.

Although, there was one highlight still to come.

MONDAY APRIL 14TH VS CHELSEA AWAY

This was probably the last time that away fans were allowed in the Shed End, as they would be allocated the opposite end of the stadium in the future.

Fourteen of us decided to meet at my mum's flat and get to the ground early.

As usual, nobody wore any colours, but because the police had formed a cordon separating the two sets of fans the previous season, we had developed a cunning plan!

As the game wasn't all-ticket, which was normal in those days, we would enter the stadium through the turnstiles reserved for home fans at the Shed End and meet up again inside.

A few other Arsenal fans, including Barry Crouch, had recognised us outside after spotting our sheepskin coats and joined in the plan.

There were now about twenty of us and we proceeded across the front of the terrace in single file, with Putney up front, looking for "Eccles", the leader of the Chelsea firm which included Jesus, Webby and "Zigger Zagger" Greenaway.

This was the days before Nightmare, one-armed Babs and the Headhunters.

Eccles was spotted screaming abuse and waving his fist at the Arsenal fans who were stuck behind the police cordon again.

Putney tapped him on the shoulder and as he turned around, Putney said, "Hello". The blood drained from the face of Eccles, as he asked, "What are you doing in here?" Putney replied, "We've come to see you," and promptly head-butted him.

The rest of us then turned as one, hitting the nearest Chelsea fan.

The Chelsea fans retreated up the terrace, leaving a huge gap, which we were now jumping up and down in, singing, "We're the North Bank, we're the North Bank, we're the North Bank Highbury".

The police couldn't intervene, as they had to hold back the other Arsenal fans, who'd recognised us and wanted to join in the celebrations.

After a few minutes of mayhem, police reinforcements arrived, which allowed Chelsea fans to regroup once the initial shock of our actions had worn off.

By a strange coincidence, one of the first Chelsea fans to charge back at us was the brother of Barry Crouch. I'd loved to have been a fly on the wall in their house that night!

We then joined the rest of the Arsenal supporters but not before somebody with a knife had slashed the back of my beloved sheepskin coat, which probably saved me from serious injury.

After the game, the police pulled everyone wearing a sheepskin coat off the tube trains at Earl's Court station.

Nobody was arrested, though obviously, the police were definitely wising up.

Apparently, Eccles was followed home sometime later after a midweek game by a group of Arsenal fans, getting a good hiding from one of them. Ironically, Chelsea weren't even playing Arsenal that night.

Arsenal finished 4th in the League behind Champions Leeds.

Man City won the FA Cup after beating Leicester City 1-0.

Swindon won the League Cup after beating Arsenal 3-1.

Milan won the European Cup after beating Ajax 4-1.

SEASON 1969-70

WEST HAM AWAY

On Monday 25th August 1969, somebody, had the not-so-cunning plan, of going to West Ham and doing what we'd previously done in the Shed End, to their North Bank.

Now West Ham were, and always have been, a formidable bunch, never shirking from anyone and I don't recall any away fans being in their North Bank in large numbers before.

The "Usual Suspects" met early without wearing any colours, entering the stadium about thirty minutes before kick-off.

We charged into the West Ham fans from the west side of the North Bank, catching them completely unaware and forcing them to retreat towards the east side, blocking other fans from coming in from that entrance.

We were about halfway across, when I distinctly remember a giant of a West Ham fan turning and shouting, "There's only a few of them!" This was the signal for them to regroup and chargeback at us. That's when I discovered that there were no exits at the back of their North Bank terraces.

Their anger at someone having the audacity to enter their territory knew no bounds, and culminated in the biggest retreat since Dunkirk.

We managed to get into the terraces on the western side of the stadium but realised they would be waiting for us outside after the game.

Luckily for us, somebody knew the back alleys that led through to Plaistow station.

Unluckily for them, other Arsenal fans were getting beaten up all over the place, such as on buses, in pubs and streets and obviously, Upton Park tube station.

We split up into smaller groups and Granty and myself managed to slip onto the tube at Plaistow, avoiding the mobs on the platforms looking for any Arsenal fans.

Foolishly, I went to get off at Mile End to change trains but Granty held me back as he could see dozens of "Hammers" fans waiting on the platform because they knew Arsenal supporters would be changing trains there.

I think we decided it was safer to get off at Tower Hill station and catch a bus home from there.

Rumour has it that for weeks afterwards, Hammers fans even went to the pubs in Hackney Road on Friday nights looking for the "Usual Suspects" but to no avail.

WEST HAM HOME

On the 4th April 1970, Arsenal played West Ham in the return League fixture at Highbury.

As we left the "Gunners" pub that day, we could see and hear the massed ranks of "Hammers" fans, waiting at the top of the steps that led up to the North Bank from the Avenell Road turnstiles.

They had obviously done their homework and organised their own cunning plan by getting into the stadium early, filling most of the North Bank.

As it would have plainly been suicidal, we all decided to avoid this entrance, and went around to enter the stadium through the Gillespie Road turnstiles instead.

THE GUNNERS PUB

We got in without any trouble, although West Ham fans had pushed Arsenal fans over to this side.

Some of us managed to get through to the middle section and saw a big blond fella marching up and down the terrace offering to take on all comers; apparently, he was one of the "Baker Brothers" from Stratford.

Anyway, despite being vastly outnumbered, Putney decided to run and head-butt him, leaving the bloke on the floor.

I couldn't believe my eyes and ran and grabbed Putney before they realised what had happened and we disappeared through the crowd.

When I later questioned his sanity, he replied, "I had to do something for my pride".

SEASON 1969-70

GLORY DAYS ARE COMING

Arsenal decided to play Swindon in a pre-season friendly at Highbury – don't ask me why!

This day was only memorable for my old mates, Putney and Spook, becoming the first Arsenal fans to be incarcerated, apparently for being drunk, in the new cages that had been built beneath the East Stand.

Arsenal drew their first home game of the season 0-0 against Leeds on Wednesday 13th August.

We were sitting in the "Gunners" pub after the game when the door opened and two familiar faces entered but quickly walked out again. Billy Bremner and Jack Charlton, two legendary Leeds players, had decided to drink elsewhere.

Looking back, it would have been great to chat with them both but that wasn't possible at the time.

AUGUST 1969. WBA AWAY.

A few days later, Arsenal won 1-0 at West Bromwich Albion and a few of us went up there in my recently bought, ex-Army Austin Champ jeep.

Upon arriving outside the ground, we noticed both sets of fans fighting and I drove the jeep up the kerb, scattering the "Albion" fans.

Granty later remarked that it was "like something out of a war film".

Two weeks later, George Hammond and I managed to accidentally set my jeep alight outside our flats, before soldiers from the nearby barracks extinguished the fire, but that's another funny story for another day. One story relating to that jeep, though, was when I first met Larry "The Lip" Graham, a fan of the Team from the Lane, at work in the late 70s, and he mentioned being chased down Drayton Park after a game at Highbury by some nutters in a jeep back in the 60s. We both collapsed with laughter when I said it was mine.

ONE MAN CLEARS THE NORTH BANK

Early in September 1969, while Arsenal were drawing 0-0 with Sheffield Wednesday at Highbury, we were all in our usual spot on the North Bank, in the centre, two-thirds of the way up, when Alfie Scully arrived.

Hoyboy asked him why he was so late and Alfie replied that he'd been working on a building site that morning and had an accident.

Hoyboy asked, "What sort of accident?" Alfie said, "I shit myself". Some of us had been listening to their conversation by now and we all started laughing.

Alfie copped the hump and said, "It's not funny. Look," then out of his coat pocket, he pulled a paper bag containing his underpants, full of dried pieces of shit. He removed the underpants from the bag and started twirling them around his head, causing bits of shit to hit anyone standing within yards of him.

Well, as you can imagine, the biggest gap seen on the North Bank since the Glasgow Rangers riot opened up, with blokes crouching down and running away with their hands covering their heads.

The police couldn't work out what was happening as there weren't any Wednesday fans in there.

Funny now, even funnier then!

CHELSEA AWAY

Also, in September 1969, Arsenal lost 3-0 away at Chelsea but not before we'd all gone into the "Rising Sun" pub opposite the ground.

When the Chelsea blokes heard we were drinking in there, they gathered outside as they probably still had the hump from the previous season.

As there was only one door, it was blatantly obvious we would have to fight our way out.

Sammy Walsh, who'd broken his ankle a few weeks previously, gave one of his crutches to Eddie Harnetty. To his credit, Sammy hobbled out waving the other crutch and we all formed up around him, using anything as a weapon and made it across the road and into the ground.

As we reached the top of the steps leading into the Shed End, the police were waiting and escorted us around the pitch to the opposite end where they'd put all the other Arsenal fans.

STOKE AWAY

Sometime during the previous season, we had given up travelling to away games on the Supporters Club coaches and depending on the numbers, we were either going in cars or hiring a van from "Godfrey Davis Van Rentals" in Euston.

These vans seated three people in the front and obviously didn't have any seats in the back, so about eight of used to sit on our coats, with only two small windows in the rear doors.

Early on a Saturday morning, Putney would hire the van for the weekend and we'd all meet outside the "Gunners" pub, where the trip meter would be disconnected.

This trip meter would be reconnected sometime on the Sunday, before the van was returned.

We travelled to a number of away games in this manner but would eventually be banned from hiring from "Godfrey Davis", as one Monday morning, when the van was being serviced, the cleaner found a "Manchester Saturday Evening Pink" newspaper inside.

As, according to the trip meter, the van had apparently only done sixty miles, we were forced to change to another company.

It was in one of these hired vans that we made the trip to Stoke to see yet another 0-0 draw.

After the game, we were calmly and quietly walking back to the van, as we were in front of hundreds, and I mean hundreds, of Stoke supporters pouring out of the Boothen End and we didn't want them to hear our accents.

Two Stoke fans walked past us, remarking to each other about how boring Arsenal were, when our mate, Terry Kelly, said to them, "You don't know what you're talking about." Now, it was the "Alamo".

These two Stoke blokes shouted to the hordes that were following, "They're Cockneys", pointing at us and we all had to leg it.

After a couple of minutes, we decided to take the next street on our left, but as we turned the corner, we realised it was a dead end, with just a high brick wall facing us.

So, I said to Putney the immortal sentence that would often be used in the future, "What are we gonna fucking do now?" His reply was, "Form a line with your backs to the wall and all hit the first ones who come around the corner".

That's what we did and as the first group turned the corner, we put most of them down. Thankfully, there were so many that the ones following behind went tumbling over them.

However, this gave us the chance to get going again, although some were actually overtaking us amid the confusion and I distinctly remember one angry fella coming alongside me shouting, "Let's get the Cockneys!" I just shouted back at him, "Yeah, Yeah!"

Eventually, they just gave up, as we split up into two's and three's, mingling into the crowd.

Another lucky escape.

After regrouping at the van, we decided to go and have a night out in Birmingham as we obviously couldn't stay in Stoke.

Off we went with Whitty, who was driving, deciding to mount the kerb while parking the van where there was a large queue of people outside a cinema waiting to see a film.

Some blokes from this queue came up to the window to remonstrate with him about his driving skills, until the back doors flew open, and when we all jumped out, they returned to the queue.

Then we went off to a pub, which I think was the "Tavern in the Town", as you had to go downstairs to the bar. I believe the IRA blew it up a few years later.

After a few beers, we decided to move on, but as we were leaving, a bouncer told Granty he couldn't take his drink with him, so Granty poured it over his head and hit him with the glass.

Now we were legging it again, with police sirens coming our way. We ran to the railway station and Whitty and myself jumped into the first taxi on the rank. The driver asked me, "Where to, mate?" I replied, "Anywhere", then the doors flew open and we were dragged out by the police.

Granty had jumped in the last taxi on the rank and was rowing with the driver, who was telling him to go to the taxi at the front. Granty then got dragged out. After arriving at the nick, the others were gradually brought in one by one.

As we were wearing either sheepskins or overcoats, we decide to swap them with each other.

After a while, the bouncer from the pub was brought in with a bandage around his head and the coppers made us all line up before asking the bouncer to identify who'd hit him.

He walked along the line and pointed at Granty saying, "I think it was him", then pointed at someone else and said, "but it was that coat".

We all started laughing and after taking our names and addresses, the coppers took us to the van, escorted us to the M1, then advised us not to return to Birmingham for at least a year.

LEAGUE CUP

Arsenal drew 1-1 away at Southampton in the 2nd Round, before winning the replay 2-0.

In the 3rd Round, Arsenal drew at home 0-0 with Everton and then lost the replay 1-0.

BLACKPOOL FA CUP

Arsenal drew at home 1-1 with Blackpool in the 3rd Round then lost the replay at Bloomfield Road 3-2 after leading 2-0.

This was the last straw for Bertie Mee and Don Howe, resulting in Terry Neill, Ian Ure, David Court, Jimmy Robertson and Bobby Gould, eventually leaving that season, with Peter Marinello being signed in January 1970 for a club-record fee of £100,000 from Hibernian.

Younger players, Charlie George, Ray Kennedy, Eddie Kelly and Sammy Nelson, were promoted to the first-team squad along with John Roberts, who'd signed in the summer of 1969.

INTER CITIES FAIRS CUP

Arsenal beat Glentoran 3-0 in the 1st Round, 1st Leg at Highbury, then lost the 2nd Leg 1-0 in Ulster.

Arsenal drew with Sporting Lisbon 0-0 in the 2nd Round, 1st Leg in Portugal, then won the 2nd Leg 3-0 at Highbury.

Arsenal drew with Rouen 0-0 in the 3rd Round, 1st Leg in France, then won the 2nd Leg 1-0 at Highbury.

Arsenal beat Dinamo Bacau 2-0 in the 4th Round, 1st Leg in Romania, then won the 2nd Leg 7-1 at Highbury.

Arsenal beat Ajax 3-0 in the semi-final 1st Leg at Highbury. Charlie George scored twice.

They then lost the 2nd Leg 1-0 in Holland.

This was a tremendous achievement, as Ajax, with talented players like Johan Cruyff, Rudi Krol and Wim Suurbier, were fast emerging as a great team that would later win the European Cup and take Holland to the World Cup Final.

This was now the first chance for my generation to finally see Arsenal win a trophy since 1953.

ANDERLECHT - APRIL 1970

April 22nd 1970 was the day when, after beating the highly rated Ajax team in the semi-final, Arsenal would play against Anderlecht in the 1st Leg of the final of the Inter Cities Fairs Cup in Brussels.

ANDERLECHT - 1970

Some of us "Original North Bank Boys" would be going with them.

During the week before this match, Charlie MacCready and Putney visited me at my home to inform me that there was a day trip being organised by 4S Sports for £12.00.

The package for this trip included flights to and from Luton Airport and Brussels, a return coach trip from London to Luton, a coach from Brussels airport to the city centre and later to the stadium, then a coach from the stadium back to Brussels airport, plus, most importantly, a match ticket.

Please remember that £12.00 in 1970 was the monthly payment on my Triumph Vitesse convertible car, therefore, I had to choose which one to pay for.

Needless to say, "The Arsenal" won.

Only a few hundred Arsenal fans went to this 1st Leg Final, as it was still a novelty to travel abroad for a football match in those days. Also, not many people could afford to spend the equivalent of a week's wages on a day out.

To put this into perspective, as Rod Moore remarked many years later, only four or five hundred Arsenal fans actually went to the1st Leg of Arsenal's first European Cup Final against Anderlecht in Brussels, due to lack of money or organised travel.

However, only ten years later, in 1980, at least twenty-five thousand went to Brussels for the European Cup Winner's Cup Final against Valencia, despite a national train and ferry strike on that day.

On the morning of the match, the coaches set off from the 4S Sports office on Kingsway in Holborn, with us all on board one of them, wearing the red football shirts that we'd borrowed from the Arsenal Supporters Club, which many of us used to play for, heading to Luton Airport.

As I've said previously, replica team shirts weren't available in those days.

It was my first flight and although the journey was only just over an hour, I started feeling sick as we were nearing Brussels airport and covered my mouth with a sick bag as a precaution.

Putney, who was sitting next to me, was told to put my table up by the stewardess as we were coming into land.

As he did this, he 'accidentally' knocked the sick bag out of my hands and I started spewing up everywhere, starting off a chain reaction from some of the other passengers on the plane.

On entering the Arrivals terminal at Brussels airport, the Arsenal fans started singing the tune of the French anthem, "La Marseillaise".

I don't know why as we were in Belgium.

Coaches then took us to a city-centre car park and we were told to enjoy the afternoon sightseeing and return by 18.00 to go to the stadium.

Well, as you can imagine, all I saw was one main street, one side street and the inside of two bars.

We were enjoying ourselves so much in the first bar, sampling the strong beers, that when the barman wanted to close at about 16.00, we wouldn't let him.

We hadn't realised the strength of those Belgian beers, as we were used to Double Diamond or Watney's Red Barrel in the Gunners.

We had been allocated a female tour rep by 4S Sports, who hadn't realised the strength of those beers either because she ended up getting instant dismissal later that day after she was caught getting too friendly with one of the blokes in the back of the coach.

GOING TO THE ANDERLECHT STADIUM

When we eventually left the bar, our West Indian mate, Bonnie, decided it would be a good idea to form a human pyramid, which turned out to be a complete disaster.

We then held an impromptu "Knees up" in the road, on the way back to the coaches.

After this, the "Munchies" set in and we bought some waffles, which we ate while watching Putney and Whitty perform a humorous cabaret act – via a revolving door, they were going in and out of a department store where they had obviously found the hat department because every time they came out, they were wearing a different hat, just like a famous Tommy Cooper sketch.

We then found another bar near the coach park and continued with our beer-tasting and singing session.

We managed to get to the coaches without being arrested and had just settled into our seats, with Whitty sitting by the window and me next to him.

While we were patiently sitting there, an officious-looking bloke got on the coach, telling us that, as he had a black belt in karate and as there had been trouble with Newcastle fans in the semi-final, anyone intent on causing trouble today would have to deal with him first.

Idiot – that was like a red rag to a bull! Immediately, most of those on our coach stood up and shouted, "He's mine". The so-called karate expert promptly jumped off the coach and disappeared.

As the driver started the coach, Whitty noticed Danny Sutherland wandering between the coaches looking for our one.

Whitty started banging on the large window but Danny was so drunk, he couldn't hear or see him.

So, Whitty grabbed the little emergency hammer that was in a bracket above the window and started hitting the glass with it. Needless to say, the window cracked and then fell out.

This resulted in one happy Whitty, one happy Danny and one very unhappy coach driver.

A short while later, the coaches were driving along a dual carriageway towards the stadium, when a carload of Anderlecht fans pulled alongside our bus, waving their scarves and fists out of the car windows.

Whitty decided that he wanted one of the scarves and promptly dived out of the gap where the window used to be; the coach was doing about 45mph at the time.

Luckily, I grabbed his trouser belt, otherwise, he would have ended up bouncing down the road, and, with the help of Eddie Prenderville and Rod Moore, managed to pull him back in.

I'll never forget the look of terror on the faces of those Anderlecht fans in the car, though.

On arriving at the stadium, there was a large group of Anderlecht fans outside, waiting for us, singing their songs while waving their flags and banners.

Now, in those days it was quite normal, at least in England anyway, for away fans to be attacked by the home fans, so we thought that we were being ambushed.

Some of us piled off the coach and started punching them, until other Arsenal supporters, who'd got to the ground earlier, shouted out to us, "Stop fighting; they're friendly".

After a few handshakes and embarrassing apologies, we entered the stadium, but not before Lenny Togwell had blagged a ticket for the Main Stand from the Arsenal Secretary, Bob Wall.

They definitely weren't too friendly inside the stadium though!

INSIDE THE STADIUM

As we entered the ground, all hell broke loose.

Arsenal fans that were already in there, were having a stone and rock-throwing fight with Anderlecht fans.

For some unknown reason, the same as the Heysel stadium many years later, there was rubble all over the terraces.

For some even more stupid reason, the Arsenal fans had been put behind the same goal as Anderlecht's most fanatical supporters, with only a wire fence that was supported by scaffold poles embedded in concrete, separating them.

Some of the Belgians were trying to climb over the fence to get at the Arsenal fans but were constantly getting knocked back until eventually, one big fella, made it to the top and one of our lot from the coach started hitting him with a long lump of wood that had been lying on the floor.

The terrace really was like a bomb site!

I remember my mate saying, "This bastard won't go down," so he kept on hitting him until, after a few minutes, he finally did, with his head covered in blood.

Just after this incident, the riot police arrived dressed all in black, with white helmets on their heads, wielding batons and carrying guns in holsters on their hips.

We'd not seen guns at football matches before.

They grabbed Putney and pulled him onto the cinder path that surrounded the perimeter of the pitch before dragging him off down the players' tunnel.

I wrongly assumed that they had taken him to the police cells.

He later told us that as he was being led down the tunnel, he passed the Arsenal team who were lined up waiting to come out for their warm-up exercises.

As he passed Charlie George, Putney said, "Hello, Charlie". Charlie recognised him but could only nod his head and grin in reply for obvious reasons.

The game started and things calmed down between the warring factions behind the goal where we were standing, as the riot police were now standing where the fence had been torn down.

ANDERLECHT & ARSENAL TEAMS
LINE UP ON PITCH – 1970

After about twenty minutes, I was distracted by laughter coming from people behind me and thought that someone had cracked a joke. Then I heard a familiar voice say, "I'm back".

It was Putney, wearing a long white butcher's coat, pushing an empty mobile hot dog stall.

He claimed to have found the stall and coat next to a hut where

78

the vendors were having a break, so he borrowed it and walked back into the stadium, past the stewards on the gate.

Needless to say, after Arsenal got beat 3-1 by a Jan Mulder and Paul Van Himst inspired Anderlecht team, the coach trip back to Brussels airport afterwards was unremarkable except for either;

A – Single headache from the result.

B – Double headache from the result and strong beer.

C – Triple headache from the result, strong beer and being hit by stones or rocks.

On arriving at Luton Airport, Whitty was still fast asleep, so when Big Bob woke him up, he told him that, "Due to an engine fault on the plane, we would have to stay the night in Brussels airport".

Much to our amusement, Whitty was now walking through Luton Airport moaning about "Belgian aeroplanes".

Peter H, one of the Holborn boys, always remembers at Brussels airport finding an unattended open duty-free drinks cabinet, full of bottles of spirits, allowing him and some of his mates to help themselves to a couple each.

Now, Arsenal only had to win the 2nd Leg 3-0, although Jeff Morris distinctly remembers Jack Kelsey telling him and his mate, Ronnie Baker, "It will be a certainty," at the airport afterwards.

FINALLY, A TROPHY

On the 28th of April 1970, after a seventeen-year wait for Arsenal and a thirteen-year wait for myself, a major trophy would finally be coming to Highbury.

On what would possibly become the noisiest and most emotional night that Highbury ever witnessed, at least by my generation, Arsenal overcame the 3-1 deficit and won the 2nd Leg 3-0.

All of the hurt and pent-up frustration of so many years poured out during the course of the match and afterwards on the pitch and in the surrounding streets.

We had gathered in the "Gunners" pub as usual, although we left early as the game was not all-ticket and we realised that every Arsenal fan was going to try to be there if possible.

We took up our usual position, behind the goal on the North Bank, ironically, about where my Uncle Billy had fought the Scouser six years previously.

I remember the Arsenal captain Frank McLintock, just before kick-off, lifting his arms and urging the fans to give as much support as possible to the team, as if we needed encouraging.

It has been well documented over the years that, on an incredibly rain-sodden, muddy pitch, Eddie Kelly, John Radford and Jon Sammels scored

ME & JOHN RADFORD
WITH FAIRS CUP – 2010

ME & JON SAMMELS
WITH FAIRS CUP – 2010

WITH EDDIE KELLY &
FAIRS CUP 2010

the three goals that Arsenal needed, with a Bob Wilson-inspired defence preventing Anderlecht from scoring in reply.

Personally, the only future feelings comparable to this magical night were when Arsenal won the League titles at the Team from the Lane and Anfield.

This one was my first trophy and at Highbury, so that's what gives it the edge, in my opinion.

Everyone who was there has their own recollections of the scenes when the final whistle went.

Absolute bedlam!

There were players on the pitch crying, there were fans on the pitch crying, there were fans on the terraces crying, there were fans in the Stands crying, there were even men with their kids on their shoulders crying, but above all, everyone was singing and shouting; the noise, what a noise!

Didn't they know it's supposed to be the "Highbury Library?"

Charlie George gave Hoyboy his shirt, and he's still got it. Incredible to think that only three years previously, Charlie had marched from the railway station with us, going to Bristol Rovers' stadium.

There were so many people on the pitch that the players had to wait until the first home game of Season 1970-71, against Man Utd in August, to do a lap of honour with the trophy.

It was hard to get into any of the local pubs afterwards, although they did stay open until the early hours, as I don't think the police wanted a riot on their hands.

Remember, most Arsenal fans still lived in Central London in those days, and so it wasn't too difficult to get home in the early hours.

I never thought, even in my wildest dreams, that it would get even better the next season.

The next, and last game of the season was away at the Lane, and I can still recall the swagger and songs of the Arsenal fans that day.

Although Arsenal lost 1-0, it was the only time in living memory that nobody from Highbury cared.

Arsenal finished 12th in the League behind Champions Everton.

Chelsea won the FA Cup beating Leeds 2-1 at Old Trafford in a replay after a 1-1 draw.

Man City won the League Cup after beating West Bromwich Albion 2-1.

Feyenoord won the European Cup after beating Glasgow Celtic 2-1.

SEASON 1970-71

FUNNY STORIES BEFORE DOUBLE GLORIES

After winning the Inter Cities Fairs Cup, everyone at Highbury was looking forward to the coming season and Putney and Spook joined hundreds of other Arsenal fans and drove up to Goodison Park for the opening game of 1970-71 against Everton.

As they got there early, they decided to wait outside the players' entrance to see the team arrive.

They called out to Charlie George as he got off the coach and he told them to wait five minutes.

Charlie then disappeared inside the stadium and, minutes later, reappeared with two tickets for the Main Stand. He signed a few autographs for some kids and then returned inside.

Spook then took the kids' books and autographed them, then handed them back, before walking off with Putney, leaving the kids wondering who the hell he was!

Arsenal drew 2-2 and Charlie George ended up with a broken ankle.

As the season progressed, most of us attended all the home games, plus many away games as well, usually travelling in a hired van.

As there was always something funny happening at these away games, I will only describe the most memorable incidents.

Anonymous Up North.

Charlie MacCready likes to tell the story, of when he went by car to a game in the north with Hoyboy, Jonah and Fred Lawman

After the game, they drove to the nearest city for a night out. They stopped and asked a local bloke if there was anything lively happening that night and he advised them to go to the Town Hall as there was a live band booked.

As they parked in a side street next to the hall, there was a doorman standing outside the side entrance having a smoke.

When he spotted the four of them, he asked, "Are you the band?" Fred said, "Yes," and the doorman said to him, "As you're early, grab a couple of beers and then you can tune up, as we've already put your instruments on stage for you".

The four of them walked in, grabbed a beer and went onto the stage where they could hear the noise of the audience through the safety curtain.

They started plucking the guitars and bashing the drums for a few minutes before they heard loud voices and a commotion at the side door.

They decided to make a rapid exit and walked past the real musicians, frantically arguing with the doorman, who was refusing to let them in.

MANCHESTER

Another incident that I recall was after a game in Manchester, when we were in the "Portland Bar" near Piccadilly, having a quiet drink and chatting to the local girls, until some bloke started verbally abusing Fred.

Now, this bloke was wearing a trendy patterned kipper tie, so Fred walked over to the barman and asked if he had any scissors that he could borrow for a couple of minutes.

Fred, with the scissors, went back to the tie-wearing bloke, said to him, "That's a silly tie," then cut it off just under the knot, before returning the scissors to the barman.

Meanwhile, the bloke with half a tie was gathering his mates together, before waiting outside for Fred.

As we left the bar, it was a madhouse with fists and boots flying everywhere and Greek Dennis was charging at the locals waving a long pole from some nearby roadworks.

Tie man and his mates soon disappeared and we went back to the van to go home.

After we'd all climbed into the back of the van, it wouldn't start and we couldn't call the hire company because we were only supposed to be in the London area.

Then Big Alex pulls out his dad's AA card and we wait for the patrolman to show up.

When the patrolman arrived, he said, "I don't fix hired vans".

Putney walked him around to the back of the van, opened the doors and said, "You'd better tell them that then!" There were eight very cold blokes looking at him, so he said to Putney, "Open the bonnet".

The van got fixed and we went home, laughing all the way.

ANONYMOUS IN THE MIDLANDS

The "Usual suspects" were drinking in a pub near the ground of a Midlands team when we realised there was a large group of the opposition fans gathered outside. It was a lovely winter's day, cold but dry with a low sun and although they knew we were in there, they couldn't see us but we could see them, silhouetted against the brightness.

After a while, one of these fans decided to enter the pub to check us out. Unfortunately for him, we were all standing in the shadows, watching him come closer with every step.

When he was within arm's reach, someone grabbed him and knocked him spark out with a knuckle duster, before dragging him into a corner.

A few minutes later, another of their fans entered the pub looking for his mate and suffered the same fate. After the third one disappeared, they left us alone. We eventually drank up and left.

When Big Bob came to see us before he sadly died in 2014, he said that he always remembered that day as being one of the funniest things he'd ever seen.

PORTSMOUTH AWAY

On January 6th 1971, Arsenal defeated Yeovil away 3-0 in the FA Cup 3rd Round and then drew Portsmouth away.

A funny incident, occurred, not funny at the time though, when we were drinking in the "Fratton Arms" pub outside the stadium at Portsmouth, before the 4th Round FA Cup match on 23rd January.

The place was packed with Arsenal fans singing and chanting, when somebody shouted that they could smell gas apparently coming from a heater on the wall.

Whitty, who was a gas fitter at the time, took out his cigarette lighter, and, holding it above his head, made his way across the bar towards the heater.

By the time he actually held the flame against the heater, shouting, "No, it's not leaking", most of the pub customers had squeezed through the doors.

More laughter!

Arsenal drew 1-1, winning the replay 3-2.

MAN CITY AWAY

On February 17th, Arsenal played away at Man City in the FA Cup 5th Round.

Due to the bad weather, this game had been postponed on the original date and was eventually played on this wet Wednesday night.

After Charlie George had scored both goals in a 2-1 win for Arsenal, four of my mates were waylaid by a large group of unhappy City fans, while walking back to the railway station.

Due to the overwhelming numbers, they chose to leg it but after a while, they were running out of steam, so they decided to stop and face the now smaller number of City fans that had followed them.

As the City fans got within arm's length, one Arsenal fan pulled out a small plastic bottle of ammonia and sprayed their faces with it, stopping them dead in their tracks, much to the surprise and relief of my other three mates. They then carried on, laughing, to the railway station.

COLOGNE HOME

On March 9th, Arsenal beat Cologne 2-1, in the Fairs Cup 4th Round, 1st Leg match at Highbury.

With about ten minutes of the match remaining, Spook decided to leave, as he had to get up very early for work the next morning.

A couple of minutes after he left, a bloke came crashing backwards through the crowd, being punched repeatedly in the face by Spook.

Some of us separated them, asking Spook what had happened. He replied, "As I walked past this bloke, he said to his mate, 'the Germans are leaving early', Well, I ain't a fucking German, so I hit him!"

We were in hysterics! The poor bloke didn't see the funny side of it though!

Arsenal lost the 2nd Leg in Germany 1-0 and were knocked out on away goals.

HILLSBOROUGH FA CUP VS STOKE

Following the 1-0 home win in the 6th Round replay against Leicester on March 15th, after previously drawing 0-0 away, Arsenal had to play Stoke at Hillsborough in the FA Cup semi-final on March 27th.

I don't recall any trouble at this match, as the police appeared to have divided the City into two halves.

We never actually noticed any Stoke fans until we entered the stadium.

They were in the Leppings Lane End and one Stand; we had the Kop End and the other Stand.

Arsenal were 2-0 down at half time and looking well beaten, when, after fifteen minutes of the second half, Peter Storey scored and the Kop End became the North Bank; sheer bedlam!

We'd all been standing about halfway up the high terrace but when everyone had calmed down, Granty and myself found ourselves at the bottom behind the goal. Granty then started screaming, "My leg, my leg, I've broken my fucking leg". I called the St John's Ambulance people over and they loaded him onto a stretcher, then proceeded to carry him around the pitch perimeter. I jumped over the railings to go with him, as he'd got the keys to his car which we'd travelled up in.

I shouted to him that I needed the keys to get home if he was detained in hospital but he won't give me them. As we were arguing, an Arsenal fan threw a Union Jack flag towards us, so I laid it across Granty as he was lying on the stretcher.

He now looked like a wounded soldier being carried from the battlefield.

By this time, I was crying with laughter and he'd got the hump.

When we arrived at the first aid hut, the medics examined him and told him that he had cramp.

Now I was going nuts at him because we were missing the game.

Storey scored again with a last-minute penalty and Arsenal had forced a 2-2 draw.

Arsenal won the replay 2-0 at Villa Park and I was finally going to see them in an FA Cup final.

LEEDS AWAY

On Monday 26th April, Arsenal travelled to Leeds for what looked like the "League Title" decider, accompanied by thousands of Arsenal fans but without me, as I was working too far away to get to King's Cross station in time for the "Football Special" train.

Apparently, this train was constantly stopping on the way and the train driver blamed the Arsenal fans for pulling the emergency cord.

At a subsequent inquiry later, he admitted he'd been responsible for the delay, as he was a Leeds fan and didn't want all those Arsenal fans to get into the ground.

As the train finally got near to Leeds, it was close to kick-off, and as the game wasn't all-ticket, when the ground appeared on the other side of a field, Hoyboy did pull the emergency cord, as he knew they'd be struggling to get to the ground in time for the start of the match.

Vic Connell and a few of my other mates jumped out with him, and they started running across the field towards the stadium. Vic recalls that after a couple of minutes, he turned around and there was nobody left on the train except the driver.

All the Arsenal fans were now running across the field and luckily, many got in but many more didn't.

Putney and Laney had hitchhiked to Sheffield to collect Charlie MacCready's car, which had been left there since he got arrested at the FA Cup semi-final for assaulting a police officer.

They got the car but had been locked out when they arrived at Elland Road.

Arsenal were beaten 1-0 by another debatable late Leeds goal, similar to 1968 at Wembley.

LEAGUE CUP

On November 9th, Arsenal lost 2-0 at Highbury against Crystal Palace in a League Cup 4th Round Replay.

Well, you had to laugh, didn't you?

MY DREAMS BECOME REALITY

THAT WAS THE WEEK THAT WAS

On Saturday 1st May 1971, Whitty got married to Helen, with many of the "Usual Suspects" in attendance, but sadly not me, as I was watching Eddie Kelly come on as a substitute for Peter Storey, to score the goal that beat Stoke 1-0 at Highbury, thereby setting Arsenal up for the historic, final League game of the season at the Lane two days later. Sorry mate, it's all about priorities!

As our Motto says, "You can change your wife, but not your football team". To his credit, he's never done either.

THE LANE. MAY 3RD 1971

For some stupid reason, the game at the Lane wasn't all-ticket.

I got to the ground at 4.00 pm, along with Granty, George, Danny, Charlie and Fred, only to find that the queue for the turnstiles was already stretching out into the High Road. Some Arsenal fans had even arrived at 10.00 am after dropping their kids off at school.

The turnstiles weren't opened until about 6.00 pm, by which time there were estimated to be 100,000 people in the vicinity of the stadium, causing massive crowd surges and crushing when they finally went into operation.

I have never been in such a crush since and could hardly breathe.

I know how those Liverpool fans must have felt at Hillsborough in 1989.

About an hour later, we were still nowhere near the turnstiles and could see the situation was getting desperate. With hardly any police in attendance to control the crowd, it was chaos.

We shoved our way out of the crush and after getting our breath back, burst through the door of a second-hand furniture shop that backed onto the stadium.

We told the elderly owner that we weren't going to nick anything and ran through to the back yard.

Bollocks! There was a thirty-foot high wall topped with barbed wire facing us.

The crowds were now besieging the ground from all four sides, stopping their season ticket holders from reaching the turnstiles that led to their seats.

Even the Arsenal team coach was stuck in the High Road until the police miraculously appeared to guide it through the main gates.

Unlike the Arsenal team, or the 50,000 supporters who did get in, we conceded defeat and returned to the "Gunners" pub and listened to the commentary on the radio.

Only Ray Kennedy's title-winning goal was shown in the Television News as there were no live football matches, apart from the Cup finals and World Cup, available on TV in those days.

The only consolation was, we could celebrate with a beer while we waited for the others to return.

On their return, I found out that Hoyboy and Spook had climbed through a window and entered the terraces from an office.

Putney and some of the others had got in at different turnstiles to the ones where we were trying, and, along with hundreds of other Arsenal fans, they all got onto the pitch and into the Main Stand at the end, with one of them even getting Bertie Mee's tie.

My brother also got in and when the game finished, as everyone seemed to be on the pitch, he decided to climb onto the cinder pitch perimeter to get some fresh air.

Unbelievably, with hundreds of Arsenal fans running amok on the pitch behind him, a copper told my brother to get back on the terraces as he wasn't allowed to stand there.

For the rest of his days, my brother would always cry with laughter when telling that story.

After an eighteen-year wait, Arsenal were Champions again.

DOUBLE WINNERS

After a fourteen-year wait, I had seen one dream finally become "Reality".

WEMBLEY. MAY 8TH 1971

After a week of almost continuous celebrations, the "Usual Suspects", along with some of the younger generation of North Bank boys such as Vic Wright, Dodger, Teddy Taylor, Edwin Childs and Peter Landers, met up in the "Greyhound" pub at Wembley.

On the way to the stadium, there were a few skirmishes amongst the two sets of supporters, mainly when desperate Scouser's were trying to nick tickets from other fans and touts.

Obviously, we all had tickets for the same end of the ground but unlike nowadays, where it's all-seater, on entering the concourse we had different enclosure numbers.

So, a few of us would go in together, then one would gather all the tickets and return to the concourse to give them to the others until eventually, we were all in the same enclosure together.

As you can imagine, our enclosure must have had nearly double the number of the other ones.

Having said that, looking at the Liverpool End, I think they must have all been doubled up.

When the teams came out, the Liverpool fans started chanting, but for once, they were drowned out by the Arsenal fans chanting continuously, "We are the Champions, We are the Champions".

As I stood there singing the FA Cup Final hymn, "Abide With Me" with a tear in my eye, I remembered when I dreamt of seeing "The Arsenal" walk out at Wembley all those years ago when I was a kid. Granty was standing next to me crying and he still cries whenever he hears that song, especially at funerals.

After Charlie George hit the winner during extra time in the 2-1 victory, another dream had finally become a "Reality".

I can still remember the silence of the Liverpool fans when, to the tune of the Beatles song "Hey Jude", Arsenal fans continuously sang "Nah, nah, nah, nah, nah, nah, nah, Arsenal" until it was reverberating all around the stadium.

We all returned to the "Greyhound" pub, for a few beers afterwards where some Scouser threw a pint of beer over me as I was celebrating.

The tension rose as I wiped my eyes, with my mates all standing next to me ready to fight, awaiting my reaction, but I happily diffused the situation by chanting "We done the Double".

To their credit, the Liverpool fans just laughed and shook our hands.

My mate, Mick Callis, recalls working at his Saturday job on that day near Petticoat Lane aged eleven, when the proprietor said that, instead of wages, he could watch the match on her brand new colour television. No contest; he watched his first Arsenal FA Cup Final in glorious colour.

Thousands of Arsenal fans took to the streets of Islington the next day to celebrate when the team paraded the trophies on an open-top bus.

Not me; I was still in bed recovering, with a massive hangover.

The celebrations lasted long into the summer.

Unluckily for me, I had moved from Westminster the year before, so I couldn't gloat over my old Chelsea-supporting mates from my schooldays and the "Cages" in my council flats.

The only sour note was that Jon Sammels was forced out of Arsenal due to, in my opinion, unwarranted barracking from some Arsenal supporters.

The Team from the Lane won the League Cup after beating Aston Villa 2-0.

Ajax won the European Cup after beating Panathinaikos 2-0.

SOME SONGS FROM THOSE GLORY DAYS

There is a team called Arsenal, the greatest of them all.

We're the North Bank, we're the North Bank, we're the North Bank Highbury.

We shall not be moved.

High Ho, High Ho.

We'll drink, a drink, a drink, to Radford the King.

Geordie, Geordie Armstrong, Geordie Armstrong on the wing.

Bertie Mee said to Bill Shankly, have you heard of the North Bank Highbury?

Some talk of Ronnie Greenwood and some of Don Revie.

If it wasn't for the coppers, you'd be dead.

Hey, Hey, Hey, Marinello.

Storey, Storey, Hallelujah.

You are my Arsenal, my only Arsenal.

I'd walk a million miles for one of your goals, Jon Sammels.

Dedicated follower of Arsenal.

We went to Chelsea on a Boxing Day.

You say Hello, but I say Fuck Off.

Come on without, come on within, come outside and get your heads kicked in.

Charlie, Charlie, Charlie, Charlie, born is the King of Highbury.

Not forgetting Granty's all-time favourite: Oh, Come All Ye Faithful.

Also, some of the songs that came later such as;

One Nil to 'The Arsenal

She wore a Yellow Ribbon.

We will follow the Arsenal, over land and sea, and Leicester.

B'Jesus said Paddy.

And it's Arsenal, Arsenal FC, they're by far the greatest team, the world has ever seen.

Ooh to, Ooh to be, Ooh to be a Gooner.

Georgie Graham's magic, he wears a magic hat.

We love you Freddie.

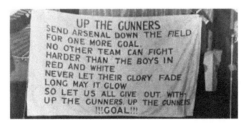

THE FIRST ARSENAL SONG

SEASON 1971-72

TROUBLE AND BALL AS ARSENAL FALL.

On August 14th, Arsenal opened their defence of the title with a 3-0 victory against Chelsea at Highbury.

When we entered the North Bank, we were surprised to see that all the Chelsea fans had been allocated the half of Clock End that was nearest the West Stand.

It was now apparent to us that separating the two sets of supporters had become standard police policy at most football grounds.

The "Usual suspects" plus a few others, decided to walk through the terraces under the West Stand as there were no seats there at that time, allowing us to enter the Clock End from that direction. However, there was one slight problem; a copper was manning the gate that separated the two terraces.

Tringy had a cunning plan, though. From his coat pocket, he produced a blue and white scarf that he'd taken off a Chelsea fan during a fight on a tube train earlier that day.

He put the scarf on and said to the copper, "We're Chelsea fans, mate, we were in the wrong end".

The cunning plan actually worked and we were in.

We also adopted the same tactics that were successfully used at Stamford Bridge a couple of seasons previously, whereby we went in single file amongst them and on a pre-arranged signal, all of us turned and hit the nearest Chelsea fan.

After the initial shock wore off, they regrouped and a mass brawl broke out.

As most of the police were stationed on the North Bank, the fighting got so intense, with people even spilling onto the pitch perimeter, that the police band had to put their instruments down and assist the few coppers that were trying to regain order.

The Arsenal Youth Team then paraded the three trophies, League, FA Cup and Youth Cup, from the previous season and we returned to an ecstatic North Bank.

WINTER 1971

In the following months, Arsenal won all four Legs of Rounds 1 & 2 in the European Cup against Stormgodset and Grasshoppers, to set up an exciting 3rd Round meeting with Ajax in March 1972.

However, in the League, up to Xmas, it was all a bit of an anti-climax after the previous season, with Sheffield United adding to our woes when they knocked Arsenal out of the League Cup in November.

ALAN BALL

Bertie Mee then made a statement of intent, when he signed the 1966 England World Cup Winner, Alan Ball from Everton, for a club-record fee of £220,000.

I was among thousands of other Arsenal fans who made the journey to Forest to see his debut in a 1-1 draw on 27th December. For many years afterwards, that day was their record attendance.

WITH BERTIE MEE – 1996

This was also the day that our mate, John Zaraski, was making his way to the stadium when a group of Forest fans confronted him, asking, "Are you a Cockney?" Now, at the time, John was a decent amateur boxer, but as he was on his own, he realised there were too many of them for him to take on.

So, mumbling and grunting, while waving his arms and hands about, in a poor imitation of sign language, he pretended to be deaf and dumb; this ruse worked, however, and they left him alone.

ELWOOD STREET

A few days after this match, I moved into Buster Wrench's house almost opposite the "Gunners" pub. Buster's parents had split up and he didn't want to leave the area. Putney had already moved in and they offered me the other bedroom.

As you might imagine, it became a madhouse, especially as Spook lived in the flats opposite and would spend more time with us than with his family, and Charlie MacCready only lived a few streets away as well.

SWINDON AWAY JANUARY 1972

Arsenal were drawn to play away at Swindon in the FA Cup 3rd Round, on January 15th.

Some of the "Usual Suspects" travelled in cars to the match, finding it hilarious when Big Alex couldn't get through the turnstiles and the stewards had to open the main exit gate to let him in. After seeing Arsenal win 2-0, we eventually ended up in a night club, where Eddie Harnetty and Peter "Schulzy" Shervill were attacked by some locals after going outside for a "puff".

By the time we arrived, they'd already seen the locals off but Harnetty had used Schultzy's portable radio as a weapon to hit a few of them with, leaving him only holding the handle, as the rest of the radio was in pieces on the ground.

Schultzy wasn't happy; we were in hysterics.

READING AWAY

It was now February 5th and Arsenal were away at Reading in the FA Cup 4th Round. We were in the pub opposite the Away supporters' turnstiles entrance. Inevitably, it was packed out and, after a few beers, I noticed Putney grabbing a soda syphon from the bar and guessing what was coming next, I ducked down under a table.

Putney spotted Hoyboy, who just made it out of the door before Putney could soak him.

A frustrated Putney then decided to spray everyone in the bar instead, causing chaos.

There was a mad scramble for the door and very soon the bar was almost as empty as the syphon, so I grabbed a hat stand and forced the last few out by using it like a lance.

The pub manager then came out from a room behind the bar, as the bar staff are all on the pavement as well, and he asked me, "What's going on?" I replied, "Two blokes have cleared the bar and now they've gone outside".

The manager then also went outside, so we bolted the pub door and started helping ourselves from the optics. Maybe we should have cleared the till as well!

Anyway, after a few minutes, there was a copper looking through the window and the manager was telling him, "There's a couple of blokes in there who've cleared the pub and locked me out".

I then repeated my often-used question to Putney, "What are we gonna fucking do now?"

I got the reply that instead of putting our backs to a wall, as we did at Stoke, we had to climb over the one in the backyard of the pub.

We then both ran around to the front of the pub and I pushed my way up to where the copper was still looking in the window. "What's happening, officer?" I asked. He replied, "A couple of lunatics have locked themselves inside". We walked across the road and entered the ground, laughing.

When Pat Rice scored his "Tasty Goal", the Arsenal fans erupted with joy as usual, with one of them banging me on the head with his flaying arms, which didn't help my splitting headache from all the free vodka.

So, I instinctively clumped him, not realising that there were three coppers standing behind me.

They dragged me through the crowd, down the terrace, over the railings and around the pitch, before taking me to Reading police station.

I was then stuck in a cell with a couple of other Arsenal fans and some "Hell's Angels", who'd come to the match to fight the Cockneys.

Everyone was ok, and we swapped a few stories. I never told them that I used to be a Mod though.

Suddenly, there was a lot of noise coming from the front of the police station; it turned out to be my mates, who'd come to get me out.

I was bailed to appear in Court on the Monday, where I got fined £20.00.

As I left the Court, I was getting into my latest car, a Triumph Vitesse convertible, when the copper who nicked me at the stadium came over and said, "You've got a nice suit on, a flash car and you've asked the judge for time to pay the fine? Typical Cockney bastard". I smiled and drove off.

I was at my mum's the day after the game, watching the highlights on the television with my brother, when I saw myself being dragged out of the crowd and marched away. My brother sat forward to get a better look, before saying, "He looks just like you". I just smiled again.

DERBY AWAY. FEBRUARY 1972

In the 5th Round, Arsenal were drawn away, yet again, this time at the Baseball Ground, home of the eventual League Champions, Derby County, on 26th February.

The "Usual Suspects" travelled to this match in a few cars and ended up in a pub near the ground, which had a large bay window with a door on either side of it.

After having a few beers, we noticed that there was a small stage located in front of the bay window, on which there was a piano and a drum kit that belonged to the resident band.

So, with Putney on the piano, myself on drums and Granty and Harnetty on air guitars, we started singing our version of "Stay With Me", the song by the Faces.

The pub was now packed and soon a large gang of Derby supporters entered through one of the doors, followed by a number of coppers.

They surged across the pub towards us, which resulted in the piano sliding off the stage and the drum kit getting knocked over.

Some of us were now throwing bottles and glasses at them, while others were exchanging punches and we ended up being forced out of the door on the other side of the bay window.

The pub suffered considerable damage but we were all ok and only Derby fans were arrested.

This incident was later described, in a book, as resembling a Wild West saloon bar fight, in the John Wayne cowboy movies.

As we entered the stadium, all we could hear were Arsenal fans singing;

Char-lie, Char-lie,
Char-lie, Char-lie,
Born is the King of
High-bury.

He lived up to that name as well, scoring both goals for Arsenal in a 2-2 draw.

After the game, we all drove to Nottingham for a night out. We ended up in a club there; I think it was called the "Penny Farthing".

It was a large three-storey building, with different types of music on each floor; Motown, reggae and rock.

We signed in using the Arsenal players' names as aliases, before dispersing through the building. By a strange coincidence, Scully and his mates were also in there, having driven over from Derby.

Most of us ended up on the rock music floor, when, after a couple of hours of drinking and dancing with the local women, Putney went off to the toilet where he found Harnetty, off his nut on speed, sitting in a sink, berating all the local blokes, telling them that they'could never take the piss out of Cockneys'.

Putney went over to him and said, "Well, Ed, one of them has taken the piss out of you, as they've turned the taps on". Harnetty was sitting in a sink full of water without noticing.

He recalls waking up in his car the next day on Ealing Common, which was rather unfortunate as he lived in Finchley at the time.

Because there were restrictions on using the floodlights and a Government-imposed three-day working week due to the miner's strike, the replay was on a Tuesday afternoon. Amazingly, 63,000 people turned up, only to see a 0-0 draw.

I went with "Bootsie" Miller on the train to Leicester, where Ray Kennedy scored the only goal of the game as Arsenal won the 2nd replay to finally defeat Derby.

AJAX. MARCH 1972

In the European Cup 3rd Round 1st Leg, Arsenal played the competition's eventual winners, Ajax, away in Amsterdam on March 8th.

My mate, Terry Jones, went to this game with "Wapping Steve" and remembers that in the city centre before the match, he saw a bunch of skinhead Arsenal fans dressed in long white butcher's coats, with red bowler hats on their heads, looking just like the thugs in the "Clockwork Orange" film, that was showing at the time.

He says that one of these skinheads stood in the middle of the road shouting, "Arsenal, Arsenal, we are here", not hearing the tingling bells of the tram, before it sent him flying onto the pavement. The skinhead wasn't seriously hurt, although Terry still reckons it was one of the funniest things he's ever seen.

Terry and his mate then got chucked out of the stadium halfway through the first half, for being drunk, and decided to go sightseeing on two bicycles they had found outside the ground. His mate then fell off his bike and ended up in hospital with concussion.

So, Terry watched the rest of the match on a television in a hospital ward. Arsenal lost 2-1.

AJAX. HIGHBURY 1972

Highbury was rocking for the 2nd Leg on March 22nd, as Arsenal only needed to win 1-0.

After a few minutes, Peter Marinello was clear on goal at the Clock End but squandered his chance.

Johan Cruyff inspired Ajax to a 1-0 win, when George Graham unluckily headed an own goal past Bob Wilson in front of the North Bank.

The legendary Johan Cruyff, actually asked Charlie George to swap shirts afterwards.

At the 1971 Player's Anniversary dinner in 2011, Spook spotted Marinello and asked me to take their photo together.

I noticed that Marinello appeared upset, after talking to another diner about something in his autobiography.

When he'd finished wiping his eyes with a napkin, I asked him, "Are you still upset about missing that sitter against Ajax at Highbury?"

Peter laughed, replying, "You bastards never let me forget that, do you?" Very nice fella is Peter.

STOKE AGAIN. APRIL 1972

Arsenal beat Orient 1-0 in the 6th Round, with an Alan Ball goal at Brisbane Road.

So, with the FA Cup still to play for, on April 15th, we all went off to Villa Park for the semi-final against Stoke City, in a van that Prenders had borrowed from where he worked.

Outside the stadium before the game, we watched as Danny punched a tout and grabbed a ticket, only for the tout to punch him back harder and take the ticket back.

More laughter.

Bob Wilson got injured during the 1-1 draw and Ray Kennedy came on as substitute with John Radford going in goal, as there were no substitute goalies in those days.

As we were going home on the M6 motorway, the engine of Prenders' company van seized up and he asks all of us sitting in the back, "What are we gonna fucking do now?"

"See you later," was the unanimous reply, as we all piled out and flagged down friendly Arsenal fans in their cars, looking for a lift back to London.

Arsenal won the replay 2-1 at Goodison Park.

Geoff Barnett replaced Bob Wilson in goal for the rest of the season.

Prenders' company replaced the engine in the van, although he had to get it towed back to London before he informed them that he'd broken down.

On March 11th 1972, Brendan Batson became the first black player to play for Arsenal, when he came on as a substitute for Charlie George in a 2-0 defeat at Newcastle.

On April 22nd 1972, he made his Highbury debut in a 2-1 victory against West Ham, when he came on as a substitute for Frank McLintock.

FA CUP FINAL 1971-72

I missed this final on May 5th, against our old mates, Leeds, as I'd gone to work in the bars in Spain for the summer with Charlie MacCready.

This meant that we had to sit in the sun outside a bar with a few beers, listening to the BBC match commentary on a radio.

Putney, Kenny Hall, Granty, Vic Connell and Sanger would later visit us for more crazy times.

Many of the "Usual suspects" never went to the final either, mainly because they were missing one token from the programmes.

Even Hoyboy never went, although he had a ticket, due to being in Bow Street Magistrates' Court for an offence unrelated to football.

When he got remanded in custody, Bonnie, who was in the public gallery, laughed and shouted to him, "Can I have your ticket?" Hoyboy gave the ticket to the court usher to give to Bonnie.

Bob Wilson never made it either. Allan Clarke made it 1-0 to Leeds and that's how it stayed.

Two days after the FA Cup final, Arsenal would draw 0-0 with Liverpool at Highbury, thereby giving Derby County the League title.

Arsenal finished 5th in the League behind Champions Derby.

Leeds won the FA Cup.

Stoke City won the League Cup after beating Chelsea 2-1 with ex-Arsenal hero, George Eastham, scoring the winner.

Ajax won the European Cup after beating Inter Milan 2-0.

SUMMERS IN SPAIN

The Original North Bank boys were now starting to split up, although we would all still see each other at most home games during the winter months.

Many had got married and become fathers, a few were in prison and Hoyboy and Scully were on the run after jumping bail in 1972.

Some of us who stayed single and out of prison went off to work in the bars and clubs in Spain for the next few summers, where I would meet the two Glaswegians, Alan and Tommo, plus Bob "Blanco" White, when, after he obtained jobs for Charlie MacCready and myself, we became the first three Englishmen to work for the "Pacha" chain of nightclubs.

The two Glaswegians, along with Charlie MacCready, are still living there to this day and Mullers and Kenny Hall later emigrated to Australia and both are now still living down under.

It was about this time that we started drinking in the "Greyhound" pub in Balls Pond Road on Friday nights and before Saturday home games. A few of us, namely Putney, Spook, Buster, Spikey, Ron Baker, Jeff Morris, Manny, Sanger, Prenderville and myself also played for the pub football team.

We were lucky that next to our house in Highbury, there was a blocked off alleyway that was long enough for two cars to park in. This allowed us to leave the "Greyhound" without worrying about getting parked near the stadium.

On one occasion, Granty was being even more annoying than usual, which resulted in him being tied to the roof rack on Whitty's van before we set off to the game. As we drove in convoy back to Highbury, there were people on the pavements pointing and laughing at a screaming Granty, who was bouncing about on the roof of the van. Health and Safety? I don't think so!

I also recall Spook dropping a fiver in the pub one Friday night, which was a night's drinking money at the time. He later heard that somebody knew who had picked it up. So, on the Sunday at lunchtime, he confronted this person, asking for the "name of the culprit".

The bloke laughed and said, "You'll have to knock me around the pub before I tell you", so Spook promptly knocked him all around the pub, with the fella eventually ending up in the, thankfully, unlit fireplace. The fiver was, miraculously, next to the till, waiting for Spook that evening.

SEASON 1972-73

STOKOE – STOKOE

To the delight of their supporters, Arsenal kicked off the League campaign by going undefeated in the first seven games.

This included a 5-2 victory against Wolves in the first home game at Highbury.

As I was still working in Spain with Blanco and Charlie, we could only read the English newspaper reports that were raving about the way Arsenal were playing, calling it "Total Football", in comparison to the "Ajax" style.

LEAGUE CUP

Arsenal progressed in the League Cup during this time, beating Everton, Rotherham and Sheffield United, only for Charlie and myself to return home from Spain just in time to see them lose 3-0 to Norwich City in the 5th Round at Highbury in November.

We sat in the West Stand that night and started the jinx, which meant that on the rare occasions when I've had to sit there over the years, I've never seen Arsenal win.

THE LANE

As we were due to play the Team from the Lane just before Xmas, some-body had the bright idea to pay a midweek visit to a pub in that area; I think it was the "British Queen".

A carload of us travelled over there and we were drinking in the bar, when a group of their fans came over and one of them asked, "Ain't you Arsenal fans?" Putney replied, "Yep, and I've come to blow your faces off", before pulling out a starting pistol and trying to stick the barrel up one of the bloke's nostrils. He didn't have time to realise that it wasn't a real gun.

Panic-stricken, they all legged it out the door and we drove back home to Highbury.

A few days later, Arsenal won the match 2-1.

FA CUP

After beating Leicester, Bradford and Carlisle, Arsenal had to play away at Chelsea.

The 2-2 draw at Stamford Bridge was the first time that a football match in England was relayed live to selected cinemas in the London area and I watched it at a cinema in Finsbury Park.

I remember Highbury being packed for the replay, which Arsenal won 2-1, to set up a semi-final against 2nd Division Sunderland at Hillsborough on April 7th.

SUNDERLAND SEMI-FINAL

Most of us went in a small convoy of cars and as Arsenal fans had been allocated the "Leppings Lane End", it was the pubs on the top of a hill in that area, overlooking the stadium, that they occupied.

After parking the cars, we were making our way to these pubs when we passed a pub that was, unbeknown to us, packed full of Sunderland supporters.

As some of us stood in the doorway, we could see and hear one of them playing a piano, while all the others were singing "Blaydon Races".

There happened to be one big fat Sunderland fan with long black curly hair and a black bushy beard, comparable to "Grizzly Adams", sitting next to the pianist.

When they had all finished singing, they turned and looked at us, and I pointed to the hairy bloke and said to the piano player, "Great playing, mate, but your monkey don't dance too good".

One of my lot dragged me out of the door, just as the Sunderland fans were coming towards us.

Another case of legging it, while laughing.

STOKOE, STOKOE

Getting into the stadium was a joke. Thousands of Arsenal fans were pouring down the hill from the pubs, about half an hour before kick-off as usual, and there was a mighty crush to get in.

This was sixteen years before all those Liverpool supporters died there and, apparently, the fans of the Team from the Lane suffered the same situation in their semi-final against Wolves in 1981.

Wasn't anybody in authority watching?

When we eventually got in, I thought we were at "Roker Park", Sunderland's ground at that time.

Arsenal had the small terrace behind one goal and the Stand above, but it seemed that Sunderland supporters had occupied the rest of the stadium.

Don't forget, they hadn't been to a semi-final for many years.

All I could hear was, Stoke-oh, Stoke-oh, Stoke-oh, repeated over and over again. I don't think I've heard noise like it at a football match before or since.

Those of us who were there that day always say they can shut their eyes and still hear it.

When Charlie George scored for Arsenal, they still made more noise than us. Unbelievable!

Charlie George and Jeff "Blockhead", Blockley, made a couple of mistakes and Arsenal were out of the FA Cup.

In the final, they beat our old mates, Leeds, 1-0 and I think only Sunderland fans were happier than us that day.

Bob Stokoe now has a well-deserved statue, outside their new "Stadium of Light".

We were all so fed up after this game that we decided to cancel our plans for another night out in Nottingham and drive straight back to London.

After a while, we decided to stop at a motorway service station in the Midlands for a break.

We were just getting out of our parked cars, admiring a row of beautiful shiny chromed motorbikes that were lined up opposite, when Fred "do things" Hill pulled in and clipped the front tyre of the first bike, causing most of them to fall over like a set of dominoes.

We calmly got back in our cars and sped off before the "Greasers" realise what had happened.

After Arsenal had just failed to win another Double, Bertie Mee decided to, in my opinion, prematurely, break up the team.

> Arsenal finished 2nd in the League behind Champions Liverpool.
>
> Sunderland won the FA Cup after beating Leeds 1-0.
>
> The Team from the Lane won the League Cup after beating Norwich City 1-0.
>
> Ajax won the European Cup after beating Juventus 1-0.

At the end of the month, some of us went back to work the bars and clubs in Spain and some carried on paying their mortgages and having kids.

Spook and Sanger came to visit Charlie and myself in Spain and we went up the coast to visit Hoyboy, Scully, Dave Pooley and Dotty in the coastal resort where they were staying.

Little did I realise at the time that I would not see Hoyboy again until the 1980 European Cup Winners Cup Final in Brussels.

I would not see Scully again for even longer, as they were both arrested in 1975.

SEASON 1973-74

END OF AN ERA

After Don Howe had left in 1971 to become manager of West Bromwich Albion and George Graham had signed for my mate, Tommy Docherty, at Man Utd in 1972, in the summer of 1973, Arsenal sold Frank McLintock to QPR, just six months before he would complete ten years' service to qualify for a Testimonial.

FRANK MCLINTOCK – ME – GEORGE GRAHAM

He inspired QPR to 2nd place in the League the following season, the highest position they've ever achieved.

Arsenal would eventually buy Terry "Henry" Mancini from QPR for roughly the same amount they received for Frank McLintock. No Comment!

Although Terry was a wholehearted player, his only memorable contribution to the history of Arsenal was scoring a goal against Wolves in 1975, which probably prevented our relegation.

On August 18th, Arsenal lost 3-1 against Wolves at Highbury in the FA Cup Third Place play-off.

I think somebody at the FA had the 'bright' idea of copying the World Cup's futile system.

MAN UTD AUGUST 1973

Because of an incident with some off-duty Spanish policemen, I had to return to London pretty sharpish.

This allowed me to go to the first game of the season on August 25th, Arsenal versus Man Utd at Highbury.

112

As Putney and Spook had got tickets in the East Stand Lower, I stood on the North Bank, in the centre, right at the back, just before the gangway that ran across from East to West, with Whitty, Rod Moore, Granty, Harnetty plus the younger blokes such as Dodger, Edwin, Teddy Taylor, Peter Landers and Vic Wright.

About half an hour before kick-off, United fans, who were massed in the Clock End, invaded the pitch and started running towards the North Bank.

Many of them were dressed like "Bay City Rollers", with wide trouser legs, tank tops and United scarves tied to their wrists.

The police and stewards formed a line across the pitch and stopped most of them from crossing the halfway line, before forcing them back onto the terraces at the Clock End, except for one big fella who was wearing a white t-shirt.

We stood there watching, as he evaded all the coppers and finally reached the bottom of the North Bank terraces. We were now straining our necks to watch, as he came up towards the middle, shoving first the kids, then the teenage fans, out of his way.

Finally, he was standing in front of our little group, where some of us were leaning on a crush barrier.

He didn't even appear to be sweating after running the length of the pitch and climbing all the way up the terraces, whereas I was feeling tired after watching him do it.

He then shouted at us, "Who's your leader?" We all looked at each other before I replied, "We ain't got one," so the United fan pointed at me before saying, "You'll do," and I said to him, "Come here then," and stepped back from the crush barrier. Meanwhile, I'm wondering, "What am I gonna fucking do now?"

To my eternal gratitude, the United fan, instead of walking around the barrier, put his head down and started to duck under it. Obviously, I immediately kicked him hard in the head and the fella tumbled back down the terrace, before disappearing beneath a flurry of boots and fists as I turned to the others and said, "What a mug!" We all burst out laughing in relief.

That's the last incident that I can recall of my last days standing in the centre of the North Bank because in the future, we would be either on the Avenell Road side or up in the East Stand, except for a very brief time in the Clock End, as the police were now getting more organised and the courts were also handing out prison sentences for football-related offences.

Off the field, a new generation of fans was now starting to emerge on the North Bank and Clock End, such as Jeffries, Jenkins, Binnsy, Mickey English, Mick Callis, Gerrish, Franco, Bill Isaac, Legsy, Kelly, Mick Doherty, Ollie Kearns, Del Hyland, Martin Cook, Gary Lawrence, the Burns brothers and the Finsbury Park boys, Russ and his mates from Hemel Hempstead, Frank with the boys from Boreham Wood and Tony Martindale with his mates from Holloway, Vidoss, Doyley and others, which later led to the nickname "Gooners" and the formation of "The Herd".

On the field, many of the '71 Double team were struggling to maintain the high standards they had set and, apparently, there was discontent due to Alan Ball earning twice as much as the others.

In August 1973, Ray Kennedy became Bill Shanklys' last signing when he was surprisingly sold to Liverpool, where he would have a fantastic career, winning many medals and 17 England caps.

The team were now very inconsistent, although there was one shining light; the emergence from the Youth team of Liam Brady, who would eventually become an Arsenal legend.

LEAGUE & FA CUPS 1973-74.

In the League Cup, Arsenal lost 1-0 at home to Tranmere Rovers, who were managed by Joe Baker's old sparring partner, Ron Yeats, in the 2nd Round.

In the FA Cup, after beating Norwich 1-0 at Carrow Road in the 3rd Round, Arsenal lost 2-0 at Villa Park in the replay, after a 1-1 draw at Highbury in the 4th Round.

In February 1974, Kenny Hall and I went on a six-day holiday to Moscow.

As Russia was still a Communist country in those days, very few foreign tourists visited there.

Now, if I don't mention that Putney had gone there a fortnight earlier, he won't forgive me.

The reason I am writing about this trip is that I managed to get myself thrown out of "Lenin's Tomb" in Red Square, much to the astonishment of the Muscovites queuing to get in and scaring the life out of Kenny Hall, who thought I was about to be sent off to the Gulags in Siberia.

I think that beats getting thrown out of Birmingham, Bristol Rovers, Bolton, Chelsea, Crystal Palace, Highbury, Leicester and Reading etc.

This only left me with two memorable highlights of the football season:

1 – In March, I got to see my favourite non-Arsenal player, Johan Cruyff, again at Geordie Armstrong's Testimonial against Barcelona, where he performed a perfect "Cruyff turn" that left Peter Storey staring into space.
2 – Man Utd got relegated. I bet my mate with the White T shirt was upset.

Arsenal finished 10th in the League, behind Champions Leeds.

Liverpool won the FA Cup after beating Newcastle 3-0.

> Wolves won the League Cup after beating Man City 2-1.

> Bayern Munich won the European Cup, beating Atletico Madrid 4-0 after a 1-1 draw.

Blanco, Charlie, Kenny Hall, Putney, Rod Moore and myself went back to working the bars and clubs in Spain.

Danny, Fred Hill and Granty would visit us for a holiday with their wives.

Franz Beckenbauer's West Germany won the World Cup, in a thrilling final against Johan Cruyff's Holland.

So, before coming home in October, Blanco and I went to see the two Johan's, Cruyff and Neeskens, guiding Barcelona to their first title in twelve years.

I remember we had seats about three rows from the front near the halfway line and as Cruyff came to take a throw-in, Blanco jumped up and shouted, "Go on, Johan". The look of surprise on Cruyff's face was a picture, as they didn't have many English-speaking football tourists in those days.

SEASON 1974-75

Many more changes were now occurring at Highbury after the previous poor season.

Bob Wilson had retired with Jimmy Rimmer coming in.

Brian Kidd was bought from Man Utd to replace Ray Kennedy.

Alex Cropley came from Hibernian to replace another ex-Hibs player, Peter Marinello.

Bobby Campbell replaced Steve Burtenshaw as coach.

In the League, Arsenal were even more inconsistent than the last season, relying on the youngsters Liam Brady, Graham Rix, Trevor Ross, Ritchie Powling, John Matthews and Brian Hornsby to make up the Squad.

Many of the home games had become so boring that Granty, Harnetty, Hutchings, Danny and myself often stayed on drinking in the "Green Hut" bar behind the North Bank, after going for a beer at half time. Alarmingly, the average Highbury attendance had dropped to 28,315.

LEAGUE & FA CUPS 1974-75

During September, Arsenal were knocked out of the League Cup in the 2nd Round by Leicester 2-1 at Filbert Street after a 1-1 draw at Highbury.

After beating York City, Coventry and eventually, after three games, Leicester, Arsenal would be beaten 2-0 by West Ham, in the FA Cup 6th Round at Highbury.

I can only remember the West Ham FA Cup game as everything else has, thankfully, faded from my memory.

The only other memorable incidents? – Chelsea got relegated.

My old mate, Tommy Docherty, brought Man Utd back up.

Arsenal finished 16th in the League behind Champions Derby County.

West Ham won the FA Cup after beating Fulham 2-0.

Aston Villa won the League Cup after beating Norwich 1-0.

Bayern Munich won the European Cup after beating Leeds 2-0.

SEASON 1975-76

Bertie Mee first sold Bob McNab to Wolves, then to the utter dismay of the North Bank, local hero Charlie George to Derby County.

Apparently, Charlie was so desperate to leave, he nearly joined The Team from the Lane.

Yet again, Bertie was relying on the young-sters coming through the ranks, such as Wilf Rostron, Frank Stapleton and David O'Leary.

However, in the League, the team was per-forming even worse than the previous two seasons and along with the kids who were try-ing to make an impression, only Jimmy Rimmer, Brian Kidd, Pat Rice, Alan Ball and the ever-reli-able George Armstrong were showing any sign of consistency.

WITH GEORGE [GEORDIE]
ARMSTRONG

In April, Terry Mancini scored his only goal against Wolves to give Arsenal a 2-1 win at Highbury, which probably prevented relegation.

I went to the 2-1 defeat at QPR for the penultimate game of the season; the rest is best forgotten.

LEAGUE & FA CUPS 1975-76

In the League Cup 2nd Round, Arsenal drew 2-2 away at Everton, before losing the replay 1-0.

Along with Buster and Putney, I went to Wolves away in the FA Cup 3rd Round to see Arsenal lose 3-0.

Arsenal finished 17th in the League behind Champions Liverpool.

Southampton won the FA Cup after beating Man Utd 1-0.

Man City won the League Cup after beating Newcastle 2-1.

Bayern Munich won the European Cup after beating St Etienne 1-0.

With the average home attendances down to 26,949, my first trophy-winning manager, Bertie Mee, would resign at the end of the season, heralding the End of an Era.

4

THE TERRY NEILL YEARS

GUNNERS GO GREEN

In the summer of 1976, Terry Neill was appointed manager of Arsenal, after leaving the Team from the Lane, to replace Bertie Mee.

He decided to build his team around the three kids from the Republic of Ireland, Liam Brady, Frank Stapleton and David O'Leary, along with the established Northern Irish Internationals, Pat Rice and Sammy Nelson.

He then made an even bigger statement of intent, when he paid a club-record fee of £330,000 to Newcastle for their top striker, Malcolm "Supermac" MacDonald.

WITH TERRY NEILL

He also bought the centre-back, Pat Howard from Newcastle, while promoting Graham Rix and David Price to the first-team squad and allowing Terry Mancini, Brian Kidd and the Double Winning players, Eddie Kelly, John Radford, Peter Storey and Geoff Barnett to move on.

Arsenal were now showing more consistency in the League, with Alan Ball, Liam Brady and Geordie Armstrong feeding Malcolm MacDonald's trusty left foot.

This was highlighted in Alan Ball's last game for Arsenal on December 4th 1976, almost exactly four years after I saw him make his Arsenal debut at Forest, in a 5-3 victory versus Newcastle at Highbury, when "Supermac" scored a hat trick against his old club.

Later the same month, Alan Hudson was signed from Stoke City, who needed the money after the roof of their main stand was blown off in a storm and they weren't insured. Therefore, we can only dream of what it would have been like to watch a midfield containing Ball, Hudson and Brady.

On the 18th December, I remember Tommy Docherty bringing his young, newly promoted Man Utd to Highbury.

He'd recently been in the papers for, allegedly, having an affair with Mary Brown, the wife of the United physio.

As he took his seat in the pitch-side dugout before the game, the North Bank started singing;

"Who's Up Mary Brown?
Who's Up Mary Brown,
Tommy, Tommy Docherty,
Tommy, Tommy Docherty".

This remains one of the funniest moments I've ever seen or heard in all my years at Highbury.

At the end of the season, he got sacked for this indiscretion. Tough! He should have signed my autograph book back in 1959.

It was about this time that a young couple used to stand on the North Bank, behind the goal.

They were nicknamed "Badger and Union Jack", because he wore a jacket covered in Arsenal badges and she waved the Union Jack flag whenever Arsenal scored.

They were the 70's version of "Old Flo and Soapy".

In the League Cup, Arsenal beat Carlisle, Blackpool and Chelsea before losing 2-1 at QPR.

I remember standing on the side of the North Bank, watching hundreds of Chelsea fans finally occupy it. I also remember going to the game at Loftus Road.

In the FA Cup, Arsenal beat Notts County and Coventry, before getting hammered 4-1 away at Middlesborough. Apparently, Arsenal fans also got hammered off the pitch as well, on that day.

Arsenal finished 8th in the League behind Champions Liverpool.

Man Utd won the FA Cup after beating Liverpool 2-1.

Aston Villa won the League Cup beating Everton 3-2 after 0-0 and 1-1 draws.

The Team from the Lane were RELEGATED!

Liverpool won the European Cup after beating Borussia Mönchengladbach 3-1.

In February 1977, I went to Wembley, to see Johan Cruyff for the last time, playing for Holland.

SEASON 1977-78

In the summer of 1977, Terry Neill made some more signings. Don Howe replaced Wilf Dixon as coach and Willie Young was bought from The Team from the Lane, who incredibly, also allowed one of the greatest ever goalkeepers, Pat Jennings, to leave on a free transfer and join Arsenal.

Later in the season, Alan Sunderland and Steve Walford were also signed with Jimmy Rimmer and sadly, Peter Simpson and Geordie Armstrong, two more of the '71 Double team, being released.

Geordie was probably the most popular Arsenal player of the '60s and '70s, if not of all time.

Now, there were reasons for Arsenal supporters to be optimistic; some quality experienced players were coming in, alongside some very talented youngsters, with Don Howe coaching them.

Arsenal were much improved in the League, with "Supermac" and Stapleton scoring regularly and Jennings as reliable as ever in goal, but they were even better in the two Cup competitions.

LEAGUE CUP

After beating Man Utd, Southampton, Hull and Man City, Arsenal lost 2-1 at Anfield to a Liverpool team that was in it's prime in England and Europe, before drawing 0-0 in the 2nd Leg at Highbury.

The 1st Leg at Anfield is remembered by many Arsenal fans for them not only being attacked on the way to the stadium but also being stripped of their jackets and coats, as the latest fashions didn't appear to have reached Merseyside at that time.

FA CUP

In the FA Cup 3rd Round, Arsenal beat Sheffield United at Bramall Lane 5-0.

This match was also memorable for when the young Arsenal fan, Denton, and his mates went into the Kop End before the game and were fighting with the United fans before being escorted out by the police and marched across the pitch towards the Arsenal fans behind the other goal.

On the way, Denton famously did a handstand in the centre circle, much to the amusement of the travelling Arsenal supporters.

On arriving back on the terraces, "Chieftain" did his party piece of throwing digestive biscuits in the air before catching them whole in his mouth.

Arsenal progressed to the semi-final after beating Wolves, Walsall and Wrexham, where they would meet the surprise team of the year, Orient, at Stamford Bridge.

The "Usual Suspects" all met up in a pub near the ground, before entering the Shed End, which brought back some happy memories of previous seasons. However, Putney and Spook were in the West Stand on account of their season tickets at Highbury.

Arsenal won 3-0 with one goal, coming from "Supermac", that I'm sure went in via two Orient defenders and a tree in Sloane Square, as it was so off-target. They all count though, don't they?

Young Johnny Collins recalls going to the 1978 FA Cup final against Ipswich from his dad's pub, the "Sebright Arms" near Hackney Road as a fourteen-year-old, with Mickey English and about forty of the "Wild Bunch". It was the first final he was allowed to go to without his dad, but after one of the fellas laid down in Hackney Road to stop a bus, he didn't think he'd even get to Liverpool Street station, never mind Wembley, as they all seemed to be nutters.

Although it was exciting, as this was Arsenal's first FA Cup final for six years, there appeared to be a feeling of complacency amongst the players and definitely among the Arsenal supporters.

Personally, I never understood this attitude, as Bobby Robson had built a very good team which had a strong defence with hard-working midfield players.

In one of the pre-match comments, the Ipswich captain, Mick Mills, apparently wrote, "This is just another trip to Wembley for Arsenal, but it's our first final and they'll get the shock of their lives". Never a truer word!

Roger Osborne scored the only goal as Ipswich won the FA Cup 1-0.

Arsenal finished 5th in the League behind Champions Forest.

Forest won the League Cup beating Liverpool 1-0 in a replay after a 0-0 draw.

Liverpool won the European Cup after beating Bruges 1-0.

SEASON 1978-79

The only signing in the summer was goalkeeper Paul Barron from Plymouth, although John Devine, Steve Gatting, Steve Brignall and Mark Heeley were promoted from the Youth team to join another free transfer from the Lane, Kevin Stead and the Australian trialist, John Kosmina.

Alan Hudson was allowed to leave and Brian Talbot would later join from Ipswich.

WITH LIAM (CHIPPY)
BRADY

During the previous few seasons, Liam Brady had been giving consistently above-average performances and, by the end of this season, he would have become an Arsenal legend.

Only Frank Stapleton would score more goals but none of his would match Liam Brady's 25-yard screamer in the 5-0 victory at the Lane.

Apart from the Lane, Arsenal also beat QPR 5-1 and Chelsea 5-2 at Highbury and away at Aston Villa 5-1, playing some fine attacking football but also hitting teams with rapid counter-attacks when necessary. The other players just couldn't quite match Liam Brady's consistent performances though.

Sammy Nelson got into trouble with the FA for dropping his shorts in front of the North Bank after scoring against Coventry in the 1-1 draw at Highbury.

LEAGUE CUP

Arsenal were beaten 3-1 away at Rotherham in the 2nd Round of the League Cup, where "Supermac" picked up a serious knee injury that would eventually end his career.

UEFA CUP

After beating Lokomotiv Leipzig in both Legs in the 1st Round, Arsenal lost away at Hajduk Split 2-1 in the 2nd Round, before winning the 2nd Leg 1-0 at Highbury.

In the 3rd Round, Arsenal lost 1-0 away to Red Star Belgrade in the 1st Leg, before only drawing the 2nd Leg 1-1 at Highbury, thereby going out on away goals.

FA CUP

In the 3rd Round of the FA Cup, Arsenal eventually overcame Sheffield Wednesday after five games, three of which were played at Leicester. This gave rise to the song;

> *"We will follow The Arsenal,*
> *Over land and sea,*
> *And Leicester".*

So, despite what some other fans think, this was always an original Arsenal fans' song.

Apparently, there were some memorable coach trips from the "Sebright" pub to these games.

DENTON

In the 4th Round, Arsenal beat Notts County at Highbury, to set up a 5th Round trip to Forest, the other team from Nottingham and the current League Champions, who were also on their way to winning the European Cup that season.

Apart from Frank Stapleton's late header to win the match for Arsenal, this game was memorable for the first meeting of us "Old Gunners" and "Denton" with his other "Young Gooner" mates.

As it was a midweek match, we travelled up the M1 in three cars in the pouring rain.

On arriving at the stadium, we discovered the place was a mud bath due to the weather and the building work that was being carried out for the new Main Stand.

Arsenal fans had been allocated a section near the halfway line and we took up a position near the back of the terrace giving us a decent view of the pitch, despite some young Arsenal fans hanging on a fence separating us all from nearby Forest supporters.

Mistakenly, we assumed that these kids would get down once the game had started.

When the teams emerged from the dressing rooms, these youngsters still hadn't budged and were completely blocking our view of nearly half of the pitch. They refused to get down, even after being asked politely, so an argument started and they were now getting pelted with coins by other Arsenal fans standing around us, who also couldn't see all of the pitch.

Suddenly, a big teenage fella, leading lots of other teenagers and some other kids, who, to us thirty-somethings looked even younger, started coming up the terraces towards us.

The big teenager, who was obviously their leader, asked, "Why are you arguing with the fans on the fence?" Someone explained that we couldn't see the pitch but this didn't seem to ease the tension between us. Yet again, I asked Putney, "What are we gonna fucking do now?" He replied, "If they come another two steps up the terrace, put the big fella down". They came forward and so the big fella went down. Now the cry went up from one of the other teenagers, "Denton's down, Denton's down!" and about six kids dragged our mate, Edwin Childs, down the terrace, giving him a few digs before we managed to pull him back. He later said that he felt like "Gulliver" in "Gulliver's Travels", surrounded by the little people of Lilliput. As the police were now moving in, we decided to move further along the enclosure. The Forest fans behind the goal in the "Trent End" were now chanting, "Forest Aggro, Forest Aggro", as the dopey idiots thought we were their supporters.

To be fair, although Denton was quite tall, he hadn't filled out like he did later, when he became a "Gooner" legend, before dying in a car crash in Moscow, while working as a minder.

I next saw him in Copenhagen before the ECW Cup final in 1994; he was a bit bigger then and, thankfully, never recognised us.

FA CUP SEMI-FINAL VS WOLVES

In the 6th Round, Arsenal beat Southampton 2-0 in a replay at Highbury, after drawing 1-1 away, to send us off to Villa Park to meet Wolves in the semi-final.

Most of us travelled up by car again for this match and saw Frank Stapleton and Alan Sunderland score the goals in a 2-0 victory that sent Arsenal to their 6th game at Wembley, including four FA Cup finals in ten years. To think that when I was a kid, I only dreamt of seeing one.

LAST GASP GUNNERS

On May 12th 1979, Arsenal would win the FA Cup 3-2, in what later became known as the 'Five- Minute Final', against Man Utd.

F.A CUP FINAL – 1979

We decided to walk down Wembley Way to the stadium, exchanging some friendly banter with United fans, until one idiot tried to nick my yellow and blue hat. I think he thought I was on my own, judging by the look of surprise when Putney and Spook stood either side of him.

Anyway, with only ten minutes of the game remaining and Arsenal cruising 2-0, thanks to Liam Brady creating goals for Brian Talbot and Frank Stapleton, Arsenal brought on Steve Walford as substitute for David Price. Now, I'm not saying it was the fault of Steve Walford but United suddenly came alive and scored two goals through Gordon McQueen, and, with only two minutes remaining, Sammy McIlroy. Panic now set in amongst the Arsenal fans, especially myself, as I was going on holiday the next day with my wife, Chris and daughter Natalie, and would miss any replay, as there were no penalty shoot-outs in those days.

Arsenal kicked off to restart the game, with the sound of the United fans' singing resounding around Wembley and some of the United play-ers still congratulating each other on the equaliser.

I think it's fair to say, United were now looking the stronger of the two teams and probably would have won the match in extra time. There's a mural on the wall of the concourse at the Emirates Stadium that repeats the words of the radio commentator at the match; "There's a minute left on the clock, Brady for Arsenal, to Rix, who hits it across the goal, Sunderland, it's there, I do not believe it, I swear I do not believe it". Nor could anybody in the stadium, or watching and listening around the rest of the world. After the game, we returned to the "Sebright" pub, before ending up in the "Venus" steak house on Bethnal Green Road. The perfect end to a perfect day.

Many years later, I met Steve Walford at an Arsenal Quiz night and when I told him, "that until he came on as a substitute in the "79 final, I had brown hair", he roared with laughter.

It was during one of these seasons in the late '70s that my QPR-supporting wife, Chris, and myself took 11-year-old Natalie to her one and only Arsenal game, when they played QPR at Loftus Road. This was memorable for Natalie shouting in panic, "You're going the wrong way!" at Paul Goddard, the QPR forward, when he kicked off for the 2nd half, as she never realised that the teams changed ends at half time.

Arsenal finished 7th in the League behind Champions Liverpool.

Forest won the League Cup after beating Southampton 3-2.

Forest won the European Cup after beating Malmo 1-0.

SEASON 1979-80

DOUBLE CUP DISASTER

Due to his recurring knee problem, Malcolm "Supermac" Macdonald, was forced to retire during the summer at the age of 29.

Despite this setback, many Arsenal supporters were now optimistic that, if two or three quality players were signed, the team would definitely be challenging for the title.

Neither Terry Neill, Don Howe or the Board of Directors felt the same way as only John Hollins was brought in and Brian McDermott, Paul

Vaessen, John Devine and one of the most underrated Arsenal players of all time, Paul Davis, were promoted from the Youth team.

The season started with Arsenal losing 3-1 to Liverpool, in the Charity Shield at Wembley.

During the season, Arsenal were pushing for the title but eventually finished eight points behind the Champions Liverpool, due to drawing sixteen games including not scoring in thirteen others.

Although Stapleton and Sunderland scored fourteen goals each, Arsenal should still have bought a top-class striker to replace "Supermac".

However, in the Cups, it was all systems go.

In the League Cup 2nd Round, Arsenal defeated Leeds 7-0, in front of an ecstatic crowd, including me, in a replay at Highbury, after a 1-1 draw at Elland Road.

Then Southampton and Brighton were dispatched at Highbury, before, in December, Arsenal lost a thrilling 5th Round replay at Swindon 4-3 after a 1-1 draw at home.

In the FA Cup, Arsenal overcame Cardiff, Brighton, Bolton and Watford to send the "Usual Suspects" off to a semi-final at Hillsborough again, and to see a 0-0 draw against Liverpool.

It would take four games to eventually reach Wembley for the 3rd successive FA Cup Final.

The first replay at Villa Park ended 1-1.

The second replay, also at Villa Park, also ended 1-1, after Kenny Dalglish scored for Liverpool in the last minute, to cancel out Alan Sunderland's first-minute goal for Arsenal.

I never made it to the third replay at Coventry where Brian Talbot scored the winner.

I did make it to the final though.

In the European Cup Winners Cup 1st Round 2nd Leg, my mate, Vic Wright, was one of the few Arsenal fans that I know who travelled to Turkey to see Arsenal draw 0-0 with Fenerbahce, after winning 2-0 at Highbury in the 1st Leg.

This game was the first of three occasions when Arsenal fans would face very hostile home supporters in Europe that season.

In the 2nd Round 1st Leg, Arsenal beat Magdeburg 2-1 at Highbury, before Vic and many other Arsenal fans were involved in serious crowd trouble at the 2nd Leg 2-2 draw in East Germany.

In the 3rd Round 1st Leg, Arsenal beat IFK Gothenburg 5-1 at Highbury, before drawing 0-0 in a relatively quiet 2nd Leg in Sweden.

My old mate, Putney, went to this match, so I'm surprised it was quiet, and outside the stadium, he saw Pat Rice, who gave him a match ticket and a pass to the Player's Lounge afterwards, where he sat chatting to his friends, Pat Rice and Sammy Nelson.

JUVENTUS HOME

Now Arsenal were up against the mighty Juventus, with legends Zoff, Gentile and Causio in their team, in the semi-finals.

I remember the date of the 1st Leg at Highbury, April 9th 1980, because that afternoon I had won the title with the team that I played for in a midweek league, in my last ever competitive game.

I mainly remember the Juventus match for when their striker, Roberto Bettega, attempted to take David O'Leary's leg back to Italy with him, after a horrific tackle in front of the East Stand.

The game ended 1-1 and so Arsenal had to go and get a win in Turin in the 2nd Leg.

JUVENTUS AWAY

Paul Vaessen came on as a substitute and scored the only goal of the game to send Arsenal into the ECW Cup Final, also creating history, by becoming the first team to beat Juventus in Turin in a European competition.

My, mate, Tony "Spandau" Moss, once told me that he'd never been so scared in his life as he was that night in Turin when the Juventus fans rioted after the match and were not taking any prisoners.

Vic Wright was, for the third and worst time in Europe that season, also caught up in the crowd trouble that night. Vic claims that at the end of the game, Arsenal supporters were kept in the stadium and all the lights were switched off; this meant that scores of Arsenal fans had to go down the stairs to the exits in complete darkness. Luckily, nobody fell over, as this could have resulted in many fatalities.

When they got outside the ground, hundreds of Juventus fans were waiting for them and he's convinced at least one had a pistol, which, thankfully, he never fired.

Apparently, some Torino fans turned up and showed many Arsenal fans a safe route to their coaches, whose windows had been smashed.

Imagine the carnage if Arsenal had played there in the late sixties.

FA CUP FINAL 1980

In the FA Cup Final, Arsenal played 2nd Division West Ham and surprisingly lost 1-0 to a rare Trevor Brooking header, in what became Liam Brady's last game for Arsenal in England.

Why do Arsenal always seem to have struggled against the underdogs in Cup Finals?

EUROPEAN CUP WINNERS CUP FINAL 1980

A few days after losing to West Ham, at least 25,000 Arsenal fans, despite a railway and Cross-Channel ferry strike on the same day, travelled to Brussels for the ECW Cup Final against a Valencia team managed by the legendary Alfredo Di Stefano.

Most of these fans went over to Belgium the day before, with the police in Ostend actually closing the city down later that night and refusing entry to any more Arsenal fans who were still arriving.

Amongst them was a coachload from the "White House" pub in Highbury Quadrant, carrying Hoyboy, Jonah, Dotty, Malcolm Froy and some others from Essex Road.

Also travelling the day before were Putney, Rod Moore, "Young Radford" Adrian and Dave Wright.

MICKEY ENGLISH & MATES – 1980

Rod remembers they decided to take the country back roads from Calais and, unsurprisingly, after a while, they got lost. In the middle of nowhere, they came to a crossroads which had no signposts, so Putney told Rod to ask someone the way to Brussels.

After a few minutes, the only people Rod saw were a large group of cyclists, so he got out of the car and stopped the first one to ask him for directions.

It turned out that this cyclist was the leader in a major race and by the time Rod let him go, he'd been overtaken by most of the others on their bikes. He wasn't happy!

On the morning of the match, I went over on a Hovercraft from Wapping Wall, on a special trip that was organised by the Arsenal Travel Club.

Arriving in Ostend, I'd arranged to be met by Prenders and Mullers, who'd arrived the day before.

We then drove to Brussels to meet Putney's carload in the "Grand Place".

When we got there, we could see that they'd obviously got there a lot earlier, as they were all very merry and had made acquaintance with a couple of women, who were the wives of British diplomats based in Brussels. These women were almost as drunk as my mates, due to trying to keep up with the pace of their drinking.

When the husbands turned up after finishing work, one of them said in a very posh voice, "Audrey, you're pissed", so we then proceeded to get the husbands drunk as well.

Rod, Putney, Adrian and Dave then decided to return to their hotel for a nap before the match. Luckily for them, their alarm clock went off an hour before kick-off and they had to get a taxi to the stadium in time to meet up with Prenders, Mullers and myself, after we'd gone straight there from the bar in the Grand Place.

Outside the stadium, there was a funfair with hundreds of Arsenal fans on the Big Wheel and other rides. There was also a large restaurant that was closed, except for one huge window, with the glass removed along one side. Beneath this window there were fridges full of bottles and cans of beer and lager. Apparently, the Arsenal supporters drank the place dry before the game.

I was quietly standing nearby having a beer, when I heard a familiar voice behind me say, "I knew you'd be here". It was my old mate Hoyboy who I hadn't seen since 1973 in Spain. He'd gone on the run in 1972 and during that time he obviously couldn't go to any Arsenal home games, although he did manage to get to some away games outside London and we've kept in touch ever since.

THE MATCH

The Heysel stadium resembled a building site, just like Anderlecht ten years previously.

As usual, Arsenal fans, like all British clubs in European finals before or since, filled at least two sides of the stadium, with only a few thousand Valencia supporters in attendance.

Nothing much happened in the 0-0 draw, until the penalty shootout, apart from David O'Leary having the Argentinian World Cup hero, Mario Kempes, in his pocket.

Everyone remembers Graham Rix missing his penalty, but seem to forget that Liam Brady and Mario Kempes missed theirs as well.

After the game, I jibbed on a ferry, as the Hovercraft wasn't leaving until later the next morning.

SOME HOYBOY FACTS

Over the years, I've read many books, articles and e-mails regarding Hoyboy, so here are the facts;

- Hoyboy is not dead, at the time of writing this in September 2020.
- Hoyboy will be 70 years old in 2020.
- Hoyboy is not 6' 5" tall.
- Hoyboy used to go to most Arsenal away games by train, as he was an expert at jibbing on.
- He mainly went to Arsenal games with two or three mates and met the rest of us at the stadium.
- He's never seen a match at the Emirates Stadium but attended the 2014, 2015 and 2017 Cup Finals.
- He never got in for the Champions League Final versus Barcelona in Paris, however, he did manage to snatch a ticket from a tout for his son. Old habits die hard!

- When they were Arsenal Youth team players, John Radford, Sammy Nelson, Tommy Baldwin and Gordon Neilson all lodged with Hoyboy's parents in Highbury.
- Hoyboy has never owned a haulage company.
- Hoyboy was once banned from standing on the North Bank in the late 1960s.
- Hoyboy doesn't live in London anymore.
- Hoyboy still has Charlie George's shirt from the 1970 Fairs Cup Final at Highbury.

Arsenal finished 4th in the League behind Champions Liverpool.

West Ham won the FA Cup after beating Arsenal 1-0.

Wolves won the League Cup after beating Forest 1-0.

Forest won the European Cup after beating Hamburg 1-0.

SEASON 1980-81

STRANGE COMINGS AND GOINGS

During the summer, the mercurial Liam Brady decided to leave Arsenal and move to Juventus, not just for more money but mainly to test himself in Italian football and also because Arsenal, unlike Liverpool and Man Utd, were not investing in top quality players.

Ironically, after he left, Terry Neill bought the prolific striker, Clive Allen, from QPR for £1million.

Losing their hero was a bitter pill for many Arsenal fans to swallow, as it would be another seven years before they would go to a Wembley Final again and they would never see another Liam Brady! Amazingly, Clive

Allen would be gone before the season started, along with Paul Barron, in a swap deal with Crystal Palace for Kenny Sansom, after only playing one friendly at Glasgow Rangers. Apparently, Don Howe thought Arsenal needed a left-back as a priority instead of a striker. Also, goalkeeper, George Wood, was signed from Everton as cover for Pat Jennings.

Before the end of the season, Peter Nicholas had also been signed from Crystal Palace with David Price going in the opposite direction. The Double Winner, Pat Rice, had left for Watford, only a year after lifting the FA Cup, and then the very last of the Double Winning squad, Sammy Nelson, played his ultimate game for Arsenal, coming on as a substitute against Aston Villa in the last game of the season in May 1981. Sammy would join Steve Gatting at Brighton.

On August 30th, I had to sit in the Lower East Stand and suffer the ultimate embarrassment of watching hundreds of fans, of the Team from the Lane, running amok on the North Bank during Arsenal's 2-0 win. This was the first time I can remember, ever seeing large numbers of them in there, although I do know that about this time, Arsenal fans had thrown a petrol bomb into the Shelf at the Lane, amazingly, without causing any injuries. So, I'm not sure which incident came first and therefore which set of fans were retaliating. In April, even Leeds fans tried their luck in the North Bank, but without success.

In September, the England goalkeeper, Peter Shilton, arrived with Forest for a League game, only a few days after crashing his car into a lamppost in the early hours of the morning with a married woman in the front seat, who he was, allegedly, having an affair with. As he was warming up before the game, the chant went up from the North Bank, "Does your missus know you're here?" Shilton just turned and smiled. The whole stadium was also laughing.

LEAGUE CUP

After needing a replay in the 2nd Round to beat Swansea 3-1 at Highbury, Arsenal then lost 3-1 away, to the "mighty" Stockport County in the 3rd Round. No, it wasn't our Youth team!

FA CUP

I went to Goodison Park with Putney, Spook and Dave Wright, for the 3rd Round match against Everton. Although we had a great view, we were so high up in the Main Stand that they had installed escalators to get the supporters up there.

Arsenal lost 2-0 with Kenny Sansom scoring an own goal. So, no Wembley this year then!

CHAMPIONS AT HIGHBURY

On May 2nd 1981, I was part of a packed Highbury crowd, including at least 16,000 of their own fans in the Clock End, jealously watching, as Aston Villa were crowned Champions of England despite Arsenal beating them 2-0 to finish in third position. There was some serious fighting between the two sets of supporters in the streets before the game and only a massive cordon of police and stewards on the halfway line prevented a full-scale punch up when the match finished.

It's just as well both sets of fans were happy that day, as who knows what might have happened?

Arsenal finished 3rd in the League behind Champions Aston Villa.

The Team from the Lane won the FA Cup, beating Man City 3-2 in a replay after a 1-1 draw.

Liverpool won the League Cup, beating West Ham 2-1 in a replay after a 1-1 draw.

Liverpool won the European Cup after beating Real Madrid 1-0.

SEASON 1981-82

When want-away striker, Frank Stapleton, was sold to Man Utd for £900,000, it left Arsenal with a huge problem in finding a top-class replacement.

After trying Brian McDermott, Paul Vaessen and Raphael Meade upfront, Terry Neill made the extraordinary decision to sign John Hawley from Hull City.

In further desperation, Terry Neill would also later offer a trial to Ray Hankin, who'd been playing in Canada with Vancouver Whitecaps.

Maybe he should have just kept Clive Allen in the first place?

Chris Whyte, Stewart Robson and David Cork were promoted from the Youth team and Paul Davis, who would eventually win every domestic honour with Arsenal, had now become a regular in the first team.

Willie Young would join Forest in December as the 1979 Cup-winning team started to break up.

In October 1981, Arsenal fans ran riot after a 2-1 defeat away at Ipswich, that left the club only five points off the bottom of the League.

In May, West Ham fans let off smoke bombs on the North Bank, before a mass brawl started with fans spilling onto the perimeter of the pitch.

FAIRS CUP

After beating Panathinaikos 3-0 in Greece and 1-0 at Highbury in the 1st Round, in the 2nd Round, Arsenal would lose 1-0 in Belgium against Winterslag and despite winning the 2nd Leg 2-1, were eliminated on the away goals rule again.

LEAGUE CUP

After beating Sheffield United and Norwich, Arsenal lost to Liverpool 3-0 in a replay at Anfield.

The two games with Liverpool were mainly memorable for three things. Firstly, when in the match at Highbury, the ex-Arsenal favourite, Ray Kennedy, had been sent off after clashing with Peter Nicholas. Secondly, in the replay at Anfield where Graeme Souness exacted revenge on Peter Nicholas, who had to be carried off with a severe leg injury, and thirdly, when Ray Hankin, whose only two appearances on trial for Arsenal were in these games, came on as a substitute at Highbury and when Pat Jennings launched a kick towards the Liverpool penalty area, Ray out-jumped everyone and headed the ball straight back into the Arsenal half.

Granty, myself and most of the crowd were in hysterics.

Needless to say, Ray's trial was soon ended.

FA CUP

Just when Arsenal fans were wondering if matters could get any worse, in the FA Cup 3rd Round, Arsenal were drawn away to the Team from the Lane and lost 1-0.

I recall coming out of the Paxton Road End, their fans were now standing on the Shelf side, and bumping into Bobby Bennett, another old North Bank boy.

He smiled and looking at their celebrating fans, said, "I wish I had a machine gun". I've not seen him again since that day, so maybe he got one!

That season, Arsenal had six scoreless draws and the manager had become Terry Nil – Neill.

The fans were getting restless at the lack of quality players being brought in to replace those sold.

This prompted rumours in the press that Arsenal were trying to buy Liam Brady back from Juventus, who'd just bought the French "Superstar" Michel Platini, and the even more ridiculous claim that Arsenal were in transfer talks with the even greater "Superstar", Diego Maradona.

Arsenal finished 5th in the League, behind Champions Liverpool.

The Team from the Lane won the FA Cup beating QPR in a replay 1-0 after a 1-1 draw.

Liverpool won the League Cup after beating the Team from the Lane 3-1.

Aston Villa won the European Cup after beating Bayern Munich 1-0.

SEASON 1982-83

Arsenal finally signed a top-quality striker, the England International, Tony Woodcock, to replace Frank Stapleton.

They also signed another striker, Lee Chapman, to replace John Hawley.

Danny O'Shea, John Kay and Colin Hill were promoted from the Youth team.

Arsenal introduced a new green and dark blue away kit to replace the traditional yellow and blue.

Spook, Putney, Bootsie and myself went to see Lee Chapman make his debut in a pre-season friendly at Chelsea; we weren't very impressed.

Many Arsenal fans who travelled to Stoke on the opening day of the new season, only to see Arsenal lose 2-1, weren't impressed either.

I was now alternating between sitting in the East Stand Lower and standing on the side of the North Bank with a few of the "Usual Suspects".

I remember watching Tony Woodcock score on his home debut in a 1-1 draw with Norwich and he would eventually finish the season with fourteen goals. This was quite impressive with such an inconsistent team.

LUTON AWAY

In November, Granty, Spook, Putney, Rod, Dave Wright and myself decided to go to the away League game at Luton.

We all sat in the section allocated to the Arsenal fans, mistakenly assuming that there would no Luton fans nearby. How wrong can you be?

Just before the two teams came out to warm up, we were all either standing up or sitting in our seats minding our own business, when a couple of Luton fans about six rows in front of us started loudly slagging off Arsenal and some of the fans that were sitting near us.

Granty and Spook then got involved in a slanging match with these idiots. After a few verbal insults had been swapped back and forth, one of the Luton fans decided to call Spook, "Joe 90", on account of his thick-rimmed glasses.

Spook asked Putney, "Who's Joe 90?" When he discovered it was a puppet in a kids programme on the television, Spook put the glasses in his pocket and he, Granty and Rod, without bothering to use the aisles, clambered straight over the six rows of seats, apologising to the people sitting in them as they went, and started clumping the two Luton blokes.

Putney, Dave and I were still sitting in our seats laughing at their antics.

A couple of coppers arrived on the scene and, after breaking up the fight, they escorted my mates back to their seats next to us.

At half time, these two Luton idiots came up the aisle and asked Spook to go downstairs to the concourse with them. Spook laughed and in his own words told them to go away, before reminding them that they'd already been rescued once by the police.

As I was sitting at the end of the row next to the aisle, the Luton blokes asked me to go downstairs with them instead. No problem, off I went, knowing I wouldn't be alone.

When we arrived on the concourse, one of the coppers from earlier was watching as they both confronted me. Suddenly, out of the corner of my eye, I saw a blur coming, and the mouthiest Luton fan disappeared from my view and ended up in a heap against the far wall with Spook ferociously punching him.

Now, there was police everywhere and after dragging Spook off the Luton bloke, incredibly, after only giving Spook and myself a lecture about retaliation, they escorted us back to our seats, where our mates were patiently waiting for us.

The two Luton idiots were led away by the police and ambulancemen.

Motto; "We might be getting older but we ain't mugs".

UEFA CUP

In September, Arsenal travelled to Russia for the 1st Round 1st Leg game against Moscow Spartak. After taking a two-goal lead, Arsenal collapsed and lost 3-2.

In the 2nd Leg at Highbury, I sat with my old mate, Blanco, in the East Stand Upper, and watched as Spartak demolished Arsenal 5-2, with one of the best performances I've ever witnessed from an away team at Highbury, inspired by Oleg Blokhin, possibly the greatest ever Russian player. They were so good they even got a standing ovation from the Arsenal supporters.

In an attempt to revive a disappointing start to the season, Vladimir Petrovic was signed in December 1982.

After watching his debut against Swansea at Highbury on New Year's Day and his subsequent performances, many fans, including myself, came to the conclusion that he was one of the most skilful players Arsenal have ever had. Strangely, he was allowed to leave at the end of the season.

LEAGUE [MILK] CUP

After beating Cardiff, Everton, Huddersfield and Sheffield Wednesday, Arsenal played Man Utd in the semi-finals. In the 1st Leg at Highbury, Arsenal old boy, Frank Stapleton, inspired United to a 4-2 victory, despite plenty of abuse from the North Bank. Although I had a match ticket and coach booked, I never bothered to make the trip to Old Trafford for the 2nd Leg, which Arsenal lost 2-1.

FA CUP

Arsenal would beat Bolton in the 3rd Round, then, after two replays, Leeds in the 4th Round before defeating Middlesbrough and Aston Villa at Highbury to reach another semi-final against Man Utd.

I went to this semi-final at Villa Park with some of the "Usual Suspects", where we sat in the Upper Tier of the Trinity Road Stand.

Tony Woodcock put a buoyant Arsenal ahead, but after Norman Whiteside of United took out the influential Stewart Robson with a nasty tackle to neutralise the midfield, United won 2-1.

Just when Arsenal supporters thought matters couldn't get any worse, on April 4th, Arsenal lost 5-0 away, to the Team from the Lane.

One glimmer of hope on the horizon? A young kid named Tony Adams had signed his first contract.

Arsenal finished 10th in the League behind Champions Liverpool.

Man Utd won the FA Cup, beating Brighton 4-0 in a replay after a 2-2 draw.

Liverpool won the League Cup after beating Man Utd 2-1.

Hamburg won the European Cup after beating Juventus 1-0.

SEASON 1983-84

During the summer, Arsenal beat off fierce competition from Liverpool and Man Utd to sign the young Celtic striker, Charlie Nicholas. Another striker? Blimey, they're like buses now; you wait ages for one and then three come along!

After Pat Jennings announced that he was retiring at the end of the season, they signed goalkeeper John Lukic from Leeds, before Ian Allison, a winger from Colchester, also arrived.

George Wood and Peter Nicholas were transferred.

Amid much hype, on August 27th, along with thousands of others, I watched Charlie make his Arsenal debut in a 2-1 victory against Luton at Highbury. In the next game away at Wolves, Charlie would score his first goal for the club in another 2-1 victory.

In typical Arsenal fashion at that time, they then proceeded to lose the next three games in September, including two home games against Man Utd and Liverpool, thereby setting the theme for the rest of an erratic season.

I went to the 2-0 away defeat at QPR, where Arsenal wore another new change kit, reverting to yellow and blue again after, thankfully, scrapping the unpopular green and blue one.

In the next away game, Tony Woodcock would score five goals in Arsenal's 6-2 win at Villa Park.

True to fashion, Arsenal would then lose five of their next six games, starting with a 2-1 home defeat to Sunderland, that set the alarm bells ringing in the Boardroom.

The Sunderland game would become memorable for many Arsenal fans, including myself, who witnessed a gangly young Tony Adams make his first-team debut. Tony obviously never impressed the Arsenal management, because a few weeks later, Terry Neill signed the equally gangly Tommy Caton from Man City, which now set the alarm bells ringing amongst the Arsenal fans.

LEAGUE [MILK] CUP

Arsenal beat Plymouth Argyle in the 2nd Round and then it was off to face the Team from the Lane in the 3rd Round.

Due to their inconsistent form, Arsenal actually went into this game as underdogs, but this didn't deter thousands of Arsenal fans from filling the Park Lane End as usual. I could only watch them from afar, as I had eventually managed to get a seat in the Paxton End, so, it was a night for keeping the gob shut and sitting on my hands.

Slight problem; Charlie Nicholas scored his first goal in thirteen games to send Arsenal on their way to a famous 2-1 victory and I was leaping about like a madman at the end of the game. Luckily, their supporters seemed too disgusted with their team to care about me.

Their goalkeeper, Ray Clemence, the ex-Liverpool player, allegedly stated that there was too much hate surrounding these Derby matches. Welcome to North London then, Ray.

This euphoria was short-lived, though, because on November 29th, Arsenal sensationally, lost 2-1 to Walsall in the 4th Round at Highbury.

Now the alarm bells wouldn't be silenced and after losing the next game at Highbury 1-0 against West Bromwich Albion, the Arsenal fans took to the streets demanding Terry Neill's sacking and singing "There's only one Liam Brady", in reference to the news that Liam wanted to leave Italy.

The fans got one of their wishes when Terry Neill was sacked, with Don Howe taking over on a temporary basis. However, they didn't get Liam Brady, as, disappointingly, he signed for West Ham.

Many years later, I would meet Terry Neill and he asked me what I thought about his eight years as Arsenal manager. I replied that he should have bought the two or three players necessary to challenge for the title after winning the FA Cup in 1979 and also that, although he bought quality players such as MacDonald, Jennings, Young, Talbot, Sunderland, Hudson, Sansom, Lukic, Woodcock and Charlie Nicholas, why did he persevere with Hawley, Hankin, Howard, Kosmina, Harvey, Chapman, Gatting, Devine, Matthews, Heeley and Meade?

He just smiled but I got the impression that the Arsenal Board might not have shared his ambitions.

FA CUP

Arsenal then lost their next two League games before Don Howe inspired them to a Xmas treat for their fans, a 4-2 Boxing Day victory at the Lane, with Charlie Nicholas getting two goals this time.

Everything was now set up for a good run in the FA Cup; problem was, nobody told Middlesbrough!

Arsenal lost 3-2 at Ayresome Park in the 3rd Round, with Arsenal supporters being ambushed afterwards in the streets on their way back to the railway station, and having their coaches bombarded with missiles from walkways above the main roads leading back to the motorway.

I wonder what would have happened if Arsenal had won?

Don Howe then signed the England International striker, Paul Mariner, from Ipswich and reinstated Brian Talbot in midfield. These changes inspired Arsenal to a seven-game unbeaten run before they, typically, lost the next three. I went to the game away at Forest, where Paul Mariner scored the only goal. After losing 4-0 at Old Trafford in March, Arsenal would then remain unbeaten for nine games until, with myself watching, losing the last game of the season 2-1 away at Watford.

This run included a thrilling 3-2 victory at Highbury against the Team from the Lane, with Charlie Nicholas scoring again, plus a 3-3 draw against a Liam Brady-inspired West Ham at Upton Park.

Arsenal finished 6th in the League behind Champions Liverpool.

Everton won the FA Cup after beating Watford 2-0.

Liverpool won the League Cup, beating Everton 1-0 in a replay at Maine Road after a 0-0 draw.

Liverpool won the European Cup, beating Roma on penalties after a 1-1 draw.

MOSCOW SPARTAK VS ARSENAL POSTER

5

THE DON HOWE YEARS

HOWE'S THAT?

In a newspaper poll of some Arsenal fans, Malcolm "Supermac" Macdonald and Laurie McMenemy were the popular choices to replace Terry Neill, with Don Howe way down the list in 10th place.

Obviously, they never read the papers in the Arsenal Boardroom as Don Howe was appointed as permanent manager.

Just like his old friend, Billy Wright, did, 20 years previously, he would promote many players from the Youth team. Alas, just like Billy Wright, another manager would later reap the benefits of this policy.

Niall Quinn, Michael Thomas, Martin Keown and Martin Hayes were now in the Youth team.

After signing another England International, Viv Anderson, the right-back from Forest would finally fill what had become a problem position since Pat Rice had left in 1981. Arsenal then began the season with a 1-1 draw against the newly promoted Chelsea, at Highbury. Remember, they were a yo-yo club before Roman Abramovich bought them.

I sat in the East Stand Lower near some of the estimated 15,000 Chelsea fans who seemed to have taken over the Clock End and much of the stadium, apart from the Upper tiers of the stands and the North Bank.

When I went for a beer at half time in the bar beneath the East Stand, I recognised some of my old adversaries from the Shed End. We just nodded and smiled at each other and left it at that.

Although Arsenal were now more exciting to watch, especially at Highbury where they beat Liverpool 3-1 and the reigning Champions Everton 1-0, the old inconsistency was still there, and so Don Howe bought another quality player, the midfielder, Steve Williams, from Southampton.

Despite his skills and all the other quality players around him, Arsenal could only finish 7th again.

LEAGUE [MILK] CUP

In the League Cup, Arsenal beat Bristol Rovers in the 2nd Round, before Putney, Spook and myself travelled to Oxford to see Arsenal lose 3-2 in the 3rd Round, where we witnessed Pat Jennings getting beaten by a long-range effort from one of the Oxford full-backs, in one of his last games before Pat would eventually retire at the end of the season, after eight years of great service.

FA CUP

In the 3rd Round, Arsenal drew 1-1 away at Hereford before winning the replay 7-2 at Highbury.

In the 4th Round, on a snowbound pitch, they lost 1-0 away at York City in front of many Arsenal supporters, including my younger mates, Vic Wright, Teddy Taylor, Dodger and Edwin Childs.

FAREWELL TO LIAM BRADY

On March 26th 1985, I went to Wembley to watch Liam Brady for one last time in competitive football, playing for the Republic of Ireland against England.

Liam Brady's last ever game at Highbury would be in the Pat Jennings Testimonial match in May.

My mate, Dodger, would swap a snowy York for a sunny holiday in Brazil, where he would visit the famous "Maracanã" stadium in Rio de Janeiro.

Granty and myself would visit our old mates, Charlie, Alan and Tommo, in an almost as sunny Spain and during our trip, we would watch Barcelona, managed by Terry Venables, beat Osasuna 2-0 at the Nou Camp.

Around this time, Constable Alex Morgan retired from singing before games and also at half time at Highbury.

Arsenal finished 7th behind Champions Everton.

Man Utd won the FA Cup after beating Everton 1-0.

Norwich won the League Cup after beating Sunderland 1-0.

Juventus won the European Cup after beating Liverpool 1-0.

OOPS! WRONG STAND

On January 19th 1985, Spook and I decided to take our revenge on Chelsea for taking over most of Highbury on the opening day of the season, when we staged a two-man invasion of their West Stand. Only joking!

After deciding to go to Stamford Bridge again, as we hadn't been there for a few seasons due to their yo-yo-ing between the divisions, I had bought the tickets from the Chelsea ticket office when passing their stadium one day.

We were approaching the West Stand before the game, when I saw a Chelsea fan that I knew from work. He told me to be careful in that stand saying, "It's full of nutters!" We just smiled at him, as we'd been to so many away grounds over the years and knew exactly what to expect.

As we got to the row where our seats were, I suddenly realised what my well-intentioned workmate meant. The stand was "full of nutters!"

We were surrounded by the most aggressive, cocky, loudmouthed football supporters I'd ever seen, and I've seen plenty, fuelled by the whisky and brandy from the bottles and hip flasks they were passing around.

Many of them weren't even teenagers; most were at least our age, if not older.

Guess where our two seats were? Yep, right in the middle of them all. So, it was time to front up and as we walked along the row, I could feel their gazes on us, as they tried to suss out the two strangers in their midst.

I'd only been sitting down for a few minutes when a very large, very drunk, bloke appeared in front of me, grabbing me by my coat lapels before claiming that I was in his seat.

I noticed Spook quickly jump up next to me, but before things escalated, as we've never been afraid to stick up for ourselves, although in this situation it would have been suicidal, I managed to show the bloke my ticket, proving that I was in the right seat.

When he realised that he should be in the seat in front of mine, he turned, grabbed the unfortunate occupant, who was another Chelsea fan, and dragged him out of the seat before telling him to "go away".

Lucky escape number one.

When the game started, they all settled down and I think some of them actually fell asleep due to all the booze they'd drunk.

The problem now was that every time Chelsea attacked or got a corner, we both had to stand up.

Then disaster; Arsenal scored and most of these "fans" were standing up looking for celebrating Arsenal supporters. Spook mumbled, "Good goal", and I just nodded in reply.

Sadly, there's always one naive idiot, as the Brummie comedian, Jasper Carrott, often tells in a similar funny story.

A middle-aged Arsenal fan stood up clapping and was immediately pummelled to the ground by the four blokes sitting near him.

The police and stewards were noticeable by their absence, and looking around me, I could sense that they thought Spook and myself were Arsenal fans.

I was only hoping none of the older ones would recognise us from our North Bank days.

Nonetheless, I still believed that we were going to get a good hiding at the end of the game.

So, when Chelsea equalised near the end of the game, and the whole stand were standing on their seats singing, Spook and myself decided to take advantage and leave the stadium.

Lucky escape Number two.

Although these were the heydays of Chelsea's notorious, aptly named "Headhunters", they never got ours!

SEASON 1985-86

My mates, including the publican, John "JC" Collins, and myself were now drinking in the "White House" pub before home games, as it usually wasn't too packed and there was ample parking space nearby.

LEAGUE

After Pat Jennings retired, John "give us a dance" Lukic became the regular first-team goalkeeper.

Rhys Wilmot became his understudy and Martin Keown, David "Rocky" Rocastle, Martin Hayes, Niall Quinn and the infamous Gus Caesar, made their Arsenal debuts.

David O'Leary and Tony Adams had formed a solid central defensive partnership. Unfortunately, the goals had dried up at the other end, with only forty-nine scored, including fourteen games without Arsenal scoring.

The form was still as erratic as recent seasons and culminated in a 6-1 defeat at Everton in November. In December, Arsenal went on a six-match unbeaten run, including victories against Liverpool at Highbury and Man Utd at Old Trafford, with Charlie Nicholas scoring in both matches.

On New Year's Day at Highbury, Graham Roberts, the captain of the Team from the Lane, ensured that Charlie wouldn't score against them again by smashing him into the advertising hoarding in front of the Schoolboy's enclosure below the East Stand, during a 0-0 draw.

I went to the return fixture in March 1986, where Graham Roberts scored the goal in their 1-0 win.

It's a pity Charlie didn't kick him up in the air earlier in revenge.

LEAGUE "MILK" CUP

Arsenal drew 0-0 at Hereford in the 2nd Round before defeating them 2-1 at Highbury.

In the 3rd Round, Arsenal beat Man City away 2-1 and then in the 4th Round they beat Southampton away 3-1, after a 0-0 draw at Highbury.

In the 5th Round, Putney, Granty, Spook and myself went to Villa Park, where, due to the horrendous traffic, mainly caused by the cars and coaches of the hundreds of Arsenal fans who'd travelled up the M1 to the game, we were forced to park in a housing estate before clambering down a muddy hill opposite the Main Stand.

After managing to get into the stadium just in time to see the two teams run out, we saw Arsenal get a decent 1-1 draw thanks to a Charlie Nicholas goal, which prompted some Arsenal fans to invade the pitch in celebration.

Despite another goal from Charlie and plenty of vociferous support from their supporters, Arsenal managed to lose the replay against Aston Villa 2-1 at Highbury.

A few weeks later, Arsenal would beat Aston Villa 4-1 away in the League. Typical of those times.

FA CUP

In the FA Cup, Arsenal beat Grimsby away 4-3 in the 3rd Round and Rotherham 5-1 in the 4th Round at Highbury before drawing 2-2 at Luton in the 5th Round. After the replay ended in another 0-0 draw, Luton won the toss to stage the 2nd replay and then won the match 3-0. I think Don Howe knew his time as manager was coming to an end, as most Arsenal fans had already realised.

ENGLAND VS SCOTLAND

As the then Prime Minister, Margaret Thatcher, had decided to ban Scottish football fans from travelling to London, more tickets became available for the English supporters for this game and so, Granty, Putney and myself went to watch the England vs Scotland International at Wembley.

As Granty is of Scottish descent, he turned up wearing a traditional Tam O'Shanter tartan bonnet.

In retaliation, Putney disappeared for a few minutes, before returning with two white caps emblazoned with the England badge.

We then sat with our shiny new caps, on either side of a fuming Granty, watching England win 2-1.

Arsenal finished 7th in the League behind Champions Liverpool.

Liverpool won the FA Cup after beating Everton 3-1.

Oxford United won the League Cup after beating QPR 3-0. I went to this final with my QPR-supporting wife, Chris. She wasn't very happy afterwards.

Steaua Bucharest won the European Cup beating Barcelona on penalties after a 0-0 draw.

6

THE GEORGE GRAHAM YEARS

GEORGE STROLLS IN

George "Stroller" Graham was appointed Arsenal manager, bringing his assistant at Millwall, Theo Foley, with him, supposedly after Alex Ferguson and Terry Venables had turned down the job.

One of the first decisions George Graham made, after noting that there was green and cream paintwork everywhere, was to ask for volunteers to paint the Arsenal stadium red and white.

George is quoted as saying at the time, "We're The Arsenal, not Celtic". Very true!

Talking of Celtic, the Glasgow giants were invited to provide the opposition in David O'Leary's Testimonial match before the season started.

Thousands of Celtic fans filled the Clock End and some of the East Stand Lower seats.

I know that for a fact, as I sat in the East Stand Lower with sixteen of them that I had collected tickets for, who drank with Granty at his local Working Men's club.

When the police entered the Clock End after some Celtic fans had burnt the "Union Jack" flag, some of the sixteen threatened to play up as well.

Now to me, they were taking a liberty; imagine if the fans on the North Bank had burnt a "Tricolour" Irish flag? So, I jumped up and said, "If you're going to play up, then start with me!" Some other Arsenal fans nearby backed me up and to their credit, Granty's mates apologised and sat down.

Sport – Politics – Religion; they don't mix in my opinion.

Next, George Graham decided to release Tony Woodcock, Paul Mariner, Tommy Caton, Colin Hill, Chris White and bizarrely, the promising youngster, Martin Keown.

In came Perry "Shut the Gates" Groves from Colchester. We gave him that nickname because he was so fast that he looked like he couldn't stop himself, before ending up either at Finsbury Park or Highbury Corner stations.

Paul Merson and Michael Thomas were promoted from the Youth team to join Martin Hayes and Niall Quinn, who were scoring regularly, since making their debuts the previous season.

LEAGUE

In September, we were all drinking in the "White House" pub before the 0-0 drawn home game against the Team from the Lane, when some of their fans, wearing replica shirts, entered through the door where I happened to be standing talking to John Landers, who's quite a big fella.

JC looked up from his spot next to the bar and shouted, "Hello, lads, you're welcome to have a drink, providing you can get past those two on the doors first". They took one look at big John and backed out of the door, with everyone in the pub, especially JC, laughing.

I remember not laughing in November, though, when we saw Arsenal win 2-0 away against Charlton in the pouring rain, where we had to stand on an uncovered terrace and the rain formed puddles in my coat pockets

Arsenal had got off to a flying start under George Graham and were top of the table at Xmas. Then, after winning 2-1 at the Lane in January, and just as Arsenal supporters are dreaming of titles, they went ten games without a League win.

Although they did recover to win most of their last eight games and eventually finish fourth, this winless run included a 1-0 defeat at Chelsea in April, where JC got a few of us tickets in their more civilised East Stand this time, behind the injured Chelsea players, Kerry Dixon and David Speedie.

FA CUP

In the 3rd Round, many of the "Usual Suspects" went to the game at a freezing cold Reading, where Arsenal won 3-1. Then Plymouth Argyle were demolished 6-1 in the 4th Round, and Barnsley 2-0 in the 5th Round, with both of these games at home.

In a highly controversial 6th Round match at Highbury, with only a few minutes of the match remaining and losing 2-1, Arsenal were push-ing for the equaliser, when the linesman below us, in front of the East Stand, flagged for an Arsenal penalty. For some unknown reason, the referee never saw the flag and waved play on, which allowed Watford to breakaway and score a third goal to seal their victory.

LEAGUE [LITTLEWOODS] CUP 1986-87

In the League Cup, Arsenal would draw 1-1 at Huddersfield, then win at Highbury against Huddersfield 2-0, Man City 3-1, Charlton 2-0, and

Forest 2-0, setting up a semi-final against the Team from the Lane, who were having a decent season, thanks to ex-Arsenal striker Clive Allen.

The 1st Leg was at Highbury and as tickets were hard to come by, I could only get two tickets from my workmate, Gerry Welling, who had three season tickets with his kids in my jinxed West Stand, but couldn't attend the game. He gave his other ticket to another workmate, Joe the Pole, who supported the enemy.

Just before kick-off, Spook and I were sitting in the West Stand Upper tier when, to my horror and his credit, Joe turned up wearing one of their scarves. You can imagine the abuse he got, even from the normally mild-mannered Arsenal fans in those seats, as he took his seat next to me.

Joe then took great delight in pointing out the large Israeli flag that was being displayed by their fans in the Clock End. I then drew his attention to the Swastika flag that some Arsenal fans had hung over the balcony of the East Stand opposite. As I've said Sport – Politics – Religion; they don't mix. True to form, I was in the West Stand and Arsenal lost and Joe couldn't stop giggling.

SEMI-FINAL 2ND LEG

On Sunday March 1st, along with thousands of other Arsenal fans, the "Usual Suspects" and myself went off to the Lane to see if Arsenal could get the two goals they needed. Disaster! At half time, Arsenal were 1-0 down, and needed two goals just to force a replay, never mind get to the final.

Then, to their perpetual embarrassment, a message was relayed over the tannoy system; "Tickets for the League Cup final will be on sale to season ticket holders on Monday". Cocky bastards!!

Apparently, George Graham used this message to motivate the despondent Arsenal players in the dressing room before they came out for the 2nd half.

Well, the Arsenal fans standing in the Park Lane End, and all around me in our section of the East Stand, certainly didn't need any motivating.

We spent most of the 2nd half standing on our seats and as mine was next to the corrugated iron wall, I was continuously banging on it whilst chanting "No Surrender". I did this so hard that the fans around me were eventually covered in the rust that was falling from the girders due to the vibration. Mind you, when the second Arsenal goal went in, nobody cared!

THE REPLAY

After losing the toss-up for the venue, Arsenal and their hordes of fans had to return to the Lane again on Wednesday March 4th for the decider. This was a game that would become one of the greatest ever nights for those that were there, and also the night when David "Rocky" Rocastle became an Arsenal legend.

DAVID [ROCKY] ROCASTLE
WITH MY NEPHEW ANDREW

With only about five minutes remaining and Arsenal losing 1-0, George Graham sent on Ian Allinson as a substitute. Within minutes, Ian scored his most important goal for Arsenal to equalise and then, incredibly, with only seconds to go and Arsenal fans still celebrating that goal, "Rocky", hit the winner in front of the delirious Arsenal fans crammed into the Park Lane End and all the rest of us standing on our seats, until the plastic gave way at that end of the East Stand.

This prompted "JC's" immortal phrase, "Grown men standing on seats singing, you twerps!"

One Nil Down, Two One Up,
Arsenal Knocked *****Out The Cup.

This song reverberated around the Lane, and the rest of the country, as finally, George Graham had given the Arsenal fans their pride back. I bet Joe the Pole wasn't giggling now!

161

LEAGUE [LITTLEWOODS] CUP FINAL VS LIVERPOOL, 1987

The "Usual Suspects" met up at Archie's "Green Man" pub in Hoxton, to board the coach that we'd hired to take us to Wembley. Arsenal were facing a Liverpool team with their talisman striker, Ian Rush, proudly stating that they'd never lost a game he'd scored in. What happened? Rush scored, but Charlie Nicholas then equalised, and after substitute Perry Groves was brought on to use his pace against the tiring Liverpool defenders, Charlie scored again from a cross by Perry. On the happy coach ride back to Archie's, 'One Nil Down, Two One Up', was being sung by all the twerps.

Arsenal finished 4th in the League behind Champions Everton.

Coventry won the FA Cup after beating the Team from the Lane 3-2.

Porto won the European Cup after beating Bayern Munich 2-1.

SEASON 1987-88

In the summer of 1987, fifteen of the "Usual Suspects", including myself and some younger mates, invested in season tickets in the East Stand Upper. We sat in two rows, John Landers with his daughter Joanne, Peter Landers, Teddy Taylor, JC with his son, Young Johnny Collins, Tony Gallagher and Lee the Gooner from Bethnal Green behind, George Hammond and his son Rikki, Eddie Harnetty, Granty, myself, Putney and Spook. Immediately to

THE 4 WHEELS – TONY ADELIZZI (WITH MOUSTACHE) DIED IN 2010

our right were four fellas who were about ten years younger than us, Clive, Roger, Craig and Tony, who we nicknamed the "four wheels", because at some time during the game, they would always sing their song;

"Four Wheels On My Wagon,
I'm Just Rolling Along.
Those Cherokees Are After Me,
Arrows Fly, In the Sky,
But I'm Singing A Happy Song".

Sadly, we would all sing this song at Tony Adelizzi's funeral in 2010.

Alan Smith, Nigel Winterburn and Kevin Richardson were brought in, while Viv Anderson, Ian Allinson, Rhys Wilmot and Stewart Robson were allowed to leave. When the season began, Arsenal didn't win any of their first three games and Charlie Nicholas was dropped, and, subsequently, never played for Arsenal again. Paul Merson made his debut coming on as substitute in the 6-0 win vs Portsmouth at Highbury and Arsenal then went twelve games unbeaten, including winning 2-1 at the Lane as usual, in a match that was memorable for being one of the funniest I've ever attended. The first "Gooner" magazine had just been published and conveniently, David Pleat, the boss of the Team from the Lane, made the front cover of this magazine and many daily newspapers after being arrested and bailed for, allegedly, kerb-crawling.

Throughout the pre-match players' warm-up, Arsenal fans in the Park Lane End were continuously chanting, "Sex Case, Sex Case, Hang Him, Hang Him, Hang Him". Then during the game, Steve Williams went to take a corner where the Park Lane End joins the Main West Stand, which contains all their hierarchy and money men. Before Steve could take the corner, an Arsenal fan threw a white blow-up sex doll onto the pitch directly in front of him. What made a hilarious incident even funnier was that the doll had a red and white bobble hat on its head. Then with all the Arsenal fans almost helpless with laughter, the doll blew towards the Main Stand and the breeze kept opening its legs. Now, to rub salt into the wound, just after a steward removed this doll, another Arsenal fan threw a black sex doll on the pitch, also wearing a red and white bobble hat. The Arsenal fans were now laughing hysterically and even Steve Williams and some of the players were also smiling. To quote a well-known journalist fan of theirs, "You couldn't make it up"!

In January, I remember seeing Arsenal lose 2-0 at Liverpool with Nigel Winterburn playing at right-back. As he was predominately left-footed, Nigel looked so uncomfortable that it came as no surprise when George Graham signed Lee Dixon from Stoke a few weeks later to fill that position.

We decided to hire a coach for this trip to Liverpool and met up at the "White House" pub. After loading up with beer and bagels, we stopped off on the M1 to pick up Harnetty and Granty.

On arriving at Anfield, the coach was directed to park up near Stanley Park, close to the stadium.

We noticed a large pub nearby named "The Arkle", and all twenty-five of us made our way inside.

Although the pub was packed, Harnetty created a path to the bar by shouting, "Make way for the Cockneys, we want a drink and we've got loads of money", whilst waving a bunch of twenty-pound notes above his head, in pure "Harry Enfield" style. As the Scousers parted to let him through, my workmate, Gerry Welling, who'd never met my mates before, asked me if Harnetty knew all the blokes in the bar. How naive can you get? After getting the beers, Harnetty then waved two match tickets in the air and declared that they were 'a fiver each for Arsenal fans or a tenner each for Scousers'. Unbelievably, two Scousers paid him a tenner each. We were enjoying our day in the "Arkle" when Harnetty announces that he wanted to "play up".

Some of the Liverpool supporters then stated, "If you want to play up, pal, we're ready". I think they'd had enough of "Flash Cockney Bastards" for one day and as the police were already waiting outside, we decided to leave and go to our seats in the Anfield Road End.

Like I said previously, with Nigel Winterburn at right-back, the team was looking unbalanced; sitting next to me in the seats, Harnetty was looking a bit unbalanced as well. At half time, he went off to the toilet and about ten minutes later I felt a tap on my shoulder from one of those long truncheons that the Liverpool Police Inspector's carry. The copper said, "Follow me," before he led me under the stand and then back up the stairs to where the Liverpool fans were sitting. Harnetty was lying on the floor with four coppers standing over him. The Inspector then said to me, "Claim him or he's ours". As I pulled him to his feet, Harnetty asked, "Shall we do the coppers?" With about six pairs of coppers' eyes staring at me, I replied, "Not today, mate". Both of us were then escorted back to our seats, where I spent the rest of the game with my arm around Harnetty's shoulders to stop him running off again, as there were now coppers stationed behind us.

Apparently, Harnetty said he took a wrong turn when he left the toilets. I think he also took something else that day.

Nearer the end of the season, Brian Marwood was signed from Sheffield Wednesday, and he helped the team to only lose once more in the remaining fourteen League games of the season.

Amazingly, Gus Caesar made twenty-two appearances for Arsenal.

Youth team striker, Kevin Campbell made his debut at Everton on the last day of the season.

FA CUP

On January 9th 1988, in the 3rd Round, Arsenal beat Millwall 2-0 at Highbury in the first-ever competitive match between the two clubs.

Everyone knows about the reputation of Millwall fans, so it was no surprise to hear they were threatening to take the famous Arsenal clock back home with them.

Now I know that they're capable of doing many things but I don't think they'd ever seen 50,000 home fans in a stadium before. Anyway, despite a mass brawl in Highbury Fields and a few scuffles in the stadium, we kept the clock.

In the 4th Round, Arsenal won 2-1 away at Brighton before beating Man Utd 2-1 at Highbury in the 5th Round, memorable for Brian McClair missing a last-minute penalty in front of the North Bank.

In the 6th Round, Arsenal lost 2-1 at home to Forest.

LEAGUE [LITTLEWOODS] CUP

In September 1987, along with George Hammond and his son Rikki, I went to Doncaster to see Arsenal win their 2nd Round 1st Leg match 3-0.

After winning the 2nd Leg 1-0, Arsenal then beat both Bournemouth and Stoke 3-0 in the 3rd and 4th Rounds, with both games played at Highbury. Only a few of us went to see the 1-0 victory at Sheffield Wednesday in the 5th Round, although this win meant another coach trip to Merseyside, against Everton in the semi-finals.

EVERTON 1ST LEG

This time the coach trip was fairly uneventful and we had great seats in the stadium, in the middle of the upper tier behind one goal. Perry Groves gave an inspired performance and scored the only goal of the game, which made it a happy coach journey home for all of us who went.

EVERTON 2ND LEG

On February 24th 1988, 50,000 Arsenal fans, who were lucky enough to be present, witnessed the night when George Graham's youngsters gave them proof that greatness was on the horizon, with a brilliant performance. Michael Thomas, Martin Hayes and the outstanding "Rocky" Rocastle scored the goals in a 3-1 victory and, at Everton's expense, established Arsenal as one of the top teams in the country again. Plus, after dancing on the pitch at the end of the game, Arsenal fans would be off to a Wembley final, yet again.

LEAGUE [LITTLEWOODS] CUP FINAL 1988

Two months later on April 24th, or "Hail Caesar Day" as Luton fans should call it, the "Usual Suspects" and some other Arsenal fans met at Archie's "Green Man" pub in Hoxton again where, after a few beers we all boarded the coach to go to Wembley.

Incredibly, the driver got lost in the back streets of Islington when he tried to avoid the traffic on Holloway Road, not realising the council had recently erected width-restricting barriers in the area.

Some of us had to leave the coach and back the traffic up so that he could get back to the main road. After a start like this, the day couldn't get any worse, could it? Oh yes, it could!

We eventually arrived at Wembley Stadium, just as the two teams were coming out onto the pitch, after abandoning the coach on the North Circular Road near where the IKEA store is nowadays. Because we were so late arriving at the ground, other Arsenal fans were in our designated seats and naturally, we all started to turf them out and there were arguments going on all over the place. During the chaos, Harnetty was head-butted by an Arsenal fan, who threatened to finish the job later. When I intervened and explained that I would be with Harnetty later, the bloke said to me, "I'll have you later as well then". I replied, "You can have me now," and hit him with a left hook which sent him flying backwards into the row of seats behind him. My mate, Dodger, later described that punch as, "worthy of Henry Cooper", who'd famously decked the then Cassius Clay with a similar punch, in the same stadium twenty-five years earlier,

A full-scale brawl then broke out with my mates fighting the other bloke's mates until they were separated by the police and stewards.

By a strange coincidence, my brother had also gone to this match, his first Wembley final since Arsenal lost to Newcastle in 1952, and he rang me the next day to inform me that when he was in the stadium, the teenager sitting next to him said, "Look at that fight in the seats above us". My brother turned to see the commotion and said, "That's my brother in the red jacket". The kid asked, "Are you going to help him?" and my brother replied, "Nope, he's doing alright".

At half time, two plainclothes police officers came up to me and said they'd seen me on CCTV punching people. As I was wearing an old red Arsenal training jacket that an ex-player had given me, I told them that I was the steward on our coach and had merely been trying to keep the fans in order. Luckily, young Rikki Hammond was sitting next to me and when the copper asked if he was my son, I replied, "Yes". Like any proper kid, nine-year-old Rikki kept quiet.

After a strong lecture about parental responsibility, the coppers departed.

Gus Caesar then tripped over to become worthy of a statue in Luton, Nigel Winterburn missed a penalty and Arsenal embarrassingly lost to Luton 3-2.

To top it all, when we finally found our abandoned coach again, we discovered a few people on it who we didn't recognise and they were ejected near Brent Cross.

When we finally made it back to "Archie's", he wouldn't let us in the pub because so many blokes had cuts and bruises and dried blood on their shirts.

JC later remarked that it was 'the worst day in football he'd ever known'!

So, was this young Arsenal team going to recover from this setback or would it spur them on to greater glories?

I think we all know the answer to that question.

Arsenal finished 4th in the League behind Champions Everton.

Coventry won the FA Cup after beating the Team from the Lane 3-2.

PSV won the European Cup, beating Benfica on penalties after a 0-0 draw.

SEASON 1988-89

POETIC JUSTICE

After the disappointment of not winning a trophy the previous season, George Graham decided to go with the youngsters in the immediate future, backed up by the experience of David O'Leary, Paul Davis, Kevin Richardson and Brian Marwood and new signing Steve Bould.

Older players such as Charlie Nicholas, Kenny Sansom, Steve Williams and Graham Rix were all allowed to move on.

Arsenal won the new pre-season "Makita Cup" tournament at Wembley, which also involved Milan, Bayern Munich and the Team from the Lane.

On the first day of the season, Arsenal sent out an even bigger statement of intent to their fans, and the rest of the country, with an emphatic 5-1 victory at Wimbledon, including a hat trick from Alan Smith. Typically, they then lost the next game at home to Aston Villa 3-2.

The Arsenal fans kept their faith in this young team, though, and turned up in their thousands at the Lane to see Winterburn, Smith and Marwood score for Arsenal in the 3-2 victory. There was another funny moment during this game, when Paul "Gazza" Gascoigne was pelted with "Mars Bars" while waiting for a corner kick to be taken in front of all the Gooners in the Park Lane End, who were chanting "you fat bastard". To be fair to him, he just smiled then picked one bar up and took a bite out of it. During the next game on September 17th, a 2-2 draw at Highbury against Southampton, Paul Davis took offence at a comment made by the Southampton player, Glenn Cockerill, and was sent off after hitting him so hard he fractured his jaw. Paul Davis thus became the first player to be tried on television evidence by the FA and received a nine-match ban and a £3,000 fine; to this day Paul has never revealed what Glenn Cockerill said to him.

Before his suspension started, I saw Paul play in and score during Arsenal's 2-1 victory against Man Utd at Villa Park in the "Mercantile Centenary Trophy" Cup final.

On his return to the team, Paul only played a handful of games before injuries ended his season.

Arsenal had now won two trophies and it was only October. Would there be more?

I went to the next game, a 2-1 defeat away at Sheffield Wednesday, after which Arsenal only lost one of their next nineteen League games and were pushing Liverpool and Norwich for the title.

In December, two carloads of, the "Usual Suspects" went to the 0-0 away draw against the surprise title contenders, Norwich City.

JC had managed to get us all seats together in the second row near the halfway line. I was a little concerned about this location because the last time I'd gone to Norwich, the Arsenal fans had been stuck in one of the corners.

My concern was nothing, compared to that of the children, wearing yellow and green hats and scarves, who were sitting all around us though!

Yep, you guessed it; in his wisdom, JC had somehow managed to obtain tickets for eight Arsenal blokes amongst the "Junior Canaries". The looks on the faces of the coppers and stewards was a joy to behold. Getting tickets in the wrong Stand or End would make JC a legend with his mates.

On February 11th, along with some of the "Usual Suspects" and hundreds of other Gooners, I went to Millwall to witness Arsenal win 2-1 on their first-ever visit to "Cold Blow Lane". My mates and I met up in JC's new pub, the "Hand in Hand", just off the New Kent Road where he'd recently moved to from the "Sebright Arms" in Hackney, as he said he "wanted a quieter life". The Elephant & Castle, quieter? Was he sure? Anyway, about midday, we were all in the pub chatting, and there were a couple of the old regular blokes, ex-dockers I believe, sitting in there. They asked us if we were all the Guv'nor's Arsenal mates? When we told them that we were, to our surprise they both launched into a diatribe of why they hated Arsenal. According to them, in the 1950s, there was a Midweek Cup competition for the reserves of all the football clubs in the London area. I think it was called "The South East Counties Cup", and as these two blokes were working in the docks at that time, they used to watch Millwall reserves on Wednesday afternoons, and one season, Millwall reached the Final against Arsenal. Typically, Arsenal put out their first team and won the cup, leaving these two blokes to carry that hatred for 35 years. We all fell about laughing, especially JC.

The old dockers then told us the story of JC's first two nights in the pub. At about 7 pm on his first night, one of the locals came in, winked at the regulars in the bar, then asked JC if he had any salt and vinegar crisps. After JC produced them, the bloke changed his mind and asked for cheese and onion ones instead. After JC swapped these, the bloke then asked him to change them for ready salted, so JC changed them yet again. On receiving these crisps, the bloke then said he'd prefer a packet of dry roasted peanuts, so again, JC changed them. Finally, the bloke asked for salted peanuts instead. After JC changed these peanuts, the bloke thanked him, smiled at all the regulars and left the pub.

At 7 pm the next evening, the same bloke came into the pub again, winked at all the regulars in the bar, then asked JC if he'd got any crisps. Without saying a word, JC leant over the bar and, with one punch, knocked the liberty-taking fella, spark out. When the bloke recovered a few minutes later, JC barred him from the pub. He obviously didn't know that JC did some boxing in his younger days.

LEAGUE [LITTLEWOODS] CUP

Arsenal defeated Hull City 2-1 away and 3-0 at Highbury in the 2nd Round and then in the 3rd Round, drew 1-1 at Anfield, with Rocky Rocastle scoring a screamer from twenty-five yards.

A sell-out crowd at Highbury had to watch a boring 0-0 draw in the replay before Liverpool won the 2nd replay 2-1 at Anfield again.

FA CUP

In the 3rd Round, Arsenal drew 2-2 at West Ham before losing the replay 1-0 at Highbury.

For some reason, Arsenal then played France in a friendly match at Highbury and I believe it was the first time that Arsenal had played a National team since the infamous "Battle of Highbury" in 1934 against Italy, but the eyes and dreams of all Arsenal supporters were now on the League title race.

LEAGUE TITLE RUN IN

Arsenal were now marching on in the League and either winning or drawing most games, with Brian Marwood reminding older fans, with performances reminiscent of Geordie Armstrong in his heyday, instrumental to the team during this time and right up until he got injured in April.

Kevin Richardson was another unsung hero, after replacing Paul Davis for most of the season.

After winning 3-1 away at Southampton on March 29th, Arsenal only had eight games left to win the title and I wasn't going to miss any of them.

On April 2nd, I went to Old Trafford with JC, Spandau and my workmate, Bernie [the radio].

As usual, JC got the tickets. Surprise, surprise, we're not with the Arsenal fans, but sitting near the front of the Stretford End by the corner flag. Not JC though; we can spot his bright yellow jacket in the Main Stand where, incredibly, he's sitting behind Sir Matt Busby.

On a wet, muddy pitch, Tony Adams scored an own goal and the media labelled him a "Donkey".

We weren't bothered though, as Arsenal got a 1-1 draw and despite Bernie attracting some unwanted attention when he forgot to keep his mouth shut after Tony Adams scored Arsenal's goal, we managed to get home safely.

At the next three games, all at Highbury, including the "Usual Suspects", we were now in full voice in the East Stand along with the rest of the stadium, as Arsenal beat Everton 2-0, Newcastle 1-0 and after a three-week break due to the Hillsborough tragedy, Norwich 5-0, to keep the pressure on Liverpool. It was during the game against Newcastle on April 15th that news was coming in of the tragedy at Hillsborough, involving Liverpool fans in their FA Cup semi-final against Forest.

I mentioned in a previous chapter about the crush hundreds of Arsenal fans, including myself, had endured getting into that same Leppings Lane End before Arsenal's FA Cup semi-final against Sunderland in 1973.

At least there weren't any fences surrounding the pitch in those days and, if necessary, we could have climbed out to escape.

This tragic event, which left many people dead, meant that Arsenal's forthcoming away game at Anfield would be rearranged as the last game of the season.

WE WON THE LEAGUE ON MERSEYSIDE

Now there were only four games left and we were still neck and neck with Liverpool.

As JC couldn't make it – he was probably upset that he couldn't get tickets with the home fans – I went by train with Bernie to Middlesbrough, where Putney meets us in his car at the station, after getting a match ticket from someone and deciding to drive up there at the last minute.

Martin Hayes scored the winner with a long-range shot as Arsenal won 1-0 and this sparked a party amongst the Arsenal fans who were being kept in at the end of the game. Many of these fans were waving plastic blow-up champagne bottles and other blow up items; no dolls this time though.

The rest of the stadium was almost empty, when, much to everyone's amusement, two drunken Middlesbrough fans tried to climb a fence separating them from the Arsenal supporters. Luckily for them, they failed.

Their actions prompted the arrival of the fattest female police Inspector you will ever see and it's not hard to imagine the abuse she got. Even the coppers were laughing.

Then, in the typical Arsenal style of never doing things the easy way, Derby won at Highbury 2-1 in the next game and the pressure was now back on Arsenal.

Now there were only two games left but if they won both, Arsenal would be Champions.

So, yet again, in front of a Highbury crowd that was on the verge of a collective heart attack, Arsenal had to rely on a rare screamer from Nigel Winterburn, to manage a 2-2 draw with Wimbledon.

After Liverpool beat West Ham 5-0, it was all down to the last game of the season at Anfield, where Arsenal had to win by two clear goals to be Champions on goal difference. Typical Arsenal, doing it the hard way! As we'd already bought tickets for the original match, Putney and myself decided to go, unless Arsenal needed to win by three or more goals. We just couldn't have lived with ourselves if they had unexpectedly got a result and we hadn't been there to see it.

We left London early as it was a Bank Holiday weekend and, as the match was on a Friday night, we knew the traffic would be heavy on the motorways. We were proved correct about this, as cars and coaches containing hundreds of Arsenal fans didn't arrive until almost half time.

We were even diverted into Birkenhead, so as to enter Liverpool through the Mersey tunnel against the commuter traffic. On arriving at the stadium, we met Hoyboy and his son and entered the stadium early. We managed to find a good spot next to a six-foot wall that separated our section from the Anfield Road End where most of the Arsenal fans were standing. If you watch the match replay, you can see Putney in his white jumper, just to the right of the Exit sign. About a foot up this wall was a ledge about six inches wide and we all stood on this in single file, holding on the top of the wall with one hand and having an uninterrupted view of the historical events that would unfold on the pitch. Just before kickoff, Paul Davis and Niall Quinn set the tone for the night, when they got a great reception as they took their seats amongst the Arsenal fans behind the goal.

The Arsenal players then ran out and presented bouquets of flowers to the Liverpool fans in the rest of the stadium, before the match got underway.

After Alan Smith scored the first goal, Denton could be seen leaping up and down on the asphalt behind the goal in celebration, before being bundled back in with the jubilant Arsenal fans.

After Mickey Thomas scored the second goal, I jumped off of the wall into all the Arsenal fans next to me and only saw the floodlights for the last few seconds of the match, while screaming my head off in sheer joy.

To our total astonishment, when we eventually left the stadium, there were Liverpool fans lined up on both sides of the pavements, but instead of giving us a battering, they were shaking our hands and saying, "Well done".

A certain ex-manager of the Team from the Lane had said earlier on television that evening, "Arsenal winning on the night, but not winning the League" was "poetic justice". Bollocks to that!!

Liverpool won the FA Cup after beating Everton 3-2.

Forest won the League Cup after beating Luton 3-1.

Milan won the European Cup after beating Steaua Bucharest 4-0.

SEASON 1989-90

After waiting eighteen years to see Arsenal become Champions again in the previous season, expectations were now running high amongst Arsenal supporters, dreaming of a new Golden Era.

Surprisingly, only Colin Pates, Siggi Jonsson and youth team striker Kevin Campbell were added to the squad. Unsurprisingly, no players asked to leave.

Due to the ban on English clubs playing in European competitions after the Heysel stadium disaster, where 49 Juventus fans died before the European Cup final against Liverpool, Arsenal could not compete for the European Cup.

However, they did have a busy pre-season; they retained the "Makita" Cup beating Liverpool, before flying to Miami to beat Independiente of Argentina 2-1, in the "Zenith Data Systems Cup".

Six days later, Arsenal lost the Charity Shield match 1-0 against Liverpool at Wembley again.

LEAGUE

On August 19th, Arsenal started their campaign to retain the League title with a 4-1 defeat at Old Trafford, despite a wonder goal from Rocky Rocastle. After playing four games in twenty-one days, including a trip to Miami, I'm not surprised!

After being unbeaten in the next seven games, Arsenal lost 2-1 at the Lane in October. Judging by the delirious reaction of the home fans, you'd have thought it was the "World Cup Final'. Unbeknown to me at the time, this would be my last ever visit to the Lane, due to the forthcoming results of the "Taylor Report" into the Hillsborough disaster, whereby stadiums would become All-Seater, severely restricting the numbers of

1980'S & EARLY 90'S MATCH TICKETS

away supporters in future. I remember getting hit on the head by a coin thrown from the Shelf causing Spook to cry with laughter. The following Xmas he sent me a card with a 10p coin inside and the message, "I told you they were a 2 Bob outfit". Earlier, before the game, we had bumped into our old teammate from our Arsenal Supporters Club days, Johnny Nash, and unbeknown to him, it was also the last game that he would see there as he sadly died in his late 40s not long afterwards. Another one of our old team, Vic Pooley, also died about that time as well.

During the rest of the season, the old inconsistencies returned and, despite only losing two home games against Chelsea and Aston Villa, Arsenal never really challenged Liverpool for the title.

LEAGUE [LITTLEWOODS] CUP

Arsenal beat Plymouth 2-1 away and 6-1 at Highbury in the 2nd Round before beating Liverpool at Highbury 1-0 in the 3rd Round. On November 22nd, along with a few hundred other Arsenal fans, I took the train to Oldham to see Arsenal lose the 4th Round game at a freezing cold Boundary Park.

Due to some trouble before the game, the drivers of the "Football Special" buses refused to return to take the Arsenal fans back to the railway. No problem; some younger Gooners simply hijacked a couple of buses who were on their regular routes and forced the drivers to divert to the station with us all on board.

FA CUP

In the FA Cup 3rd Round, Arsenal beat Stoke City 1-0 away. This day was only memorable for JC, Putney and Spook deciding to eat in the cafeteria of a large store full of people doing their weekly shopping. The set menu was pie, chips and peas and JC told the waitress that he wanted two pies, because he always had "Double, Double" when he was in a pie and mash shop in London.

The waitress then told him that he must have the set menu containing only one pie.

So, he ordered two dinners for himself and when they arrived, he took the pie off one plate and put it on his plate so that he'd now got his two pies. Apparently, all the shoppers eating their dinners and the waitress couldn't believe that someone would pay for two dinners, just to get another pie and they were all staring at JC and muttering to themselves about 'flash Cockneys' with too much money.

Although, it made perfect sense to me!

In the 4th Round, Arsenal drew 0-0 with QPR at Highbury before losing the replay 2-0 at Loftus Rd.

UNOFFICIAL CHAMPIONS OF BRITAIN

As a consequence of the ban on English teams competing in Europe, Arsenal were invited by the Scottish Champions, Glasgow Rangers, to play a match for the Unofficial Championship of Britain, at Ibrox Park on December 19th 1989.

Apparently, Arsenal fans were advised against attending this game by the British Government and so Arsenal turned down the allocation of tickets that Rangers offered them.

My Rangers-loving, "Jockney" mate, Granty, had a cunning plan though.

He had a friend in Glasgow who'd ordered a new car from Putney's company, so he offered to deliver it to him, as long as he bought us two tickets for the game.

We drove up the day before the match, delivered the car to the buyer, who insisted on paying for our flights back to London before showing us around his farm and stables where he kept his ponies and donkeys that he let local handicapped children use as part of their therapy treatment.

As we were walking around the farm, the fella was pointing to different animals and saying, "I've got a goat, I've got a goose, I've got a pig," etc. When I asked him if he had a "Duckdoo", he replied, "What's a Duckdoo?" I immediately started flapping my arms around while saying, "Quack, Quack, Quack". He loved it. One-nil to the Cockneys!

This fella then took Granty and myself to get our match tickets from the Rangers-supporting landlord of the "Hecla Arms" pub in Drumchapel. For those of you who haven't been there, Drumchapel is the sort of place where they have scars on their faces, and that's just the women.

After having a couple of beers and claiming our match tickets, we got a taxi to meet Russell, an old Glaswegian workmate of Granty's, who'd recently retired and moved back up there.

He was in his local pub in Duntocher, and as it was December, they were having the Old Age Pensioner's Xmas dinner. Inside, there was a singer getting everyone to join in singing all the traditional old songs.

This singer then went around the bar asking people to sing, solo, a song of their choice.

Now, Granty and I only knew the words of one old song, "Come Round Any Old Time". Obviously when it was his turn, that's what Granty sang. Then the singer stuck the microphone in my face and asked this panic-stricken Cockney boy to sing a wee song.

I could only think of one other old song I knew, and I just managed to sing the first line of "Maybe it's because I'm a Londoner", before Russell bundled me out of the door, saying, "You can't sing that in here". After standing with my beer, on the pavement for a few minutes, I returned to the bar where everyone was laughing about what had happened, and we spent a lovely evening with them.

Cockneys One, Glaswegians One.

The next day, we went to the match and discovered that our seats were in the middle of the Main Stand.

We were sitting there minding our own business, when a kid leant over from the row behind me and asked me to get the fella in the row in front of me to sign his programme.

It turned out the bloke in front was none other than Ally McCoist, who was not playing through injury. He smiled when he heard my accent before signing the kid's programme.

Good job it wasn't my old mate, Tommy Docherty, then?

Arsenal won 2-1 and were declared the "Unofficial Champions of Britain".

After a few more "bevvies" with Russell, we left his house the next morning and flew home.

Arsenal finished 4th in the League behind Champions Liverpool.

Man Utd won the FA Cup, beating Crystal Palace 1-0 in a replay after a 3-3 draw.

Forest won the League Cup after beating Oldham Athletic 1-0.

Milan won the European Cup after beating Benfica 1-0.

SEASON 1990-91

YOU CAN STICK YOUR 2 POINTS

In an attempt to revitalise the squad, George Graham bought goal-keeper David Seaman from QPR for £1m, plus the skilful Swedish winger, Anders Limpar and centre-back Andy Linighan, with David Hillier, Andy Cole and Alan Miller being promoted from the Youth team and Martin Hayes, Gus Caesar, Siggi Jonsson and John Lukic all moved on to other clubs.

Stewart Houston replaced Theo Foley as Assistant Manager and two Arsenal legends, Pat Rice and Geordie Armstrong were brought in as coaches.

Sadly, two other legendary Arsenal players, Jack Kelsey and Joe Mercer both died.

Arsenal lost 2-0 to Sampdoria in the Makita Cup Final at Highbury.

LEAGUE [RUMBELOWS] CUP

My old schoolmate, George Hammond and I went to see Arsenal beat Chester City away 1-0 in the 2nd Round 1st Leg, when this game was played at Macclesfield's ground because Chester's stadium wasn't up to the required standards. Arsenal won the 2nd Leg 5-0 at Highbury and in the 3rd Round, I went to see Arsenal win 3-1 at Maine Road against Man City before I, unfortunately, had to witness Arsenal losing 6-2 to Man Utd at Highbury in the 4th Round.

FA CUP

Arsenal beat Sunderland 2-1 in the 3rd Round at Highbury, then drew 0-0 at home, 1-1 away, then 0-0 at home again, before finally beating

Leeds away 2-1 in the 4th Round. In the 5th Round, Arsenal beat Shrewsbury away 1-0 and then in the 6th Round, Cambridge United 2-1 at Highbury.

In the semi-final, Arsenal surprisingly lost to that other team from up the A10, the Team from the Lane, 3-1 at Wembley, which killed our hopes of another Double, but thankfully, we wouldn't have to wait too long for our revenge.

LEAGUE

The omens were looking good after Arsenal won 3-1 away at Wimbledon in the first League game, just like they did in their previous Championship-winning season.

They would only lose one League game all season, away at Chelsea in February, and only concede eighteen goals, mainly due to the solid performances of the famous back five, David Seaman, Lee Dixon, Steve Bould, Nigel Winterburn and Captain Fantastic, Tony Adams.

In October, Arsenal won 1-0 at Old Trafford, where twenty-one play-ers, Seaman being the exception, got involved in a brawl after Nigel Winterburn and Anders Limpar had been singled out for some "special" treatment by United players.

At the subsequent FA inquiry, Arsenal were docked 2 points and Man Utd one point. Arsenal fans reacted to this perceived injustice with a new song, "You Can Stick Your Two Points Up Your Arse".

In November, I went with my wife, Chris, and her boss, both QPR fans, to Loftus Road, where we all sat in the Main Stand surrounded by QPR season ticket holders. I had promised my wife that I would be on my best behaviour and all was calm, until, after getting some merciless abuse from QPR fans in the Loft End regarding his drink driving offences, Tony Adams decided to give them a double V sign after Arsenal scored to equalise. Then, with the game in the balance, Arsenal were pushing for the winner, when, after a corner, the ball was bouncing about the QPR goalmouth and I instinctively jumped out of my seat and screamed at the top of my voice, "Get the fucking ball in the goal, will ya!" My wife was mortified and her boss was staring straight ahead, unlike all the other QPR fans who were wondering how this lunatic got into their Main Stand. Once a Gooner, always a Gooner.

Arsenal eventually won 3-1 and my wife declared that she would never go to another football match with me. Every cloud ....

Her diplomatic boss later told her that He didn't hear me, but that I was very enthusiastic.

In December, Tony Adams was sent to prison for 3 months for those drink driving offences and

David O'Leary and Andy Linighan shared the duties of replacing him.

In January 1991, Arsenal drew 0-0 at the Lane, but without hundreds of Gooners, including myself, who couldn't get a ticket due to the new restrictions on away supporters.

On March 3rd, JC and I drove to Anfield to see Arsenal win 1-0, with a Paul Merson goal, against the current Champions, who, incidentally, wouldn't be Champions again for thirty years.

Arsenal then beat Aston Villa 5-0 at Highbury, where David Platt went in goal after Nigel Spink was injured and I was thinking that If Arsenal ever bought David Platt, hopefully, it wouldn't be as a goalkeeper.

Our next trip was to Sheffield United in April, where Arsenal won 2-0, despite Vinny Jones trying to dismember Anders Limpar with some dubious, to say the least, tackles.

After the game, as we were walking back to the car, JC was talking about our chances of winning the League, when a passing twenty-something United fan heard our conversation and started loudly ranting about how his dad told him stories of "Lucky Arsenal". He continued his rant saying, "You've only had two shots all game and won 2-0", while JC just stood there smiling, waiting for the fella to stop before he replied, "Our goalie won't even have to put his shorts in the wash tonight," and the young bloke was now waving his arms around in anger and walked off, muttering to himself about "Bloody Cockneys".

In a break from the stress of the League campaign, I watched Arsenal play Liverpool in a Testimonial match for the ex-player of both clubs, Ray Kennedy, who had suffered from Parkinson's Disease for many years. On the morning of the match, my mate, Spandau, informed me that Ray was staying at a hotel in Bayswater, so naturally, I popped around there for a chat and photo with Ray.

With the title in sight, Putney and I drove to Sunderland on May 4th, in his brand new bright yellow Volvo car. When we arrived in Sunderland, Putney wanted to find a car wash and I asked him Why, as we still had to drive back to London later. He replied, '"Because we're Flash Cockney Bastards". After getting the car washed, we drove into the car park of a large Victorian-style pub, which had a big bay window with a door on either side of it and as we parked up, I noticed lots of Sunderland fans with their faces pressed up against the windows watching us.

Putney and I strolled into the bar and, after getting a beer and some sandwiches, we engaged in conversation about football with the extremely friendly locals, who loved our stories about the 1973 'Stokoe, Stokoe' semi-final at Hillsborough. After a while, Putney told me to "drink up, as we're leaving to see the sights of Sunderland" and we shook hands with all the fans, wished them well, and told them where we were going before we went outside through one of the two doors.

As I was walking towards the car, Putney said, "Where are you going? Follow me," and we walked back into the pub through the door on the other side of the window.

All the Sunderland fans that we had just been talking to turned around to see us standing there and one of them said, "We thought you were going to see the sights?" Putney replied, "We have, there's fuck all here!" The Sunderland fan spluttered, "You flash Cockney bastards!" Putney smiled, looked at me and said, "I told you". Arsenal drew 0-0 and the title was getting closer.

Two days later, most of the "Usual Suspects" were in the "Robinson Crusoe" pub in Highbury Quadrant, where we watched Liverpool lose at Forest in the earlier game on television. This meant that Arsenal were Champions again, even before they kicked off, before beating Man Utd 3-1 later that night

CHAMPIONS – 1991

at Highbury, which was also memorable for a drunken Jimmy "Barnsey" Barnes and his mate taking penalties against each other at the Clock End before the game until they were arrested, but in court, the Magistrate let them off. "We Won The League In The Robinson Crusoe" was our chant and all of our gang were there again on the Saturday, when Arsenal beat Coventry 6-1 before Tony Adams received the League Champions trophy for the 2nd time in three years, while reverberating around the stadium was the song, "You Can Stick Your 2 Points Up Your Arse!"

The Team from the Lane won the FA Cup after beating Forest 2-1.

Sheffield Wednesday won the League Cup after beating Man Utd 1-0.

Red Star Belgrade won the European Cup, beating Marseille on penalties after a 0-0 draw.

SEASON 1991-92

VIENNA – LISBON – WREXHAM

The Main topic amongst Arsenal fans during the summer was the board's decision to replace the iconic North Bank terraces with a two-tier stand.

This decision was taken mainly in response to the "Taylor Report" into the Hillsborough disaster, that would make seating in football stadiums compulsory. It also made financial sense to the club, as the capacity would be severely reduced and this new stand would help maintain the financial income. Well, that's what the Arsenal board said, allegedly. The original design had the new stand connected to the old East and West stands with covered seating areas, but these eventually had to be omitted to allow the wind through in order to protect the pitch.

As if all this wasn't controversial enough, a Bond Scheme was announced, to help fund the building costs. JC, Putney, Teddy Taylor and myself each bought a Bond in the new North Bank Upper Tier, and I have to admit that the club were true to their word and the Bond eventually became a good investment for the supporters who purchased them.

The Arsenal Vice-Chairman, David Dein, got a lot of stick from many supporters at the time but would later redeem himself in the eyes of many Arsenal fans when, a few years later, he brought in Arsène Wenger and some world-class players.

Ray Parlour, Neil Heaney and Steve Morrow were promoted from the Youth team and Jimmy Carter was signed from Liverpool.

Arsenal drew 0-0 in the Charity Shield match against the Team from the Lane at Wembley, where a certain Andy Cole played only his second game for Arsenal before he was sold to Bristol City.

LEAGUE

After only winning two of their first seven League games, Arsenal then won 4-1 against Crystal Palace at Selhurst Park, where, because of the restricted parking in the area, JC left his car on someone's drive because it looked like they were away on holiday, although they'd only gone shopping, and weren't very happy when they returned home.

FC AUSTRIA VS ARSENAL –
EUROPEAN CUP 19991

In the next game, Arsenal won 6-1 against FK Austria in the European Cup before a 5-2 victory against Sheffield United in the League at Highbury. So, after seeing his team score fifteen goals in three games, what does George Graham do? Obviously, he buys another striker. Not just any old striker though, but Ian Wright from Crystal Palace, who would become one of the greatest strikers in Arsenal's history.

The chant goes 'Ian Wright, Wright, Wright' because he was so good the Arsenal fans named him three times, and he made his League debut at Southampton on September 28th and promptly scored a hat trick. He also scored on his Highbury debut in the 3-2 win against Chelsea on October 5th.

He finished the season with twenty-four goals in thirty games, winning the Golden Boot award, after scoring another hat trick during the 5-1 victory, again against Southampton, in the last game of the season and sadly, also the last game in front of the old North Bank terraces where many of the "Original North Bank Boys", including Hoyboy, Putney, Spook, Tringy, Rod Moore, Granty, Harnetty, Gary Davies, Lenny Togwell, Teddy Taylor, Dodger, Edwin Childs, Peter Landers, Vic Wright and myself, all decided to stand for one last time, eventually leaving after the game with a few tears in our eyes, but with so many happy memories of our younger days.

In November 1991, the Norwegian full-back, Pal Lydersen, was signed, and although he only played for the club sixteen times, he would later become a significant part of Arsenal's history.

In January 1992, Michael Thomas, who had already played a significant part in Arsenal's history, was sold to Liverpool. In February, JC, Jim Kane, Teddy Taylor and myself went to Notts County and saw Arsenal win 1-0 and although it was freezing cold, we had, sensibly, fortified ourselves with plenty of glasses of port or whisky before the game.

LEAGUE [RUMBELOWS] CUP

Ian Wright made his Arsenal debut on September 25th in the 2nd Round game at Leicester, where he scored in the 1-1 draw. He also scored in the 2-0 victory against Leicester at Highbury.

In the 3rd Round, Arsenal lost 1-0 at Coventry.

QUIZ NIGHT

We entered a team in the first Arsenal Quiz Night and came 3rd, although the highlight for most of us was meeting George Graham, Frank McLintock, Bertie Mee and Tony Adams.

EUROPEAN CUP

As I previously stated, Arsenal beat FK Austria 6-1 in the 1st Round 1st Leg at Highbury. Then for some obscure reason, Putney drove Hoyboy and his son, JC and myself to Vienna for the 2nd Leg.

This trip is memorable for two classic JC stories. The first was when we arrived in Vienna and we went to meet JC's contact in the Hilton Hotel to collect our match tickets.

After getting the tickets, JC spotted a high-sided armchair in the lobby and told us that he was going to take a nap in it, despite the fact that he'd slept almost all the way from Calais. So off he went and, after a few minutes, he was fast asleep again. The rest of us were having a beer in the bar, when a bellboy appeared with a little sign on a board that said "Dr Weber". Obviously, we directed him over to where JC was sleeping. The bellboy then started ringing a little bell next to JC's ear but got no reaction. The kid then spotted us all laughing and, in full view of everyone in the bar and lobby, gave us double-handed V signs. Then the waiter brought our drinks bill on a small silver tray and so we also sent him over to the sleeping JC, where he put the tray on a table next to his seat.

We then decided to leave JC in the land of nod and go and get something to eat. While we were in the restaurant, we all started laughing when Putney pulled out the euros that we'd all put in the whip earlier, because this meant that JC didn't have any money to pay the bar bill with. About an hour later, we returned to the hotel and find JC standing outside waiting for us. After he got in the car, he told us he'd had a lovely kip, then we asked him how he'd paid the drinks bill. He replied, "What drinks bill?"

ANOTHER MAGIC MOMENT

On the drive home after the game, which Arsenal lost 1-0, JC slept most of the way again, except that every time he woke up, he stated that Arsenal would "never win anything with Andy Linighan in the team". In the early hours of the next morning, we stopped at a garage somewhere in Germany. We left JC to fill the fuel tank up with petrol, while the rest of us went inside to fill up with food and drinks. Putney was using his limited knowledge of schoolboy German to converse with the totally non-English-speaking bloke behind the counter, when suddenly, the door opened and JC s standing there. He said to the German, "Hello, mate, do you like football?" The German bloke shook his head and looked bewildered because he didn't understand English, never mind a Cockney accent. So, JC started kicking an imaginary ball and the German nodded his head and said, "Ya, der Fussball". JC then asked him, "Do you know how Spurs got on?" Apparently, the Team from the Lane had played the night before and we all now collapsed on the floor laughing because JC was deadly serious, which is what made him so funny.

One final tale from Vienna, was when we were in the restaurant, Putney and myself had each bought one of the beautiful beer glasses we had drunk from, which we wrapped in towels and put in the car boot. When Putney dropped me off in England, he reminded me to take my beer glass with me. On opening the boot, I noticed one of the glasses had broken, so I picked up the other one and as I walked away, looked back and told him, "That's a shame, mate, your one's broke". The look on Putney's face was a picture!

LISBON

In the 2nd Round, JC and I flew to see Arsenal play Benfica in Lisbon on October 23rd 1991.

Playing such a famous club as this in the European Cup is what I had dreamt of for many years and I couldn't believe my luck because while we were waiting in the Departures Area at Heathrow the night before the game, I spotted one of the greatest football players of all time, Franz Beckenbauer, and approached him for a chat and a photograph. He laughed when I thanked him for earning me a few quid for winning the World Cup

WITH FRANZ BECKENBAUER – 1991

as manager of Germany the previous year, then he said to me, "But you are English." I pointed to my heart and replied, "That says England," then I pointed to my head and said, "but that says Germany". He'd been to a reunion with the England 1966 World Cup winners.

On the morning of the match, JC and I were sitting at the table in our hotel waiting for breakfast, when JC looked at the roll and croissant on his plate and asked me, "What's this shit?", I told him, "It's a Continental breakfast". "Well, I don't want that" he replied, and then, as he looked up, he saw a little old woman, wearing a white apron pushing a trolley with all the dirty plates on it, and just as she was about to disappear into the kitchen, JC shouted, "Dear, dear, excuse me dear, this no good, I want eggs and bacon". The old girl laughed, waved and went through the door. I said to him, "You've got no chance; she doesn't understand English". I was totally gobsmacked when, five minutes later, she put a plate of eggs and bacon in front of him on our table and after thanking her, all JC said to me was, "They all understand eggs and bacon, mate". Later, JC and I went to the "Estadio da Luz" stadium to have a look around and while we were standing outside, our mate Dodger arrived in a taxi to get himself a ticket at the Box Office. We then found an open gate and had our photos taken on the pitch and in the empty stands without anybody intervening.

ON BENFICA PITCH WITH
JOHNNY "JC" COLLINS

When we were finished, I left JC standing outside the stadium, while I went through a large wooden door and found myself in a hallway with framed pictures of old Benfica teams. The security bloke just smiled and watched me studying them. When I came out, JC told me that the Legendary Benfica player, Eusebio, had just walked past him and I missed a chance to get my photo with him. I never did find out if he was having me on! Arsenal drew 1-1 and most Arsenal fans were confident of finishing the job at Highbury.

In the 2nd Leg, despite a rare Colin Pates' goal, Benfica totally mugged Arsenal with their counter-attacking football and for Arsenal fans, including myself, our European Cup dream had turned into a nightmare. Still, there's always the FA Cup, ain't there?

WREXHAM

On the infamous day of January 4th 1992, JC, Jim Kane and I drove to Wrexham to see Arsenal in the 3rd Round FA Cup match.

The night before the game, Granty, who had travelled there to stay with an old mate of his, called me to say that the local police had announced that as only local people would be allowed in the pubs before the game, he had another cunning plan, whereby his mate would vouch for the rest of us in his local pub near the ground. So, when we arrived at about 1 pm, we gave the name of Granty's mate to the bouncers on the door and one of them called him to the door to identify us. No problem, we were in. When we walked into the bar, it was packed with locals and we managed to find a space under the solitary television that was fixed on the wall. As it was probably the biggest game in Wrexham's history, everyone was eagerly watching the pre-match interviews with the managers and players. JC then looked around at all the Welshmen and, totally oblivious to what was going on, said, "Hello, lads, you don't mind if I switch this over, do you, as I've got one running in the 1.30 at Haydock," before reaching up and switching the channels on the television.

I almost choked on my beer and made a quick note of where the exits were. All the Welsh blokes were standing in silence with their mouths open, looking at this Cockney nutcase, while Granty's mate was shell-shocked. JC didn't bat an eyelid. The horse never won and nor did Arsenal.

The ex-Man Utd player, Mickey Thomas, got his revenge for the 1979 FA Cup Final defeat when he scored the first goal for Wrexham with a devastating free kick that eluded the Arsenal defence. Then Steve Wilkins got the winner after Alan Smith had equalised, before, in the final few minutes, Paul Merson had what looked like a perfectly good goal disallowed for offside and Champions Arsenal had lost 2-1 to the team that had finished bottom of the League the previous season.

It was a long miserable journey home in the car, especially with Danny Baker on the radio, constantly mocking the "Big Boys" of Arsenal, which had JC threatening to bash the living daylights out of him, if he ever saw him down the Old Kent Road.

Arsenal finished 4th in the League behind Champions Leeds United.

Liverpool won the FA Cup after beating Sunderland 2-0.

Man Utd won the League Cup after beating Forest 1-0.

Barcelona won the European Cup after beating Sampdoria 1-0.

MEETING MY BOYHOOD HERO – NOVEMBER 1992

After spotting an article in a newspaper, announcing that there was going to be an Appreciation Dinner in Edinburgh for Joe Baker, our favourite Arsenal player from the days of the early sixties when we were schoolboys, Spook and myself decided to travel up there and try to meet him.

We rang the organiser, Mr Victor Paris, to order two tickets and on hearing my accent he said, "You must be Arsenal fans". They'd had no official reply from Arsenal, although the club later did send a signed shirt to be auctioned. We drove up north the day before the dinner and stayed the night with an old mate of ours before crossing the border the next morning. On arriving in Edinburgh, we booked into our hotel and then took in some of the sights of the city in the afternoon.

WITH MY BOYHOOD HERO
JOE BAKER 1992

We then went to the "Sheraton Hotel" where the function was, arriving nice and early, suited and booted and wearing our Arsenal club ties, as requested by the organiser.

The official time for arriving was 7 pm but Victor had told us to get there at 6 pm as, unbeknown to us, he'd arranged for Joe Baker to arrive early to meet us before all the other guests showed up.

We were invited into the "Hospitality Room" to be greeted by Joe and his family, where, after pinching myself a few times to make sure I wasn't dreaming, I presented Joe with a framed photo of the moment that he knocked down the Liverpool captain, Ron Yeats, at Highbury in 1964.

Joe was highly delighted with this present but his brother, Gerry, laughed and said, "Oh no, he's got the proof now, he'll be driving them all mad down the Golf Club".

I also gave Joe a copy of "The Arsenal Player by Player" book, that contained his scoring records and inside the cover, I had written the words from a Pink Floyd song, "Remember when you were young, you shone like the sun, shine on, you crazy diamond".

Joe then had a chat with both of us about football past and present and his career at Arsenal, before he had to speak to his special guests who were now arriving.

As we looked around the room, we could see it was filling up with Scottish football legends such as Billy McNeill [Celtic], Jim Baxter and Ralph Brand [Rangers], Alex Young [Hearts and Everton], Pat Stanton [Hibs] and then Denis "The Lawman" Law arrived.

The whole room turned to greet him and it was as though a Scottish King had arrived. Denis came straight over to Joe, who was still talking to the pair of us, shouting "Giuseppe,

WITH DENIS LAW – 1992

Giuseppe, my old pal Giuseppe" and gave him a hug. Joe then introduced Spook and myself to Denis as the two Arsenal lads who'd come all the way from London. Denis was amazed at this information, especially as the only other Englishman at the function was Johnny Haynes, the ex-Fulham legend who actually lived in Edinburgh, but never had a pass for the Hospitality Room.

I don't think they'd forgiven him for the 9-3 hammering England gave Scotland in 1961; only joking!

Denis laughed when I told him that if I'd had the money, I would have bought him for Arsenal as well as Joe in 1962. Imagine those two upfront with George Eastham and Geordie Armstrong.

I reckon I could've played in goal and Arsenal would still have scored enough goals to win.

ALAN [SPOOK] ING – BILLY MCNEILL – ME
1992

Spook and I then made our way around the room, chatting and having our photos taken with all the other famous ex-players. Meanwhile, we noticed another fella taking photos with a proper professional-looking camera, and we asked him if he was the official press photographer. We both laughed when he replied, "No,

I'm just a Hibs fan with a nice camera around my neck and I bluffed my way in past the security guy".

John Coyle, the fake photographer, sat at our table for the dinner and I still exchange Xmas cards with him to this day. When we entered the function suite for dinner, I couldn't believe that there were 300 people sitting in there. When Joe Baker led his special guests in, he immediately came over to our table and shook our hands, and again thanked us for coming. The compere then introduced the "two Arsenal fans" to the rest of the diners and we received a standing ovation.

After the dinner came the speeches and auctions of football memorabilia and the first item to be auctioned was one of Joe's England caps in a glass frame. Spook turned to me and said, "I'm going to get Joe a few quid," before, to my horror, jumping up and offering £500. I said to him, "We ain't got £500 between us!" "Don't worry," was his calm reply. About 45 seconds later, someone offered £600 and I could stop looking for the exits.

WITH JIM BAXTER – 1992

We ended this memorable evening with our "Boyhood Hero" back in the Hospitality Room, after taking Johnny Haynes in with us as our guest, talking to Joe and Jim Baxter about England vs Scotland games in the Sixties before presenting them both with our Arsenal ties.

SEASON 1992-93

TELL YOUR MA, YOUR MA

Before the season started, George Graham broke the heart of David "Rocky" Rocastle and many thousands of Gooners by selling him to Leeds United.

A few weeks later, another popular player, Perry Groves, was sold to Southampton. Every Arsenal fan now held their breath in anticipation of what "Superstar" was coming in to replace them.

Disappointingly, to say the least, it was the Danish International, John Jensen, a decent wholehearted player but somewhat lacking the pace and skill of Perry, never mind the legendary Rocky.

Mark Flatts, Paul "Cut Yer" Dickov, Scott Marshal, Gavin McGowan and Ian Selley were promoted from the Youth team, while Martin Keown would rejoin Arsenal from Everton later in the season.

PERRY GROVES

I recall that Perry was the subject of one of the funniest moments I've ever seen at Highbury, when during a game, Perry was injured in front of the West Stand towards the Clock End. When the St John's ambulance first aid men arrived on the scene, they loaded him onto a stretcher and proceeded to carry him off and then around the perimeter of the pitch to the tunnel.

The game restarted and play was down the North Bank End and the stretcher-bearers had reached the corner flag at the Clock End and had decided to take a sharp turn. while undertaking this manoeuvre, they inadvertently tilted the stretcher and the helpless Perry Groves fell off. Perry then jumped up off the ground and started berating the four hapless ambulance men, leaving all the fans that had seen the incident, including myself, in hysterics.

To be fair to Perry, if you read the last line of his autobiography book, it shows he's a true Gooner.

PREMIER LEAGUE

This was the first season of the new Premier League and, not surprisingly, after losing the first game 4-2 against Norwich at Highbury, Arsenal had an unremarkable season, only scoring forty goals, which was half of the previous season's total and even losing 1-0 away and 3-1 at Highbury, against the Team from the Lane.

We even had to suffer the ignominy of looking at a mural with painted faces on it where the demolished North Bank used to be, however, in the Cup competitions, the team, unlike the mural, came alive.

LEAGUE "COCA COLA" CUP

On September 22nd 1992, in the 2nd Round 1st Leg, Arsenal drew 1-1 with Millwall at Highbury.

On October 7th, in the 2nd Leg, Arsenal again drew 1-1 at Millwall before winning 3-1 on penalties.

For this game, the ever-reliable JC managed to get seats for Spook and myself in the stand, where we were surrounded by school kids until we had a word with a steward and managed to get transferred to another section.

DERBY COUNTY 1992

Arsenal played Derby County at the Baseball Ground in the 3rd Round on October 28th.

True to form, JC somehow got two tickets for him and me in the Derby season ticket holders stand behind the goal, where we had a great view of the pitch and all the Arsenal fans in their section nearer the halfway line.

About thirty minutes before kick-off, I was quietly sitting down reading the programme, when JC decided to talk to the two blokes sitting in front of us. "Hello, mate, you've got a bit of class up here tonight, ain't yer, the best you've seen since Charlie George was playing for you," was his opening line.

The Derby blokes were not impressed and ignored JC, while I was more concerned that anyone within earshot now knew that there were two Cockney fellas sitting near them. "Miserable bastards, ain't they?" JC said to me. I replied, "They don't like us up here, mate". During the game, Derby scored from a penalty, and about five minutes later, Kevin Campbell equalised with a twenty-yard screamer into the goal in front of us, which caused JC to immediately leap out of his seat, throw his cap on the floor and shout, "You lot won't see a better goal than that up here all season!" Pandemonium; now the whole stand knew we were Arsenal fans and some of the more aggressive Derby fans were starting to climb over the seats towards us, with one of their larger blokes running up the aisle and screaming abuse and waving his fists at JC.

JC's reaction? He turned to me and said, "They're a bit hostile, ain't they?" I told him, "Hostile? They're gonna fucking kill us!" Now I appreciate that JC had done a bit of boxing when he was younger, but this was like standing next to Davy Crockett at "The Alamo".

JC was now telling the stewards "to get a grip of all these nutcases looking for trouble" and I had to remind him that, although the stewards were holding the Derby fans back for the moment, they lived locally and were not going to help us when we left the stadium at the end of the match. Luckily for us, Derby got a corner about fifteen minutes from full time and I could see salvation and I grabbed JC and pulled him down the stairs to get away from the still-angry mob safely.

As we left the stadium, I asked a copper for directions to the car park. The copper then asked me, "Why were you two Arsenal fans sitting in that stand reserved for Derby season ticket holders only?" I could only point at JC and reply, "Ask him, 'cos he got the poxy tickets". JC just smiled and then moaned at me all the way home about missing the remainder of the match. What a character he was, and he is still sadly missed by all of his family and friends.

Arsenal won the replay 2-1 at Highbury.

YEOVIL

In the FA Cup 3rd Round on January 2nd 1993, JC and I travelled to Yeovil to watch Arsenal win 3-1 with an Ian Wright, Wright, Wright hat trick. As this was such a memorable day for Yeovil Football Club, they were even selling commemorative baseball caps of the occasion and it was especially memorable for me, because JC had actually managed to obtain two seats in the Arsenal supporters' section, although he did get warned by the police for "inappropriate language".

On January 6th Arsenal won 1-0 at Scarborough in the League Cup 4th Round and although JC and myself had tickets, we didn't travel to this match because of the weather that was forecasting fog across most of the north of England and, as JC wasn't the best of drivers in normal conditions, there was no chance of us going in the fog.

On January 12th, Arsenal beat Forest 2-0 in the League Cup 5th Round at Highbury.

On January 25th, Arsenal drew with Leeds 2-2 in the FA Cup 4th Round at Highbury.

On February 3rd, Arsenal beat Leeds 3-2 in the FA Cup 4th Round replay at Elland Road.

On February 7th, Arsenal beat Crystal Palace 3-1 in the League Cup semi-final Ist Leg at Selhurst Park.

Most of the "Usual Suspects", including myself, went to this game on a very wet Sunday afternoon.

On February 15th, Arsenal beat Forest 2-0 in the FA Cup 5th Round at Highbury.

On March 6th, Arsenal beat Ipswich 4-2 in the FA Cup 6th Round at Portman Road.

Tickets for this match at Ipswich were very hard to come by, but as we were season ticket holders, Putney, JC, "the four wheels on my wagon" boys and myself got our allocation. We met Hoyboy and his son in the city centre pub that was owned by the ex-Arsenal player Alan Sunderland, who during the previous weeks in the media had invited all Arsenal fans to visit his pub and obviously hundreds turned up. When he eventually ran out of beer and lager, we had to drink cider instead.

You have to remember that most of the Arsenal fans in the seats were season ticket holders and didn't usually get involved in any trouble at the games.

Therefore, it came as a complete surprise to us when we could see fans from both teams fighting in the street as we came down the stairs to the exit, where, apparently, an Ipswich fan had hit the first couple of Arsenal fans with a metal pole as they left the stadium, which left them bleeding on the pavement. The police were now involved but we could see a very tall Ipswich fan sneaking away after he'd been shouting abuse and offering to fight some other Arsenal fans and I thought we'd all ignored him until, as we're walking through the car park, I noticed that Hoyboy and Putney were missing and when I asked young Hoyboy, "Where's your dad?" he replied, "He's gone with Putney to have a word with that tall Ipswich fan".

Now, like you, I know what "having a word" means and just as I found them, Putney was crouching down and reaching through the legs of the Ipswich fan trying to grab his nuts from behind, while Hoyboy was laughing as he watched him.

When the tall fella felt Putney's hand between his legs, he spun around and caught him off balance and Putney toppled over. I was then standing immediately in front of the bloke who appeared about a foot taller than me and obviously he thought it was me who'd grabbed him, as Putney was still on the floor.

As the tall bloke raised his fists, my natural instinct was to jump up and head-butt him. He then fell to the ground screaming that his nose had been broken.

Just my luck as, unbeknown to me, a copper had crept up behind me and as he grabbed me, I managed to slip away and the others then blocked him from chasing after me.

When they arrived back at the car, JC was in hysterics claiming he never knew I could run that fast.

Another quiet day out?

On April 10th, Arsenal beat Crystal Palace 2-0 in the League Cup semi-final 2nd Leg at Highbury.

WE'RE ON OUR WAY TO WEMBLEY PART ONE

On April 4th 1993, before Arsenal played the Team from the Lane in the FA Cup semi-final at Wembley, about twenty of the "Usual Suspects" met up in a hotel near Boreham Wood for a breakfast that Putney's company kindly paid for, although they never actually knew it!

Tony Adams won the "Donkey Derby" with a header, and Arsenal fans had got their revenge. The anthem, "We only waited two years" reverberated around Wembley and beyond.

WE'RE ON OUR WAY TO WEMBLEY PART TWO

On April 18th 1993, Arsenal beat Sheffield Wednesday 2-1 in the League [Coca Cola] Cup Final.

Steve Morrow will always remember this day, as not only did he score the winning goal but he dislocated his shoulder after Tony Adams dropped him during the celebrations at the game's end.

However, two of our lot will always remember it as being the day that Hoyboy's sister baked a "Cannabis Cake" for all of us but we never got to taste it, as Hoyboy and Harnetty sneaked off to the car park where the greedy bastards ate most of it between them. Naturally, they were "off their nuts" in the stadium, with one of them actually lying on the floor at one stage, but the rest of us didn't need any help to reach a state of "Nirvana" after Arsenal lifted the trophy.

We all went back to JC's pub to celebrate and when Putney's wife, Janet, came to drive him home, she took one look at all of us drunks and said, "If only your wives could see the state of you all now". Teddy Taylor replied with our legendary motto, "You can change your wives but not your football team!"

Spook and I stayed the night in one of the spare rooms upstairs in the pub. No problem with that, until we woke up in the early hours needing a piss and as I went to open the bedroom door, I forgot that JC's Rottweiler dog, Bruno, was patrolling the corridor. Spook, who is terrified of all dogs, told me to shut the door just as Bruno arrived, and we lay on our beds for a while, listening to him pounding on the door, before we decided that it was safer to piss out of the window.

There's another little story about JC in that "quiet" pub at the Elephant & Castle. One Sunday evening, he went upstairs to his bedroom and found a burglar ransacking the bedside cabinet drawers. Obviously, JC started fighting with him and Bruno could hear the commotion but was locked in a spare room as the pub was open and nobody in the bar could hear anything because of the music. Although JC's mum and mother-in-law were watching television in another upstairs room, they had just turned the sound up to drown out the noise of the fighting. After a fight that apparently lasted for fifteen minutes, the would-be burglar tried to escape by climbing out of the window but JC pulled him back in again. The burglar eventually escaped, empty-handed and minus a shoe, by hitting JC over the head with a table lamp.

When JC returned to the bar, nobody had heard a thing and the two mums were still watching their television.

FA CUP FINAL 1993

What a touch! JC had got four tickets in good seats for this game! There was only one problem, though; he wanted Putney, Spook and myself to sit with him, even though we already had ours due to our season tickets.

FA CUP FINAL 1993 –
SPANDAU'S BANNER ON RIGHT

He convinced us to give our tickets to some of our mates who hadn't got any, as he wanted to sit with us sensible blokes.

So, on FA Cup Final day, May 15th 1993, four sensible blokes, thousands of red and white-shirted Arsenal fans and thousands of blue and white striped-shirted Sheffield Wednesday fans marched down Wembley Way and when they arrived at the stadium, all the Arsenal fans turned right and all the Wednesday fans turned left, with four red and white-shirted, sensible Arsenal fans in the middle of them. Yep, the legendary JC had even out-performed himself this time with his "Creme de la Creme" moment, as unbelievably, we were now sitting with the Sheffield Wednesday season ticket holders. As we were queuing on the steps to enter the stadium, two very drunk Wednesday fans suddenly spotted our

Arsenal shirts and one of them said to Spook, "There'll be trouble inside the ground with you lot". Spook replied, "If there's gonna be any trouble, then we'll have it right now here on these steps". The two blokes wisely returned to the queue.

When we got onto the concourse inside the stadium, there were obviously thousands of Wednesday fans in their blue and white striped replica shirts, drinking and singing their songs while gazing, incredulously, at the four blokes in red and white shirts who were walking through them. We were getting so much abuse that one woman said to me, "You fellas are ever so brave to walk through here". I replied, "No love, that nutcase got us the tickets in your end," and pointed at JC, who had by now zipped his yellow jacket up to the collar after muttering, "Fuck this for a game of soldiers".

When we reached our seats near the halfway line, JC was raving about the great view of the pitch and I must admit that the seats did have a great view – of the Arsenal fans and my mate Spandau's banner at the other end of the stadium!

WITH IAN WRIGHT 1993

Ian Wright scored as Arsenal and Sheffield Wednesday drew the match 1-1.

FA CUP FINAL REPLAY 1993

Five days later, on Thursday, May 20th, Arsenal beat Sheffield Wednesday 2-1 to win the FA Cup with another goal from Ian Wright and a dramatic winning header from Andy Linighan in the last minute of extra time.

This game was memorable for the following reasons;

1 – My brother finally saw, in person, Arsenal winning a Cup Final at Wembley.
2 – JC was proved wrong, after always saying that Arsenal wouldn't win anything with Andy Linighan in the team.

3 – Teddy Taylor said at the end of the match, that due to the stress of supporting Arsenal, "None of us would make old bones". Sadly, in his case, he was proved right, as two years later, he died of a brain tumour aged 42, although thankfully, most of the rest of us have now made it into our seventies.

4 – As it was a Thursday, I had now seen Arsenal win a trophy on every day of the week.

5 – Arsenal became the first team to win both the League and FA Cups in the same season.

"Tell Yer Ma, Yer Ma,
To Put the Champagne on Ice.
We're Going to Wembley Twice,
Tell Yer Ma, Yer Ma."

Disappointingly for him, Anders Limpar missed both finals due to injury.

Arsenal finished 10th in the Premier League behind Champions Man Utd.

Marseille won the Champions League that had replaced the European Cup after beating Milan 1-0.

3 ORIGINAL NORTH BANK BOYS – [JONAH WITH BEER DIED IN 2016]

SEASON 1993-94

EUROPE – WE CAME, WE SAW, WE CONQUERED

The season got off to a bad start with David O'Leary eventually retiring after making a record 722 appearances and scoring eleven goals in his career at Arsenal.

It then got slightly worse when Eddie McGoldrick was signed from Crystal Palace, before matters got even worse than that when, after drawing 1-1 in the Charity Shield match with Man Utd, David Seaman strode up to take the last penalty in the shoot-out decider and, for reasons known only to himself, he calmly passed it to Peter Schmeichel in the United goal and then, to add insult to injury, he turned and laughed at the crowd in the stadium. Someone should have told him that Arsenal don't play friendlies with certain clubs, such as United. I vowed never to attend another Charity Shield game again, believing that if the players didn't care, why should I?

Unbelievably, it got even worse when, in the opening game of the League season, in front of the new North Bank Stand, Lee Dixon scored an own goal in Arsenal's 3-0 defeat by Coventry.

Things just had to get better soon and they did. Colin Pates was transferred and Arsenal won 1-0 at the Lane, thanks to a goal from Ian Wright, to begin a run of only one defeat in twelve games before the old inconsistency returned as Arsenal drew seventeen games in the League.

Alan Miller, Mark Flatts, Neil Heaney and Paul Dickov all made their debuts during the season.

LEAGUE [COCA COLA] CUP

In September, JC and I went to see Arsenal beat Huddersfield 5-0 in the 2nd Round 1st Leg match as neither of us had ever been there before. The occasion was also memorable for JC driving up most of the motorway at 55mph in the middle lane, as, in his words, "It's safer here", despite having the radiators of large lorries almost in the boot of his car for most of the journey. Amazingly, he also obtained tickets in the Arsenal section of the stadium.

Arsenal and Huddersfield then drew the 2nd Leg 1-1 at Highbury.

In the 3rd Round, Arsenal drew 1-1 with Norwich before winning the replay 3-0 at Carrow Road.

Arsenal then lost 1-0 against Aston Villa in the 4th Round at Highbury.

FA CUP

Arsenal beat Millwall at the New Den in the 3rd Round with a last-minute Tony Adams goal.

Unsurprisingly, this sparked a mini riot after the game in the surrounding streets, where Teddy Taylor, Spook and myself, along with hundreds of other Arsenal fans, were herded by the police towards Surrey Quays station. This was no big deal except for one thing; we had parked nearer Peckham, about two miles in the opposite direction. So, the three of us, using another cunning plan, slipped away from the police escort and started walking back towards the stadium, only to be almost mown down by three mounted coppers who were chasing some Millwall fans that were still following the Arsenal fans. We then diverted through a housing estate that was straight out of a "Charles Dickens" novel – I swear it still had gaslights – to finally reach the Old Kent Road and the motor before we eventually got back to JC's pub in time for last orders.

In the 4th Round, Arsenal drew 2-2 away at Bolton before losing the replay 3-1 at Highbury.

So, as there wouldn't be any chance of retaining the FA and League Cups at Wembley this season, everything hinged on a good try at winning the European Cup Winners Cup instead.

Arsenal finished 4th in the Premier League behind Champions Man Utd.

Man Utd won the FA Cup after beating Chelsea 4-0.

Aston Villa won the League Cup after beating Man Utd 3-1.

Milan won the Champions League after beating Barcelona 4-0.

EUROPEAN CUP WINNERS CUP 1993-94

ODENSE

In the 1st Round in September, Arsenal started their ECWC campaign by beating Odense 2-1 in Denmark, without knowing that they would end the campaign in the same country in May, before the two teams drew 1-1 In the 2nd Leg at Highbury.

STANDARD LIEGE

In the 2nd Round, 1st Leg Arsenal beat Standard Liege 3-0 at Highbury before winning 7-0 in the 2nd Leg in Belgium, where even Eddie McGoldrick managed to score a goal.

Apart from the scoreline, this night was memorable for the "Curly Whirly Turd" that mysteriously appeared on a toilet seat.

Putney drove Hoyboy, young Hoyboy and myself to Liege for this game and after an unremarkable afternoon in a bar near the ground that only had one record, "Blueberry Hill", worth listening to in the jukebox, we entered the stadium and sat near the halfway line in front of the Main Stand.

Just before halftime, I needed a piss, so I left to go and find the toilets before the queues formed, as these toilets were very basic; a single metal urinal trough and three closets.

While I was having a piss, I heard someone loudly speaking or swearing, in what I assumed was Belgian and as I turned around, I notice that all three closet doors were open and the toilets were full to the brim with shit. Obviously, they hadn't been emptied or cleaned since the last match at the stadium the previous weekend, so naturally, when I got back to my seat, I warned the other three about the filthy state of the toilets. Hoyboy now decided that he needed a shit and so off he went with his son and when they returned about twenty minutes later from the opposite direction, he had a big smile on his face, confirming that the toilets were as bad as I told him and suggesting that Putney should also have a look. Putney declined the offer, but when the game finished, we decide to have a piss before returning to the car. When we entered the toilet, someone was trying to get some poor soul in a wheelchair into one of the closets but when they opened the door, I could see that a large curly-shaped turd had been deposited on the toilet seat lid by a previous occupant, and Hoyboy was in hysterics.

I will leave you to decide who that previous occupant was; I just know that it wasn't Putney or me!

TORINO

In March, some of us flew to Milan the day before Arsenal's 3rd Round 1st Leg 0-0 draw with Torino, but for some unknown reason, our hotel was also in Milan.

On arriving, we decided to visit the San Siro stadium, the home of both Inter and AC Milan before sightseeing in the city and drinking in a bar.

The next day, a coach picked us up and we were taken straight to the Delle Alpi stadium that Torino shared with Juventus.

TORINO FANS IN STADIO DELLA ALPI VS ARSENAL 1994

I remember that back in the 1980s, a poll was taken in a newspaper on whether Arsenal and the Team from the Lane could ever share a stadium like these Italian clubs. Apparently, their fans said yes, but Arsenal fans said NEVER!!

Outside the stadium, Spook spotted a burger stall and we grabbed one each. Stupidly, I asked for some sauerkraut on mine and this almost led to disastrous consequences later on inside the ground.

When we were queuing up to enter the stadium, the police were confiscating trouser belts and cigarette lighters from the Arsenal fans for so-called safety reasons.

Absolutely ridiculous, because when we finally got in, there were giant red flares being held up by Torino fans at the opposite end of the stadium.

THE BUBBLE

About halfway through the second half of the game in Turin, I started to get a weird feeling in my stomach and what felt like a large bubble started winding its way through my intestines. I now realised that the sauerkraut was beginning to have an effect on my body.

Spook was standing next to me and I said to him, "I've got this bubble moving through my guts and I can only hope that it's a fart and not a turd".

A few minutes later, Spook was quietly chuckling away to himself when the bubble finally reached the departure lounge. Phuut! it was out, but thank goodness it was only a silent but incredibly deadly fart.

Moments later, Teddy Taylor, who was standing directly behind me, was covering his nose and mouth with his hands and screaming, "What's that fucking smell?". Spook was now doubled up with laughter as I told Teddy, "I can't smell anything". The trouble was that anyone within five metres of us was coughing and spluttering and moving further away, including the Italian police who'd been guarding us.

Needless to say, I've never eaten sauerkraut again, although it wasn't as bad as leaving a turd on a toilet seat lid, like some, allegedly, anonymous person did in Liege.

Arsenal won the 2nd Leg 2-0 at Highbury and now we were off to another semi-final.

PARIS

We hired a coach to go to the semi-final 1st Leg against PSG in Paris. As tickets for this match were hard to come by, Putney arranged for someone at his company's Paris office to purchase them on our behalf. There was only one slight problem; our fifteen tickets in the stadium were in the Main Stand directly opposite where the Arsenal fans were located, although I have to admit that, for once in his life, JC was not involved in getting these tickets.

When we boarded the coach in London, I noticed that two of the "4 wheels" boys were wearing their best clothes and this was because the night before we left, I had told them we would go clubbing after the game. They weren't too happy when they realised it was a wind-up.

When we arrived at Dover for the ferry crossing, the customs agents couldn't believe that there was no booze on the coach. As we knew they would obviously search for some, we hadn't loaded any on board, however, we did when we arrived in Calais.

After arriving in Paris, we had the usual drinking session in the afternoon, where Spook made friends with an African bloke, "Ganja Man", who was dressed in camouflage combat clothing and you can imagine the piss-taking Spook suffered.

When the time came, we made our way to the stadium via the Metro and Spook insisted on following the route of his newly acquired subway map. As many of you will already know, the Paris Metro is just like the London Underground, easy to follow with different colours for each line and so, after about ten minutes of watching Spook studying his map and still getting us on the wrong line, I snatched it from him and tore it up, leaving him speechless for once.

Then, as we were walking through one of the subway passages, Hoyboy's son spotted a tramp who bore a remarkable resemblance to JC. Immediately, we all started singing, "There's only two Johnny Collins, there's only two Johnny Collins" and JC was not amused and refused my request to have his photo taken with his new twin brother, which only made us sing even louder and longer.

When we came out of the Metro station near the stadium, it was just like the old days. PSG fans were congregating, looking for a fight with any Arsenal fans they could find, but we just bunched up together and walked right through the middle of them. They probably thought we were too old to bother with. Mind you, I think they might have got a shock if they had started on us.

However, we did hear later that there was some serious fighting

PSG FANS IN PARC DE PRINCE VS ARSENAL 1994

between the two sets of fans elsewhere, with many Arsenal fans being locked up in an empty warehouse by the police for the duration of the game.

BRIAN MOORE

When we finally got to our allocated stadium entrance, there was pandemonium. The officials started panicking because they realised they had fifteen Arsenal fans with tickets for the Main Stand and I had to produce a letter on headed notepaper from Putney's company stating that all of us were their staff on a specially sponsored company trip to Paris for the match. This cunning plan worked and we were eventually escorted to our seats by police officers carrying machine guns.

After they left us, we went out onto the concourse for a couple of beers, then, a few minutes later, we said hello to the television commentator, Brian Moore, as he walked past us. After five minutes, Tony Adelizzi and I followed him through the same door and then climbed up the ladder to the television gantry, where Brian was sitting doing his pre-match notes. Once he got over the initial shock of seeing us again, Brian was as good as gold and we both had our photos taken with him.

IN THE TV GANTRY WITH
BRIAN MOORE – PARIS 1994

Inside the stadium, the PSG fans sang a powerful rendition of the Bob Marley song "Buffalo Soldier", before David Ginola scored for PSG and Ian Wright (who else?) scored for Arsenal in a 1-1 draw and if I remember correctly, this was the night that the anthem "One Nil to the Arsenal" was first sung.

In the 2nd Leg at Highbury, Kevin Campbell scored the goal that sent Arsenal to the ECWC Final but tragically, Ian Wright got booked and would now be suspended for the match against Parma.

WONDERFUL, WONDERFUL COPENHAGEN.

On May 4th 1994, Arsenal beat the Italian team Parma 1-0 in Copenhagen to win the European Cup Winners Cup Final. About 25,000 Arsenal fans travelled to Denmark for this game, including many of the "Usual Suspects" past and present. Poor old JC was one of the few of our lot who didn't make the trip as he'd recently suffered a heart attack and his doctors had advised him not to travel. We arrived in Copenhagen the day before the match and, after checking into our hotel, we all went out for a few beers.

We were in a bar near the famous "Tivoli Gardens" with many other Gooners, when a bloke appeared in the doorway and, due to his size, nearly blocked out all of the light. Edwin Childs, who you might remember had been bashed by all the "Lilliputian" youngsters at Forest in 1979, said to me, "That's Denton". I could only reply, "I hope he doesn't remember us". Thankfully, he didn't!

COPENHAGEN – 1995

MATCH DAY

The next morning, some of us went off to do some sightseeing, while the others visited the Tivoli Gardens or looked for a bar.

Spook, Granty and myself discover the famous "Mermaid" statue in the river next to a park and we manage to drape it with an Arsenal shirt

COPENHAGEN MERMAID
IS A GOONER

without any of us getting wet before, in the early afternoon, we all met up again, and after grabbing a snack, we descended on the outside bar of a pub next to the old harbour. There were now about twenty of us, as we'd also met up with Gary Davies and Lenny Togwell, so we almost filled this separate section and Granty asked the barmaid to pour twenty beers. When she'd almost finished pouring, he told her to start again and then just keep them coming. Eventually, she had to get another barmaid to assist her as she couldn't keep up with us. Well, it was hot! After a couple of hours, our old mate Rod Moore turned up with his family and we asked him, "How did you know we were here?" He replied, "I could hear you all from three streets away".

Later in the afternoon, a Swedish bloke, who'd been sitting at a nearby table with his mate having lunch, loudly declared that he was fed up listening to our swearing, as all he could hear was, "Fuck you, Fuck this, Fuck that, Fuck him, Fuck her, Fuck, Fuck, Fuck!" He then asked us, "What have you to say to this then?" As one, we all replied, "Fuck Off". Then just as the waitress brought him his dessert of two small balls of ice cream, this idiot said, "Another word I keep hearing is bollocks; what is bollocks?" We all pointed at his dessert and again, in perfect unison, shouted, "That's bollocks".

Funny now; even funnier then.

INSIDE THE STADIUM

As the Parken Stadium was only a couple of miles away, we decided to walk there from the bar and long before we got there, all we could hear were groups of Arsenal fans singing as they also made their way to the ground. The scenes were similar to the streets outside Highbury before a home game. When we got into the stadium, it was even more like Highbury as three sides of the ground were full of Arsenal fans, including the whole of the covered stand behind one goal, and the few thousand Parma fans were located out in the open behind the opposite goal.

I even bumped into my old mates, Spandau and Jim Patterson, plus Vic Wright and Barry Baker from the Arsenal Supporters Club.

Throughout the game, the Arsenal supporters continuously sang their new anthem, "One Nil to The Arsenal" and were justly rewarded when Alan "Smudger" Smith scored the only goal, as an Arsenal team without Ian Wright, Martin Keown, John Jensen and Anders Limpar but including Ian Selley, Steve Morrow and substitute, Eddie McGoldrick, somehow overcame the highly-rated favourites, who had Gianfranco Zola, Faustino Asprilla and Tomas Brolin in their team.

At the end of the game, Granty, who'd disappeared with the hump at half time when one of the others sat in his seat, returned and with a tear in his eye, remarked, "I'm so happy, but I was all on my own". He was immediately nicknamed "Macauley Culkin".

After the game, Spook and I saw Johnny Jensen and I had my customary photo taken with him. Unfortunately for Spook, I then ran out of film as there weren't any digital cameras at that time.

Unfortunately for John Jensen, somebody nicked his wallet when he was in a nightclub celebrating.

The next morning, as we were all in the hotel lobby waiting to go to the airport, I saw Peter Landers reading the back page of a newspaper. The front page happened to have the photo of a familiar face wearing a Viking style helmet. I asked Peter, who jointly owned a shop in Smithfield meat market, if one of his staff, Ray Head, had phoned in sick in the last few days. Peter replied, "No, he's taken some days off that he was due; why do you ask?" After I told him to look at the front page, Peter just burst out laughing, as there was Ray wearing his Viking helmet.

This day is one of my favourite memories of all the trips with my mates, especially as none of us dreamt that it would be Teddy Taylor's last Arsenal Cup Final.

None of us dreamt that it would also be George Graham's last Arsenal Cup Final and trophy, although many Arsenal fans did realise they wouldn't see Anders Limpar in an Arsenal shirt again.

SUMMER 1994

Arsenal bought another Swedish player, Stefan Schwarz, to replace Anders and promoted Lee Harper, Vince Bartram, Scott Marshall, Paul Hughes and Stephen Hughes from the Youth team.

TONY ADAMS TESTIMONIAL

In the summer of 1994, Tony Adams received a well-deserved Testimonial match at Highbury but for some strange reason, this fixture was squeezed in between the pre-season tournament and the first League game of the season at home.

For some even stranger reason, the opposition were Crystal Palace when, for a man of his stature, it should have been either Milan, Barcelona or Ajax at least, and sadly, but not

GRANTY – TONY ADAMS – GEORGE

unsurprisingly, the attendance was very low as many people were still on holiday.

219

However, Arsenal fans were confident of more trophies to come in the following season, not realising how those dreams would be shattered in such incredible circumstances.

SEASON 1994-95

MONKEY – MILAN – MONEY

Arsenal opened their League campaign with a 3-0 victory against Man City at Highbury, then never won again in the next five games and this pattern would be repeated throughout the season and would eventually result in Arsenal's lowest League position for seventeen seasons, especially as they also only managed to score more than one goal in a match on another twelve occasions.

In November, Paul Merson admitted to having drink, drugs and gambling addictions before he went into rehabilitation until February. In an attempt to increase the firepower, George Graham signed John Hartson, Chris Kiwomya and Glenn Helder in January 1995.

The only highlight on the pitch was when, on New Year's Eve, Johnny Jensen finally scored his first goal for Arsenal after 98 games, in a 3-1 defeat to QPR at a cold, wet, miserable Highbury. The whole stadium erupted in prolonged celebrations that must have gone on for about fifteen minutes, and any onlooker would have thought Arsenal had just won the League, which demonstrates just how tedious the football had become.

Off the pitch, Hoyboy turned up in the "Crusoe" for one home game with his brother-in-law and his mates. Apparently, Hoyboy had told them I was a bit of an "Anorak" regarding Arsenal's history and his brother-in-law was going to test me, as he'd been doing a bit of research all that week.

After agreeing that the loser would buy the next pint and with everyone listening intently, especially Hoyboy, who was almost standing on my shoulder, he asked these questions;

B-I-Law – Who were Arsenal's first opponents at Highbury?
Me – Leicester Fosse.

B-I-Law – What was the score?
Me – 2-1 to Arsenal.

B-I-Law – Who scored the goals?
Me – Andy Devine and George Jobey.

B-I-Law – What happened to Jobey later in the game?
Me – He got injured as was carried off.

B-I-Law – How was he carried off?
Me – On a cart.

B-I-Law – Whose cart was it?
Me – The local milkman's in Gillespie Road.

B-I-Law – What was the milkman's name?
Me – Griffiths.

The brother-in-law turned to Hoyboy and everyone else in the pub and said, "This guy's unbelievable", before going to the bar to get my pint.

Hoyboy then said to me, "I knew all those answers except the name of the milkman. How did you know his name?" I replied, "I never knew it either, so I took a gamble that he wouldn't know it, and just gave him a Welsh-sounding name as I knew all the dairies in London used to be owned by Welshman in those days". Hoyboy had to go outside as he was laughing so much and has never told his brother-in-law the truth to this day. By the way, the milkman's name was David Lewis.

OLD? FAT? – HAVE THAT!

The only other incident worth recalling occurred during the 1-1 draw against the Team from the Lane in April at Highbury, when, after they scored in front of their fans at the Clock End, a twenty-something fan of theirs stood up behind me in the North Bank Upper Tier and started singing. Obviously, he was getting pelted with all sorts of objects that were also hitting me and Teddy Taylor and so I suggested that if he wanted to celebrate, he should go up the other end where his mates were. He just sneered at me and said, "Come downstairs, you fat, old bastard". At this, I just smiled and, without leaving my seat, grabbed his belt and yanked him over my head and with two punches knocked him out as he was lying on my lap. Teddy Taylor then helped me to put him back in his seat next to his terrified mate who was now claiming to be an Arsenal fan.

By now, about half the stadium was watching and within minutes, the police and stewards arrived demanding to know what had happened.

I calmly explained that I was a season ticket and bond-holder, with my name on my seat and this idiot had sat behind me and threatened me. By now, the young bloke had recovered and so the police carted him away. When we later got back to the "Crusoe", Tony Adelizzi asked us if we'd seen the commotion where we sat up in the stands. Teddy Taylor just pointed at me and laughed.

LEAGUE CUP

In the 2nd Round 1st Leg, Tony Eames and I went to Hartlepool and saw Arsenal win 5-0.

I used to like going to these League Cup away legs as they gave me the chance to visit the grounds of the smaller clubs that Arsenal didn't usually play against but sadly, this system was dropped after the following season and many smaller clubs would lose a much-needed payday.

Tony Eames wanted to go to Hartlepool to find the "Hanging Monkey" and in case you're wondering, legend has it that during the Napoleonic Wars, a French ship was sunk off the coast near Hartlepool and the only survivor was the mascot, which happened to be a monkey. As the monkey obviously couldn't speak English, never mind anything else, when he was put on trial, the xenophobic locals assumed he was French and hung him as a spy. Incredible but true!

We were met at Newcastle railway station by a couple of my old mates and went off to the Bigg Market for a few beers. When Tony asked them what they wanted to drink, they both replied, "A pint of Scotch, please". Tony looked at me and said, "Is this going to be a silly day out?" Laughingly, they explained that 'Scotch' is the name of the beer up there. Later in the afternoon, we drove the short journey to Hartlepool and set off in search of the monkey. After visiting the Marina, which only had one old boat moored up in it – well it's not exactly Monaco, is it? – we ventured into the Hartlepool United Supporters Club bar, home of the "Monkey Hangers", where much to the delight and amusement of the four of us, in a corner of the club, hanging from the ceiling, was a toy monkey. I had my photo taken with it but as Tony lifted it onto his shoulders for his photo, the monkey fell off the hook and he now had to try and get it fixed back on without annoying the locals, who were now all staring at him.

Later on, as we were standing outside the ground, the Arsenal team coach arrived and we had our photos taken with David Seaman, Lee Dixon and Ian Wright, before going inside the ground, where we discovered the best meat pies I've ever had at a football match, without sauerkraut on them, obviously. They were the size of a small plate. The cold rain came in horizontally from the North Sea, which was only a couple of hundred yards away, and soaked all of us Arsenal fans standing on an uncovered terrace, even though It was still only September.

In the 2nd Leg, Arsenal won 2-0 at Highbury.

Arsenal drew 0-0 away at Oldham in the 3rd Round before winning the replay 2-0 at Highbury.

Arsenal then beat Sheffield Wednesday in the 4th Round at Highbury before losing to Liverpool 1-0 at Anfield in the Quarter-Final.

FA CUP

In the 3rd Round, Arsenal drew 0-0 away at Millwall before losing the replay 2-0 at Highbury.

So, after never having played Millwall before in a cup tie, Arsenal played them three years running.

EUROPEAN SUPER CUP – MILAN

In February 1995, I achieved another of my ambitions when I saw Arsenal play against Milan in the famous San Siro stadium, in the first, and so far, only time that Arsenal have played in the European Super Cup.

I went to this game with Gary Davies and his, sadly, now-deceased mate, Stephen "Yog" Cordrey, where we found an "Irish" bar in the City centre and when I ordered the drinks, the barman asked me, "Are you Arsenal fans over here for the match?" When I replied "yes", he told me

WITH MALCOM [SUPERMAC]
MACDONALD – MILAN 1995

INSIDE SAN SIRO –
MILAN VS ARSENAL 1995

that the ex-Arsenal player, Malcolm "Supermac" MacDonald, was in the downstairs bar being interviewed by the Arsenal supporting journalist, Amy Lawrence.

Naturally, I went off to find them and luckily, Amy had just finished the interview. I invited Malcolm to join us in the bar upstairs and Yog was especially happy as, being a bit younger than Gary and myself, "Supermac" had been his hero. We bought Malcolm a few pints and he told us some stories about his time at Arsenal and what a great club it was.

When I told Yog to ask his hero Malcolm a question, he was so nervous, all he could say was, "How do you have a shit in these Italian toilets, where there's only a small hole in the floor and two indentations for your feet?" Gary and myself cracked up and Malcolm replied, "with a good aim"! You won't be surprised to know that before Malcolm left us, we had the obligatory photo shoot. Later, outside the stadium, we bumped into Charlie George and had the chance of another photo. Before entering the stadium, the fog came down, but not enough to stop us from seeing Arsenal lose 2-0.

One funny moment before the start of the game was when, a very optimistic ice-cream seller stood behind the goal in front of the Arsenal fans shouting, "Ice cream, ice cream, lovely ice cream."

In total unison, the Arsenal fans all sang;

"Just one Cornetto,
Give it to me,
Delicious ice cream,
From Italy".

To everyone's amusement, the ice-cream seller responded by waving his arms about as if he was conducting the singing.

EUROPEAN CUP WINNERS CUP 1994-95

Arsenal beat Omnia Nicosia 3-1 in Cyprus and 3-0 at Highbury in the 1st Round.

In the 2nd Round 1st Leg, they beat Brondby 2-1 in Denmark before drawing 2-2 at Highbury.

On February 21st 1995, Arsenal sacked George Graham for allegedly taking a £285,000 bung involving the transfer of Pal Lydersen and Stewart Houston was appointed as Temporary Manager.

As only George Graham knows the truth regarding this matter, I can merely thank him for my memories of the trophies and the opportunities he gave me to see "The Arsenal" play in some of the most famous stadiums in Europe.

On March 2nd, in the 3rd Round 1st Leg, Arsenal drew 1-1 with Auxerre in France, thanks to a superb performance from David Seaman and a goal from Ian Wright, who also scored the only goal in the 2nd Leg at Highbury.

SAMPDORIA

In the semi-final, Arsenal beat Sampdoria 3-2 at Highbury with goals from the unlikely source of David Hillier and, even more surprisingly, a brace from Steve Bould.

On April 20th, Arsenal travelled to Italy for the 2nd Leg and Putney, with his son Jordan, Gary Davies and myself went the day before, with a group that was recommended but not organised by Chris Knott. In fact, it wasn't organised very well at all as this trip included flying to and from Milan, then a coach to

SAMPDORIA VS ARSENAL – 1995

and from Genoa, two nights in a hotel and match tickets. That was the theory, but this was the reality. No return flights from Milan, no coach from Genoa back to Milan, the hotel was thirty minutes away by road from Genoa, hotel accommodation had not been paid for and the match tickets were counterfeit.

Gary and I didn't find out about any of this until we arrived at the hotel the next day as we'd hired a car in Milan and gone to visit my cousin Annabelle and her family at her home in Florence where she's lived for many years.

Her husband, Alberto, insisted on showing us the stadium of his beloved "Viola", Fiorentina FC to me and you, before some more sightseeing, dinner, vino and an overnight stay. Gary and I then drove down to the hotel which was supposed to be in Genoa but was so far down the coast and up in the hills that I think Florence might have been nearer. When we finally arrived, Putney and Knottsy explained the bad news that none of the trip had been paid for, apart from the flights to Milan and the coach from the airport to the hotel. Unluckily for Knottsy, some of the other Arsenal fans on this trip had mistakenly believed that he'd organised it and he had turned them over for the money, so they gave him a few clumps the night before and, according to Knottsy, threatened to throw him over the balcony.

The day before, when Putney had discovered the hotel wasn't paid for, he and Jordan checked into another nicer hotel near the Marina.

Surprisingly, this Marina had a few larger, more expensive boats than the one at Hartlepool and Gary and I checked into this hotel as well. Knottsy came in the car to Genoa with us but checked into a hotel there instead, as he would be getting a flight back to London from that airport.

While Knottsy was checking in at the Hilton Hotel, we had a drink in the bar and met Ron Atkinson and Brian Moore who would be commentating on the match later.

After the obligatory photos, we made our way to our allocated entrance at the stadium and it was total chaos; all forty of the blokes who were on our trip were being refused entry with their dodgy tickets. Eventually, an official from the British Consulate arrived and, after some prolonged discussions, we were escorted inside by the police, where, because we didn't have a seat, as many of us had the same seat number on our tickets, we were made to stand at the back of the stand behind the seating area. No problem; most of the Arsenal fans stood up during the game anyway.

We found out later that some of these fans appeared to have had an even worse time than us when they travelled with the Official Arsenal Travel Club. By all accounts, when their coaches arrived in Genoa from the airport, they were herded into a temporary parking area with high fences near the docks, and were forced to wait there all day without access to food, drink or toilets.

Arsenal lost 3-2 despite a Stefan Schwarz long-range free-kick and the usual Ian Wright goal before, in the penalty shoot-out, Paul Merson hit the winner after David Seaman had saved two of Sampdoria's attempts.

The stewards and police now decide to treat the Arsenal fans to the customary one-hour wait, but I had a cunning plan. I had bought a

Sampdoria scarf as a souvenir for the son of a mate of mine and so I draped it around my neck and walked past a steward in front of Putney, Jordan and Gary, who were bunched up behind me. The cunning plan worked and we drove back to the "Lord Nelson" bar near our hotel in Chiavari, where we were treated to drinks and snacks by a, presumably, wealthy local, who unsurprisingly, by the time he'd finished drinking with us happy souls, had to be carried home by his mates.

The next morning, Gary and I woke up with what can loosely be described as "The Runs".

After some breakfast, we all drove back to Milan airport in the hire car and then discovered that there were only full-price tickets available on the last flights to London later that night.

Putney now had an even better cunning plan, as he put them on his company credit card.

Footnote: When Knottsy got back to London that evening, he decided to ring my wife and ask to speak to me. When she replied that I was supposed to be in Italy with him, he told her that there had been a bit of trouble out there and then hung up.

My wife then sat up half the night trying to decide whether I was in hospital or prison.

HOUSTON'S ALAMO – PARIS 1995

IT STARTED WITH A KISS TOUR

On May 10th, Arsenal lost 1-0 to Real Zaragoza in the European Cup Winners Cup Final in Paris.

The afternoon before, about twenty-five of us had met up at a hotel in Brentwood where our hired coach would be picking us up to take us to Paris. After a few beers, as we were all boarding the coach, Putney decided to thank the hotel manageress for their hospitality with a kiss on the cheek. Well, judging from her reaction, you'd have thought he'd violently raped her, as within minutes, the staff were blocking the coach from leaving and the police arrived with blue lights flash-

WITH GEORGE & PETER
SYMES – PARIS 1995

ing. Putney then had to apologise profusely to this lady and I had to sit on Hoyboy's lap as he wanted to "have a word" with the coppers and the hotel staff. Nightmare, and we hadn't even left the hotel car park yet, never mind the next 280 miles to Paris!

All was sorted and we arrived at our French hotel without any further incidents. The next day, we walked along the wide footpath beside the river Seine and found a nice bar near the Eiffel Tower, which we decided would be our HQ for the afternoon. Some of the youngsters went off sightseeing with their dads while the rest of us made ourselves comfortable before amazingly, Rod Moore turned up again with his family just like he did

PARIS 1995 - JAMIE TOGWELL –
GARY DAVIES – LENNY TOGWELL
[LENNY DIED IN 2020]

SPANDAU'S BANNER – PARIS 1995

in Copenhagen. Then my mate, Spandau, arrived with his kids, Jordan, Ben and Charlotte, plus his famous "Arsenal" banner, which was immediately draped over the railings outside. I think the bar owner enjoyed us spending our money in there just as much as we did, before we later took the Metro to the stadium where the police had formed a barrier across the access roads and were checking match tickets and searching everyone.

These procedures meant that thousands of Arsenal fans had to filter through the police lines almost in single file and it was causing a large hold-up, so, while we were waiting, we started singing;

> "One Johnny Collins, there's only one Johnny Collins,
> one Johnny Collins, there's only one Johnny Collins".

and then, "We all live in a Johnny Collins world, a Johnny Collins world".

To JC's and our utter amazement, hundreds of Arsenal fans joined in. After about ten minutes, one bloke, who'd been singing his head off, said to my nephew, "Who the fuck is Johnny Collins?" and those of us who heard him could hardly walk for laughing.

Inside the stadium, Granty and Harnetty finally turned up after flying in from Luton airport, but not until after they'd joined in with a French family singing "La Marseillaise" a few times, at a birthday party in a bar near the stadium.

Unfortunately, Nayim, the ex-player from The Lane, also turned up and scored the winner in the last minute of extra time, with a shot from the halfway line that caught David Seaman off his line.

To cap it all, Arsenal fans were tear-gassed by the French police when they tried to leave the stadium after being told to wait, while Zaragoza were presented with the trophy.

My mates and I then went back to our hotel and drowned our sorrows with a few beers.

Harnetty slept in the bath, more comfortable than the sink in Nottingham, and Granty slept on the floor of our hotel room.

The next morning, as our coach home wasn't due until the afternoon, rather than have any more booze, Spook, my brother, his son and I decide to visit the grave of Jim Morrison, the legendary singer of the Doors rock band, in Père Lachaise cemetery.

On the coach journey home, we received the devastating news that our dearly loved old mate, Teddy Taylor, had been diagnosed with a malignant brain tumour and only had a few months to live.

So, the "It started with a kiss" tour sadly finished with a tear.

At the end of season 1994-95, Arsenal finished 12th behind Champions Blackburn Rovers.

Everton won the FA Cup after beating Man Utd 1-0.

Norwich won the League Cup after beating Sunderland 1-0.

Ajax won the Champions League after beating Milan 1-0.

Stewart Houston left the caretaker manager's seat.

Tragically, Teddy Taylor left us all in August, aged 42.

Tribute to Teddy Taylor.

In fondest remembrance of our mate, Teddy.
You will live as long as we live,
because the memories of you will be told and retold,
just like your favourite, Paddy's song,
over and over and over again.

TEDDY TAYLOR – MYSELF –
MICKEY (PUTNEY) CHILDS – JC

7

THE BRUCE RIOCH YEARS

Bruce & Bergkamp

Bruce Rioch was appointed as manager with Stewart Houston as his assistant and, not long afterwards, I happened to be driving past the stadium one evening when Bruce came out of the main door and started walking towards the car park beneath the Clock End. After welcoming him to Highbury, I asked what Arsenal fans could expect from his team. He replied that he, "wanted a couple of wingers to put in lots of crosses for the strikers". I then asked what his policy would be if Arsenal scored first. When he replied that he'd want the team to go looking to score more goals, I said that Arsenal fans would start panicking and would prefer another defender to be brought on, as we were only used to winning 1-0. At that, Bruce just laughed and made his way home.

He never mentioned that Dennis Bergkamp, one of the greatest players in the history of Arsenal, would soon be joining from Inter Milan and apparently, Bruce tried to sign Andrei Kanchelskis from Man Utd as well but that never materialised, although David Platt did join from Sampdoria, but thankfully, not as a goalie!

Stefan Schwarz went to Fiorentina and Kevin Campbell joined Forest, Chris Kiwomya moved on and two of the most underrated players in Arsenal's history, Paul Davis and Alan Smith, retired.

DEBUTS

For the first time in my life, I went with a few thousand other Arsenal fans to Southend's Root's Hall stadium to see Dennis Bergkamp make his Arsenal debut in a pre-season friendly, before I also saw his and David Platt's Highbury debuts in another friendly against Inter Milan.

Bizarrely, Kevin Campbell would score a goal at Highbury for Forest before Dennis Bergkamp scored one there for Arsenal, but looking back, I don't think any Gooner is bothered now though.

I celebrated with thousands of other Arsenal fans at Highbury when Dennis finally scored his first goal for the club after 646 minutes and 10 seconds of playing time, during his seventh League game in a 4-2 victory against Southampton on September 23rd.

Despite Bruce Rioch's hopes of Arsenal playing more attacking football, they actually ended up scoring fewer goals than in the previous two seasons, although they did qualify for the UEFA Cup after beating Bolton 2-1 with goals from David Platt and Dennis Bergkamp on the last day of the season at Highbury, so I think that was a case of money well spent then!

In April, some fans of the Team from the Lane had actually turned up for the 0-0 draw, and there was some serious fighting and seat-throwing in the Clock End between the two sets of supporters after the game, which spilled out into the surrounding streets.

LEAGUE [COCA COLA] CUP

Arsenal travelled, without me, to Hartlepool in the 2nd Round 1st Leg and won 3-0.

In the 2nd Leg at Highbury, they won 5-0.

In the 4th Round, JC, George and Rikki Hammond and myself drove to Barnsley to see Arsenal win 3-0 in such atrocious weather that the Barnsley stewards handed out plastic ponchos to all the Arsenal fans in the uncovered seats behind one of the goals where the rain was coming into our faces horizontally from the nearby moors, and this was later recorded as the wettest Arsenal game ever. In the 4th Round, Arsenal beat Sheffield Wednesday 2-1 at Highbury.

I was in hospital during January 1996 when Arsenal beat Newcastle in the 5th Round 2-0 at Highbury, with David Ginola getting sent off after elbowing Lee Dixon in the face, and I also missed both the semi-final 1st Leg 2-2 draw against Aston Villa and then the 2nd Leg 0-0 at Villa Park, which is remembered by many Arsenal fans for the unusual animosity shown to them by the Villa fans, especially as Villa had qualified for the final.

FA CUP

As I was still in hospital in January 1996, I missed the 3rd Round 1-1 draw at Highbury against Sheffield United.

This day was memorable for my mates because the actor, Sean Bean, turned up in the "Crusoe" pub with some other Sheffield United-supporting pals and was enjoying some friendly banter about his "Dick Van Dyke" style of Cockney accent before Putney then decided to pull his favourite stunt of spraying everyone in the pub with a soda syphon before leaving. As Putney was walking out of the pub, a big Sheffield United supporter with no hair at all, not even any eyebrows, was sitting by the door and said to Putney, "If you ever come to Sheffield, go to such and such tavern and you'll get plenty of grief in there". Harnetty looked at the hairless and eyebrowless fella and said, "How will we recognise you?" as everyone cracked up laughing.

Despite the soda-syphoning incident, Sean Bean and his mates happily returned to the pub after the game.

Arsenal lost the replay 1-0 and apparently, there were some serious arguments in the dressing room afterwards, that, allegedly, culminated in Ian Wright asking for a transfer, causing Arsenal fans to become very concerned with what was happening behind the scenes.

Due to my recuperation, I didn't return to Highbury until the 3-1 victory against Man City in March.

Arsenal finished 5th in the Premier League behind Champions Man Utd.

Man Utd won the FA Cup after beating Liverpool 1-0.

Aston Villa won the League Cup after beating Leeds United 3-0.

Juventus won the Champions League, beating Ajax on penalties after a 1-1 draw.

"DIXIE"

Another JC story was when he ordered a brand-new car from Putney's company and was told when to come and collect it. When the car arrived from the factory, Putney asked the mechanic to remove the front bumpers and insert some car horns inside before fixing them back on, and the mechanic then wired these horns up to the reverse position on the gear stick. When JC and his wife, Joannie, drove home in their shiny, brand spanking new car, as they reversed onto their drive, they suddenly heard the tune "Dixie", "Da da da da da da da, da da, da da", loudly repeating and JC said to Joannie, "Can you hear music?" He then reversed a bit further and the music of "Dixie" blared out again. By now, his neighbours were coming out to see where all the noise was coming from.

JC then drove to his local Car Spares shop and asked the assistant behind the counter, "Do you know anything about motors? Every time I put my car in reverse, music comes out of the engine". The assistant thought he had a lunatic in the shop and told JC to fuck off.

JC then rang Putney, who had already informed his secretary to tell all callers he was out for the afternoon, and Putney then listened in while JC was ranting away at her about being stitched up.

PRE-SEASON 1996

Towards the end of July 1996, JC, Knottsy, myself and Soldier Dave, who was a regular customer in JC's pub, flew to Glasgow to see Arsenal play Celtic in a friendly; no, we didn't burn a flag!

On the day of the match, we visited Hampden Park and Ibrox, where we bumped into the Rangers players, Brian Laudrup, Richard Gough and Andy Goram, before we had a look in the Rangers club shop, except Dave, who was a Catholic and still had family living in Glasgow and refused to enter it with us in case he was spotted. JC was also a Catholic but nothing ever bothered him. Like I've said before, sport, politics and religion don't mix, in my opinion.

We then had a few "bevvies" in the Celtic legend, Billy McNeill's pub, which made Dave happy, before going to Celtic Park, where, near the stadium, we discovered a little bar that was straight out of the 1930s;

no music, no glass-fronted fridges, dark wood panelling, tobacco-stained walls, a big old clock on the wall that, judging by the dust on its motionless hands, obviously hadn't worked for years, and a landlady who bore a strong resemblance to the ex-heavyweight boxer, Joe Bugner.

I can still recall our conversations with her to this day;

Landlady, on hearing our accents – "What are youse doing in Glasgow?"

JC – "We've come to see the match, love!"

Landlady – "What match would that be then?"

Me – "The one that all those people passing the window wearing green and white hooped shirts are going to."

Landlady – "What do youse all want to drink?"

Knottsy, who had his jumper, trendily at the time, draped over his shoulders – "I'll have a cold bottle of "Becks" please".

Landlady – "A cold bottle of what?"

Me to Knottsy – "Have a look around, you idiot; we ain't exactly in Covent Garden, are we?"

Knottsy – "Sorry, love, I'll have half a pint of draught lager instead, please".

JC – "I'll have half a pint of draught lager as well please, love".

Landlady – Once she'd got over the shock of being called love on three occasions in one day, glared at me and said – "And what do youse want?"

Me – "A pint of draught lager, please".

Landlady – "A whole pint? Are you sure you can manage that?"

Then she gave me such a look of contempt that I thought I was back at school, although I think she was slightly relieved because I'm not sure she had three half-pint glasses in the bar.

After a while, the bar began filling up with the Celtic equivalent of the older Rangers fans who'd terrorised Highbury back in 1967 and we decided to drink up and leave before Knottsy came out with another classic remark and got us killed.

Paulo Di Canio inspired Celtic to a 2-1 victory and we, safely, spent the evening in our hotel bar.

DAVID DEIN

On the flight home the next day, I was sitting immediately behind the Arsenal Vice-Chairman, David Dein and his daughter.

After introducing myself as a season ticket and bond-holder, I told him how despondent I was about the situation as the season hadn't even started yet, and

WITH DAVID DEIN – GLASGOW 1996

he told me that there were two players coming in soon; one was a decent player but the other one would, in his opinion, become an Arsenal legend. However, obviously, he couldn't name them to me.

Now, I might be a bit of a cynic but I don't think these two players were ever on Bruce Rioch's radar and maybe Dennis Bergkamp and David Platt weren't either! This begs the question, was Arsène Wenger already involved in transfer dealings at Arsenal while completing his contract in Japan, which didn't expire until October?

After we had a conversation regarding all the old players at Arsenal that we had seen when we were both kids in the '50s, Kelsey, Clapton, Herd, Bloomfield, Haverty etc., I then asked David Dein if he could remember how many games Arsenal had played in the season 1979-80 when they lost the two Cup Finals. He immediately replied, "70". I then explained that this was the correct answer that I had sent to a previous "Arsenal" magazine but they had given the prize, a complete new kit, to someone else who'd given a different number and I'd complained to the editor as I wanted the prize for my 3-year-old grandson. David Dein then told me to contact his secretary and promised that he would send me a kit, which to his credit, he did.

A few days later, Arsenal beat Glasgow Rangers 3-0 and then, in a tournament in Florence. they lost to Fiorentina 2-0 and Benfica 3-1.

Bruce Rioch was sacked on August 12th and Stewart Houston was appointed caretaker manager again but left in September when he was overlooked for the permanent manager's job.

On August 13th, Arsenal played Northampton Town in a testimonial for Dave Bowen and, as I'd never been to Northampton's stadium before, I had arranged to meet my mate, Spandau, and his sons, Ben and Jordan, before the game, where I related the story of my chat with David Dein on the plane, causing Spandau to laugh and say, "I suppose you're his mate now, then?"

Moments later, there was a commotion in the car park and we all turned to see David Dein and the Arsenal Chairman Peter Hill-Wood, strolling across the car park, surrounded by camera crews and journalists who were pestering them both for news regarding the future Arsenal manager's name.

They were both trying to ignore everyone and so I nudged Spandau and said, "Watch this". I then pushed through the throng of media people and approached David Dein, holding my hand out, before saying "Hi, David, thanks for the kit". He immediately shook my hand and replied, "Hi, Eddie, it's nice to see you again". Spandau was completely gobsmacked! "Fucking hi Eddie?" was all he kept repeating out loud to himself as we made our way into the ground.

Poor old Spandau, he never forgot that magic moment until the day he died.

Ben and Jordan never forgot the sight of me walking around the pitch perimeter to go home five minutes after kick-off either, as I'd now added Northampton to my list of stadiums that I've seen Arsenal play in and wasn't prepared to suffer another friendly.

According to the newspapers, Arsenal fans, me included, wanted my favourite non-Arsenal player, Johann Cruyff, as the next manager.

According to the Arsenal board, we were getting Pat Rice as caretaker until a certain relatively unknown Frenchman named Arsène Wenger would be arriving in October.

As promised, David Dein's two players, Rémi Garde and the future legend, Patrick Vieira, arrived and George Graham's last signing, Glenn Helder, went on loan to Benfica.

TONY [SPANDAU] MOSS [DIED 2017] &
HIS CHILDREN

8

THE ARSÈNE WENGER YEARS

ARSÈNE ARRIVES

Before the match against Chelsea at Highbury on Wednesday September 4th, Arsenal confirmed that Arsène Wenger would soon be the new manager and Spook and myself were asked to comment on camera about his appointment by ITV London news outside the stadium. We then went to the "Crusoe" pub to watch our interview along with our mates.

Imagine the stick Spook got when, after showing mine, they deleted his comments. Hilarious!

Arsenal only lost one of their nine Premier League games, 2-0 away at Liverpool, before Arsène Wenger officially took charge, with Pat Rice as his assistant, for the 2-0 victory against

MATCH TICKETS – LATE 90'S

243

Blackburn Rovers at Ewood Park in October 1996 and they would then lose only once in the next eight games, even reaching top spot in November, before finally finishing in third place, which was their highest League position for six seasons.

Patrick Vieira made his debut when he came on as a substitute for David Platt during the Ian Wright hat trick-inspired 4-1 win against Sheffield Wednesday on September 16th at Highbury and his appearance prompted JC to remark, "It looks like we've bought a Harlem Globetrotter now".

The team might have finished even higher if some of their best players hadn't missed games after being been sent off, and another two points were also lost when, in a highly controversial incident during the penultimate home game of the season against Blackburn Rovers, Chris Sutton forced a corner by putting David Seaman under pressure from the resulting throw-in, after Arsenal had put the ball out of play due to an injured player needing treatment and, for this misdemeanour, he was subjected to abuse from Arsenal fans in the following seasons. More points were dropped when Arsenal only won one of their last four games, although fans could see a big improvement and were excited when the young Frenchman, Nicolas Anelka, was signed from PSG early in 1997.

UEFA CUP

In the 1st Round 1st Leg, Stefan Effenburg inspired Borussia Mönchengladbach to a 3-2 victory with a stunning performance, which was probably the best display Highbury had seen in European competition by an individual since Oleg Blokhin in September 1982 with Moscow Spartak, before Arsène Wenger watched the 2nd Leg in Germany, where Pat Rice was still in charge, when Arsenal lost 3-2 again.

LEAGUE [COCA COLA] CUP

Arsenal drew 1-1 away at Stoke City in the 3rd Round before winning the replay 5-2 at Highbury.

In the 4th Round, Arsenal lost 4-2 against Liverpool at Anfield.

FA CUP

In the 3rd Round, Arsenal drew 1-1 with Sunderland at Highbury before winning 2-0 in the replay.

Arsenal then lost 1-0 in the 4th Round at Highbury against a Leeds United team managed by George Graham. Same old George, same old score!

SUMMER 1997

During the season, Arsène Wenger had assessed the playing staff and decided on the following changes:

Out went – Andy Linighan – David Hillier – Eddie McGoldrick – Glenn Helder – Ian Selley – John Hartson – Matthew Rose – Paul Dickov – Steve Morrow and, surprisingly, Paul Merson.

In came – Alberto Mendez – Alex Manninger – Christopher Wreh – Giles Grimandi – Luis Boa Morte – "Manu" Petit – Marc Overmars and Matthew Upson.

Arsène Wenger also realised that, with a change of diet and certain training methods, he could prolong the careers of the "Super Six", David Seaman, Lee Dixon, Steve Bould, Tony Adams, Nigel Winterburn and Martin Keown, who had made up the superb defensive partnerships of recent seasons.

NIGEL WINTERBURN'S TESTIMONIAL

After 30 years, Glasgow Rangers were invited to Highbury again for this match and apparently, it was a very calm evening as all their nutters from 1967 were about 80 years old by then. I missed this game as I'd taken my wife, Chris, to see "El Classico", Barcelona versus Real Madrid in the Nou Camp and also visit Charlie MacCready and my Glaswegian mates, Alan and Tommo.

CAMP NOU – BARCELONA VS
REAL MADRID – MAY 1997

Arsenal finished 3rd in the Premier League behind Champions Man Utd.

Chelsea won the FA Cup after beating Middlesbrough 2-0.

Leicester City won the League Cup, beating Middlesbrough 1-0 in a replay after a 1-1 draw.

Borussia Dortmund won the European Champions League after beating Juventus 3-1.

MERSON – MAIDENHEAD – MIDDLESBROUGH

Recalling the transfer of Paul Merson to Middlesbrough has provided a link for two funny stories.

MAIDENHEAD

One day, in the winter of 1993, I got a phone call from JC telling me that his son was playing for Tooting & Mitcham the next evening at

Maidenhead stadium, near where I live, and so I arranged to meet JC behind the dugout at the ground. However, due to the heavy rain and the rush hour traffic, I arrived about ten minutes after kick-off and there was no sign of JC on the terraces or his son, Young Johnny, on the pitch or in the dugout. About five minutes later, JC turned up moaning about the traffic on the M4. He started moaning even more when I told him his son wasn't playing and he then strode down to the dugout, leant over the fence and asked the Tooting & Mitcham manager, "Where's my Johnny?" He then came back to me moaning even louder and said, "The soppy bastard got sent off after five minutes for kicking the opposition goalie and he's still in the shower".

JC's moaning had now increased to a different level, as the rain was pouring down even heavier and everyone either had the hood up on their coats or were sheltering under an umbrella, or both.

A few minutes later, despite the hoods, JC somehow spotted one of the Premier League's top referees, Alf Buksh, standing a few steps in front of us. That was the last straw; the kettle had now boiled and steam was coming out of JC's ears, as this was the referee who apparently disallowed a blatant penalty for Arsenal after about five minutes, for a foul on Paul Merson in a 0-0 draw at the Lane a couple of seasons previously. On that occasion, JC had told me that he'd, unsurprisingly, got two tickets from Teddy Sheringham in the section where their players' families and guests sit. He'd known him since Sheringham was a kid and I had declined this offer, saying that we'd probably get arrested if we're sitting amongst their fans. JC still insisted everything would be ok, as we were two sensible blokes but I wasn't having any of it, as I know only too well how passion and tribal loyalty takes over during these "Local Derby" matches. The outcome? JC decided to go on his own, Alf Buksh denied "Merse" his penalty, JC lost his temper, their fans started abusing him, the police were called, JC lost the plot completely, the police threatened to eject him if he didn't stop swearing, JC responded by shouting at the coppers, "Carry me out! Carry me out!" and the coppers carried him out.

Then, after the game, Teddy Sheringham arrived in the players' lounge looking for his guest, only to be told, "Your guest was escorted from the stadium earlier".

With steam still coming out of his head, JC started berating poor old Alf about the disallowed penalty and Alf couldn't believe that this lunatic had recognised him and mumbled, "You Arsenal fans never leave off about that, do you?" JC ended the conversation by telling Alf that he was "the worst referee he's ever seen". Don't you just love JC? I know I did.

MIDDLESBROUGH

My wife and I once attended a party of a workmate of mine who, mainly thanks to his wife having a highly paid job, lived in a very affluent area of Surrey. At this party, my rather pretentious, workmate introduced me to one of his neighbours who had originally come from Middlesbrough before making his fortune and, as he couldn't get to see his favourite team very often, this bloke had bought a private box at Crystal Palace.

My deluded workmate had recently attended a game at Palace in this box with his neighbour and was extolling to me the delights of, "how this is the only way to watch a football match".

With his 'Boro-supporting neighbour listening, I explained that the best way to watch a football match was by standing on the terraces at a Northern ground, with the cold rain coming horizontally into your face, your fingers going numb in the puddles inside your coat pockets, three sides of the stadium singing "We hate the Cockney bastards" and your team are 1-0 up, whereby the "Middlesbrough Millionaire" put his arm around my shoulders and said, "This is a proper fan", while my workmate just stood there in total shock with his mouth open. What a prick!

DOUBLE DELIGHT – SEASON 1997-98

On August 9th, JC and I went to see Arsenal draw the opening game of the season 1-1 away at Leeds United. This has since been recorded in some articles as the hottest ever day for an Arsenal match and therefore, I can have the unenviable claim for attending Arsenal away games involving extreme weather records:

- Hottest – Leeds United 1997.
- Coldest – Oldham/Glasgow Rangers 1991.
- Wettest – Barnsley 1995.
- Postponed at noon due to Snow – Sunderland 1965.
- Postponed 15 minutes before kick-off due to Fog – Man Utd 1961.

The Leeds game was the start of a twelve-match unbeaten run which included a superlative hat trick from Dennis Bergkamp in the 3-3 draw at Leicester City, Ian Wright scoring his record-breaking 179th goal in a 4-1 win against Bolton at Highbury, Nigel Winterburn scoring a rare goal with the winner in a 3-2 victory at Chelsea and Dennis Bergkamp conspiring with Marc Overmans to send Arsenal to the top of the table with a 4-0 victory against West Ham at Highbury.

UEFA CUP

In September, Arsenal were surprisingly eliminated from Europe by PAOK Salonika after losing the 1st Round Leg 1-0 in Greece and only drawing 1-1 at Highbury in the 2nd Leg.

I then went with my wife to visit my cousin Annabelle and her family in Florence, where Alberto, her "Viola"-supporting husband, took me to see the Fiorentina players training and I managed to have the obligatory chat and photo with Stefan Schwarz and Rui Costa.

On November 1st, JC and I went to Pride Park to see Derby County beat Arsenal 3-0 in the League. The only thing memorable about this day was that we'd parked on the drive at JC's brother-in-law's house near the stadium and, with Arsenal losing 3-0, we decided to leave early and avoid the traffic. When we got back to the house, we discovered that a mate of the brother-in-law had blocked our car in with his careless parking. Steam kettle time, but this time it was me and not JC. We were now stuck until this idiot mate returned and, to make matters worse, he didn't come back until about forty minutes after the final whistle. When JC went out to give him a bit of verbal, his brother-in-law stood in the doorway to stop me joining him. He later told JC that he thought I was going to kill his mate. Imagine, Arsenal get slaughtered and we can't get off home. You've all been there no doubt?

LEAGUE [COCA COLA] CUP

In the 3rd Round, Arsenal beat Birmingham City 4-1 and then beat Coventry City 1-0 in the 4th Round with both games at Highbury.

Arsenal beat West Ham 2-1 at Upton Park in the 5th Round, before beating Chelsea 2-1 in the semi-final 1st Leg at Highbury. Some of the "Usual Suspects" and myself went to Stamford Bridge in February for the 2nd Leg, where Gianluca Vialli had just been appointed manager and Mark Hughes appeared to be on a one-man mission to take out the entire back four of Arsenal in the first twenty minutes. This combination inspired Chelsea to a 3-1 victory and ended any further Arsenal involvement in that competition.

As Arsenal had also only won three of their last seven League games up to the New Year and were now twelve points behind Man Utd in the League, certain sections of the media were asking if David Seaman, Tony Adams and Ian Wright were still top-class players?

1998

FA CUP

The criticism increased when, on January 3rd, Arsenal only drew 0-0 against Port Vale at Highbury in the FA Cup 3rd Round and, as I'd never been there before, I went with Andrew Miller to Vale Park on the 24th to see Arsenal win the replay 4-3 on penalties after a 1-1 draw.

The team's response would silence all their critics and send the Arsenal fans into Dreamland.

In the 4th Round, JC and I drove to Middlesbrough to see Arsenal win 2-1. By a strange coincidence, the ex-Arsenal player, Paul Merson, and the future Middlesbrough player, Ray Parlour, both scored. Even stranger was the fact that JC had got us tickets sitting with the Arsenal fans.

In the 5th Round, Arsenal drew 0-0 against Crystal Palace at Highbury before winning the replay 2-0 at Selhurst Park in front of many of the "Usual Suspects", including myself.

In the 6th Round, Arsenal again drew 0-0 at Highbury, against West Ham this time, and then, after a 1-1 draw, and despite Dennis Bergkamp being sent off, won the replay on penalties thanks to an inspired performance from Alex Manninger at Upton Park.

This was the third FA Cup game this season when Arsenal had won the replay away after drawing 0-0 at home, and they would eventually win the trophy without winning a game at Highbury.

On April 5th, Putney borrowed a Limousine from his company and, along with his son Jordan, JC and myself, travelled in style to the FA Cup semi-final against Wolves at Villa Park. There, through his business contacts, Putney had also got us into a private box almost on the halfway line, with a great view of the pitch and my mate Spandau's famous banner, amongst the Arsenal supporters in the upper section of the Holte End. I would now sample a football match in the same circumstances as my pretentious workmate with the neighbour from Middlesbrough, who I wrote about previously.

SPANDAU'S BANNER –
FA CUP FINAL – 1998

When we pulled up in the official car park, there were hundreds of Wolves fans queuing up to enter the stadium. On seeing our "posh" car, they all turned to see who the famous occupants might be and imagine their surprise when JC got out first and gave his customary greeting of, "Hello, lads, do you fancy your chances today?" whereupon, all the Wolves fans turned away, wondering who he was. Another silly but hilarious moment.

When Christopher Wreh scored what turned out to be the only goal, as we were stuck inside this box behind a glass window, we weren't really part of the celebrations, and to me, this was not the way I was used to watching football, so to try and get some of the atmosphere, I pulled myself up by hanging onto the slatted window and cheering through the gap. Slight problem – those slats are only meant to be air vents and it obviously snapped, resulting in Putney's company eventually receiving a letter demanding payment for the broken window and banning them from having another private box at Villa Park in future. I never wanted to go in one again anyway!

After the game, we decided to have a few beers in the car until the traffic eased off and we were still sitting there when the Arsenal players came out to get onto their coach to go home. As you can imagine, I don't miss an opportunity like that and so I managed to get photos with Marc Overmars and Patrick Vieira.

PREMIER LEAGUE

Since losing 3-1 against Blackburn Rovers at Highbury on December 13th, Arsenal had gone seventeen games unbeaten in the League, including a 1-0 victory at Old Trafford and a 4-1 revenge win in the snow at Blackburn, and would be Champions with two games to spare if they could beat Everton in the next game.

Chelsea won the League Cup after beating Middlesbrough 2-0.

Real Madrid won the Champions League after beating Juventus 1-0.

ARSENAL WIN THE PREMIER LEAGUE, FA CUP & WORLD CUP

On May 3rd, in front of an ecstatic packed Highbury, Arsenal demolished Everton 4-0 with Tony Adams surprisingly turning striker when he latched on to a Steve Bould pass to score the fourth goal with a left-foot thunderbolt in front of the North Bank, to put the icing on the cake.

After watching the new Champions' lap of honour, all the "Usual Suspects" then returned to the "Crusoe" for a few beers to celebrate.

Arsenal then lost those two games in hand 4-0 at Liverpool and 1-0 at Aston Villa but so what?

On May 16th, Arsenal won the FA Cup by beating Newcastle United 2-0 and, therefore, completed the second double in the club's history.

Our old mate, Kenny Hall, had flown back from Australia for a three-week holiday a few days previously, and six of us had chipped in to buy him a ticket in the Arsenal End for the match, as a surprise. Coincidentally, the last FA Cup final he went to before emigrating was when Arsenal beat

Liverpool to win their first double in 1971, so maybe he should return more often!

One of the most memorable moments of the day was when, as the two teams were lined up waiting to be introduced to the dignitaries, the Arsenal fans out-sang the "Geordies" for once, by booming out;

> *"Vi – ei – ra, Oh oh oh oh,*
> *He comes from Senegal*
> *He plays for Ar – se – nal*
> *Vi – ei – ra, Oh oh oh oh".*

After Tony Adams lifted the trophy, my mates and I returned to Highbury for a few beers to celebrate seeing two doubles in our lifetime. Arsenal had never even achieved this when I was ten years old playing Subbuteo.

Dennis Bergkamp missed the FA Cup semi-final due to suspension and then, unluckily, missed the final as well due to injury and Ian Wright was an unused substitute in the final and was not happy about it and joined West Ham soon after. The consolation for Dennis was winning everyone's Player of the Year award.

WITH PATRICK VIEIRA –
VILLA PARK 1998

WORLD CUP 1998

Since 1966, West Ham fans have proudly claimed that they won the World Cup due to Bobby Moore, Geoff Hurst and Martin Peters being in the victorious England team.

On July 12th 1998, France won the World Cup for the first time, after beating Brazil 3-0 with Patrick Vieira and "Manu " Petit in the team and

Nicolas Anelka also in the squad, along with two future Arsenal players, Thierry Henry and Robert Pires and, as Vieira and Petit had just won the Double with Arsenal, maybe this special achievement means that Arsenal have also won the World Cup.

David Suker, another future Arsenal player, was the Tournament's top scorer with six goals.

David Seaman, Tony Adams and Martin Keown were in the England squad that lost to Argentina on penalties, before Dennis Bergkamp scored the Goal of the Tournament for Holland in the last minute of extra time to knock out Argentina in the next round.

QUIZ NIGHTS

The Arsenal Supporters Club team, Vic Wright, Emilio Zorlakki, Peter Kirkwood, Henry Laghi and myself, retained their title of the Radio 5-sponsored "All-London Football Quiz Champions", and on another occasion, I came second answering questions about Arsenal in the televised "Sports Anorak of the Year" quiz, hosted by Rory Magrath.

PHOTO DAY

I took my grandchildren, 4-year-old Guy and 2-year-old Hollie, to have our photos taken with the trophies at Highbury and I only just managed to save the FA Cup from serious damage, after Hollie almost knocked it to the floor when trying to climb into it, much to the photographer's anxiety.

GOONER GRANDKIDS GUY & HOLLIE – 1998

SEASON 1998-99

LEGENDS ARRIVE & DEPART

In the summer of 1998, the Arsenal legend, Ian Wright, had joined West Ham and David Platt had retired, with Nelson Vivas coming in and Arsène Wenger admitting that he was now looking for a top-class striker.

Arsenal beat Man Utd 3-0 in the Charity Shield and everyone at Highbury was anticipating more success in the coming season, especially in the Champions League, where Arsenal would play all their home games at Wembley. Although this decision undoubtedly made sense financially due to the regular attendances of 73,000, many Arsenal fans believed that it removed any advantage for the team, as the opposition players all seemed to relish playing at such a famous stadium.

CHAMPIONS LEAGUE

On September 30th 1998, Arsenal won their first-ever Champions League game at Wembley 2-1 against Panathinaikos with goals from defenders Tony Adams and Martin Keown.

In the next game, Dennis Bergkamp scored in the 1-1 draw with Dynamo Kiev, which I watched with my cousin Albie Ward's son Barry, before he emigrated to Australia the next day and, to our amazement, we were spotted by Ben, the son of one of my other cousins, Bert Leach, amongst all the thousands of fans as we left the stadium, and Ben has since emigrated to Australia as well.

In the final Group game at Wembley, Arsenal lost 1-0 against Lens and were knocked out, which poses the question that maybe Arsenal might have made more money by staying at Highbury and progressing further in the competition?

LEAGUE CUP

In the 3rd Round, with a team mainly comprising youngsters, Arsenal beat Derby County 2-1, before, in the 4th Round, using almost the same youngsters with whom Arsenal lost 5-0 at Highbury versus Chelsea's first team. Against most Arsenal fans' wishes, Arsène Wenger would still persevere with this tactic of using the kids in the future and ultimately would never win this trophy.

FA CUP

In the 3rd Round, Arsenal beat Preston North End 4-2 at Deepdale and, as the game had been switched to a Monday night, I didn't go, even though I had never been to that stadium.

In the 4th Round, "Manu Petit" collected the 19th red card since Arsène Wenger had arrived at Arsenal, during the 2-1 victory at Wolves, and in the 5th Round, Arsenal beat Sheffield United 2-1 in a replayed game at Highbury, after winning by the same score in the original match with a controversial goal when Arsenal players had, "done a Chris Sutton", and pressurised the United defenders when the game had restarted after an injury.

In the 6th Round, Arsenal beat Derby County 1-0 and would now play Man Utd at Villa Park.

Putney arranged a company car again but no private box this time, thank goodness! And as JC hadn't arranged the tickets either, we all managed to sit together in the Arsenal section and watched Nelson Vivas get sent off in the 0-0 draw.

Most of the "Usual Suspects" went to the midweek replay at Villa Park again, and after Dennis Bergkamp missed a penalty, Arsenal were beaten 2-1 when Ryan Giggs weaved his way through their famous defence to score a dramatic winner in extra time.

One funny story from when we were in a pub before the game, was when Knottsy arrived with his son, Christian, and proceeded to tell us about his experience in Kiev at the recent Arsenal game against Dynamo. He told us that when he was talking on his phone, a teenage Ukrainian had stood close to him, so he moved away, only for the fella to move next to him again, so Knottsy crossed the road and the fella followed him there also. So, Knottsy shouted at the teenager, "Can I help you?" at which point the fella ran away. While Knottsy was eagerly awaiting our reaction, thinking we were impressed with this story, I said to him, "You know why the bloke ran away, don't you? He was a Chicken Kiev!" Everyone was now in hysterics and Knottsy stormed out of the pub with the hump and that made it even funnier! A truly magic moment.

PREMIER LEAGUE

Mainly due to drawing too many games and some key players getting suspensions after being sent off, Arsenal were never really challenging for the League title until the New Year, despite not losing a game until the end of September, in the last minute against Sheffield Wednesday at Hillsborough where Paulo Di Canio was sent off for shoving the referee to the ground. The team's erratic form even prompted the following quote from Arsène Wenger; "Perhaps we've given our fans too much by winning the double; as once you've eaten caviar, it's difficult to go back to sausages".

In January, Freddie Ljungberg was signed and Arsène Wenger found the striker he needed when Kanu joined the club. These two signings gave Arsenal the boost they needed and they went top of the table for the first time that season after scoring five against Wimbledon and six versus Middlesbrough before winning 3-1 at the Lane to really put the pressure on Man Utd. Incidentally, the game at the Lane was the first time Highbury had staged a live screening of a match and this enabled a few thousand fans, including myself, to sit in the North Bank End and enjoy the victory.

Unfortunately, a few days later, a late winner from Jimmy Floyd Hasselbaink in the 1-0 defeat at Leeds gave the advantage back to Man Utd.

Oddly, the Leeds fans celebrated this goal as though they'd won the League themselves, and yet they've always claimed that they hated Man Utd more than any other club, although somehow, I don't think Arsenal fans would celebrate beating Leeds if it meant the title going to the Lane, or maybe that's just me being old school?

So, it was now all down to the last day of the season and Arsenal needed to win at Highbury against Aston Villa while the Team from the Lane had to win at Old Trafford.

Surprise, surprise, Arsenal got the required win against Aston Villa and, true to form, the Team from the Lane kept their supporters happy by losing to Man Utd, despite scoring first.

> Arsenal finished 2nd in the Premier League, one point behind Champions Man Utd.
>
> Man Utd won the FA Cup after beating Newcastle United 2-0.
>
> The Team from the Lane won the League Cup after beating Leicester City 1-0.
>
> Man Utd won the Champions League after beating Bayern Munich 2-1.

So, Man Utd won an unprecedented treble and the Team from the Lane won a cup. Nightmare!

SUMMER 1999

Arsène Wenger now decided that changes were required in certain positions and out went Diawarra, Rémi Garde, Luis Boa Morte, the ever-reliable Steve Bould, and for £21m, Nicolas Anelka to Real Madrid.

In came Davor Suker, Sylvinho, Stefan Molz, Maurice Volz, Oleg Luzhny, Jermaine Pennant and the future Arsenal legend Thierry Henry from Juventus.

CHARITY SHIELD 1999

In August, Arsenal won the Charity Shield beating Man Utd 2-1 at a soon-to-be-demolished Wembley stadium.

This game was memorable for my grandson, Guy, as it was his first time at an Arsenal game, because, although he was only five years old, I wanted him to be able to say in the future that he had been to the Original Wembley stadium. It was also the first time that he heard the word "wanker", when an Arsenal fan sitting near us was shouting it at Teddy Sheringham, who was holding up three fingers to denote United's treble the previous season, in reply to the abuse from the Arsenal fans, for being an ex-player at the Lane. When Guy asked his Nan what the word meant, she told him to ask Grandad and when he asked me, I was caught on the hop and said that it was someone from Manchester. For many years afterwards, we dreaded him meeting a proper Mancunian when on holiday somewhere, and asking if they were a wanker!

SEASON 1999-2000

PREMIER LEAGUE

After Arsenal confirmed that they would be moving to a new stadium within the next few years, I decided to sell my bond and used the money to take my wife to visit my old mates, Kenny Hall and Johnny "Mullers" Mullard, in Australia.

However, before we went, I did see Thierry Henry for the first time against Bradford City and Davor Suker score his first Arsenal goal against Aston Villa, in games at Highbury.

While I was away, Martin Keown and Freddie Ljungberg were sent off in a 2-1 defeat against the Team from the Lane and Patrick Vieira was sent off for kicking Paulo Di Canio, who scored both goals when Arsenal lost 2-0 at West Ham before Oleg Luzhny also got sent off at Wimbledon.

Despite a Kanu hat trick in the pouring rain at Chelsea when Arsenal came back from 2-0 down to win 3-2 with only fifteen minutes to go, Arsenal eventually finished eighteen points behind Man Utd.

FA CUP

Arsenal beat Blackpool 3-1 in the 3rd Round but then lost away at Leicester 6-5 on penalties after a 0-0 draw in the 4th Round.

LEAGUE CUP

After beating Preston 2-1 in the 3rd Round, Arsenal then lost 5-1 on penalties to Middlesbrough after a 2-2 draw in the 4th Round.

CHAMPIONS LEAGUE

Arsenal started their campaign with a 0-0 draw against Fiorentina in Florence and, although I would have liked to have gone and visited my cousin, inconveniently, I was in Australia, although before I went on holiday, I did manage to visit my "Uncle Billy" who'd been escorted out of Highbury against Liverpool all those years ago in 1964, as he was seriously ill and would sadly die before I returned.

Arsenal then beat AIK Solna 3-1 at Wembley before going to Barcelona and drawing 1-1, despite Gilles Grimaldi getting sent off and the ex-Real Madrid player Davor Suker suffering plenty of abuse from the Catalans.

Hoyboy, his son, Granty, Spook, Roger Taylor and Tony Adelizzi all went to the game in the Nou Camp with our old mate Charlie MacCready, who had obtained the tickets, while I watched the game on television at 4 am with Kenny Hall in his house in Sydney.

Arsenal then lost the return game 4-2 at Wembley.

I returned home in time to go to Wembley with Hoyboy and his son for the game against Fiorentina on October 27th, where the Argentinian striker, Gabriel "Battigoal" Batistuta scored the only goal of the game to knock Arsenal out at the Group stage in front of 70,000 disappointed "Gooners".

In my opinion, this was probably the best Arsenal team that I'd ever seen, containing at least six world-class players, and would now enter the UEFA Cup as a consolation.

Arsenal entered this competition in the 3rd Round and won the 1st Leg against Nantes 3-0 in France, before only managing a 3-3 draw in the 2nd Leg at Highbury, before in the 4th Round, Arsenal beat Deportivo la Coruna 5-1 in the 1st Leg at Highbury and lost the 2nd Leg 2-1 in Spain.

In the 5th Round, Arsenal beat Werder Bremen 2-0 in the 1st Leg and progressed to the semi-finals despite losing the 2nd Leg 4-2 in Germany.

In the semi-final 1st Leg, Arsenal beat Lens 1-0 at Highbury before winning the 2nd Leg 2-1 away.

Apparently, there was some serious fighting between the rival fans before the final in Copenhagen which Arsenal lost to the Turkish team, Galatasaray, 4-1 on penalties after a 0-0 draw, and therefore, Arsenal had been beaten in every Cup competition with a penalty shoot-out.

Arsenal finished 2nd in the Premier League behind Champions Man Utd.

Chelsea won the FA Cup after beating Aston Villa 1-0 in the last final at the Old Wembley stadium.

Leicester City won the League Cup after beating Tranmere Rovers 2-1.

Real Madrid won the Champions League after beating Valencia 3-0.

On December 17th 1999, just before the start of the next century, my mate, the "Legend that was JC", departed this world aged 61, after suffering another heart attack.

I had first met him in 1974 when he managed the "Goldsmith's Arms" and I had my stag night in his next pub, the "Sebright", in 1977. We travelled all over Britain and Europe together watching our beloved Arsenal and I have so many happy memories of this lovely character who is still sadly missed by all his family and friends. RIP mate!

In February 2000, another legend, Sir Stanley Matthews, also died and allegedly, in 1954, the then Arsenal manager Tom Whittaker offered Blackpool a blank cheque for him but they turned it down.

SEASON 2000-2001

During the summer of 2000, the doors of the Marble Halls were opening and closing faster than the ones at Harrods, as out went Marc Overmars, "Manu" Petit, Stephen Hughes, Davor Suker and another long-serving legend, Nigel Winterburn.

In came Robert Pires, Lauren, Sylvain Wiltord, Edu, Igor Stepanovs and from the Youth team, Ashley Cole.

Allegedly, Arsène Wenger was prepared to sell Ashley to Crystal Palace but Liam Brady threatened to resign from his role in charge of Youth Development in protest if he did. Despite moving to Chelsea in controversial circumstances later, in my opinion, he's still the best left-back that I've ever seen play for Arsenal, with all due respect to Kenny Sansom and Nigel Winterburn.

Another ex-Arsenal legend, Ian Wright, scored on his debut for Glasgow Celtic to maintain his impressive record of scoring on all of his debuts for every team he played for but the omens for a successful season weren't looking too good when Arsenal came bottom of a tournament in Amsterdam behind Ajax, Barcelona and Lazio.

PREMIER LEAGUE

The hopes of Arsenal fans were not raised any further by the 1-0 defeat at Sunderland on the opening day, with ex-Gunner Niall Quinn scoring the winner and Patrick Vieira getting sent off.

However, Lauren scored on his debut in Arsenal's 2-0 victory against Liverpool, even though Patrick Vieira was sent off again in the first home game, and the team had improved so much that they were unbeaten throughout September and October. Then, after Thierry Henry had scored a wonderful thirty-yard chipped goal in a 3-0 win against Man Utd at Highbury, Arsenal were joint top of the table.

In November, Arsenal lost away at Everton and Leeds and were trailing behind Man Utd again, and the inconsistency continued when, after Ray Parlour had scored a very rare hat trick against Newcastle in a 5-0 home win early in December, only a Patrick Vieira equaliser in the last minute at the Lane spared the Arsenal fans' agony, before five days later, Arsenal lost 4-0 at Anfield.

On Boxing Day, Thierry Henry scored a hat trick in the 6-1 victory against Leicester at Highbury.

On January 1st 2001, in an event even rarer than a Ray Parlour hat trick, Charlton Athletic beat Arsenal for the first time in forty-four years with a 1-0 win at the Valley, and in February, Arsenal went to Old Trafford, realistically needing a win to have any chance of becoming Champions. They lost 6-1 and Igor Stepanovs joined Gus Caesar in the Arsenal "Hall of Shame" with such a poor performance that even Gus would have been ashamed of it.

On another sad day in March, another Arsenal legend, David "Rocky" Rocastle, tragically died of cancer aged 33 and surprisingly, to be fair to them, the fans of the Team from the Lane observed the minute's silence at Highbury for "Rocky" before the game which Arsenal won 2-0.

On the last day of the season, Matt Le Tissier scored the winner for Southampton in their 3-2 victory against Arsenal in the last ever game at The Dell, but the title had long gone before then.

CHAMPIONS LEAGUE

In the group stage, Arsenal won their first three games, Sparta Prague away 1-0, then both their games at Highbury, Shakhtar Donetsk 3-2 and

Lazio 2-0 before drawing 1-1 with Lazio in Rome and beating Sparta Prague at Highbury and finally, losing away to Shakhtar Donetsk 3-0.

LAZIO VS ARSENAL – 2000

I took my wife, Chris, for a five-day holiday to Rome to coincide with the Lazio game and, as it poured with rain on the night of the match, she was not impressed!

However, I was impressed to see some of the great players in the Lazio team such as Peruzzi, Nesta, Mihajlovic, Simeone, Veron, Inzaghi, Crespo and Nedved.

After the game, Chris and I shared a taxi back to the city centre with an American couple who were amazed at the aggressive behaviour of both sets of fans in the ground. According to them, in the USA, everyone takes a picnic to their football [soccer] games and there's no trouble. I explained that if it had been the final, at least another 30,000 Arsenal fans would have been in there.

In the next Group Phase, Arsenal lost the first game 4-1 against Spartak Moscow in Russia before drawing 2-2 with Bayern Munich at Highbury and winning 1-0 versus Lyon in France, and then in the return games at Highbury, Arsenal drew 1-1 with Lyon and then beat Spartak Moscow 1-0 before qualifying for the knock-out stage despite losing 1-0 to Bayern Munich in Germany.

In the knock-out phase, Arsenal beat Valencia 2-1 in the 1st Leg at Highbury but lost 1-0 in Spain and were eliminated on away goals.

LEAGUE CUP

In the 3rd Round, Arsenal's youngsters and squad players lost 1-0 against Ipswich at Highbury.

FA CUP

After beating Carlisle 1-0 at Highbury in the 3rd Round, Arsenal then beat QPR 6-0 at Loftus Road in the 4th Round, Chelsea 3-1 at Highbury in the 5th Round and then Blackburn Rovers 3-0 also at Highbury in the 6th Round.

In the semi-final at the ridiculous venue of Old Trafford, Arsenal beat the Team from the Lane 2-1, thanks to Robert Pires.

CARDIFF – 2001

After dominating for most of the game, with Thierry Henry bizarrely missing some clear-cut scoring opportunities, Arsenal lost the FA Cup final 2-1 to Michael Owen's two late goals for Liverpool.

Hoyboy and his son stayed at my house the night before the match and we drove to Cardiff the next day, where we met up with some of the other "Usual Suspects" including Putney, Spook, Prenders, Fuzzey, Gary Davies, Lenny Togwell, John, Joanne, Robert, Peter and Mark Landers plus three of the "4 Wheels", Roger, Clive and Tony in the city centre where a certain North Bank legend left shoppers and football fans alike gagging for air after he had used the public toilets in a Shopping Mall.

We then descended on "Henry's" bar for the pre-match drinking session before leaving for the ground and much to everyone's dismay, my new friend, David Dein, waved to me and said, "Hello", as we passed him by outside the stadium entrance.

Arsenal finished 2nd in the Premier League behind Champions Man Utd.

Liverpool won the FA Cup.

Liverpool won the League Cup beating Birmingham 5-4 on penalties after a 1-1 draw.

Bayern Munich won the Champions League beating Valencia 5-4 on penalties after a 1-1 draw.

The Arsenal Supporters Club Quiz team, Vic Wright, Peter Kirkwood, Emilio Zorlakki, Henry Laghi and myself, retained the Radio 5 Live-hosted "Barnardo's" trophy for the third consecutive year, against twenty-five different teams from all over London, including teams containing Nick Hornby, Frank Skinner, David Baddiel and the ex-Arsenal player, Alan Smith. "Anoraks are us!"

AFSC QUIZ TEAM WITH
ALAN SMITH – 1996

SEASON 2001-2002

TREBLE DOUBLE TO THE INVINCIBLES

Before the season started, Nelson Vivas and Sylvinho were transferred and John Lukic retired and in came Richard Wright, Giovanni Van Bronckhorst, Francis Jeffers, Inamoto, Jeremy Alladiere and, on a free transfer, Sol Campbell, the captain of the Team from the Lane. His move so upset many of their fans that they even hung effigies of him from lamp-posts near their stadium before Sol also got some horrendous abuse when he returned to the Lane with Arsenal in November.

As this was the first season since I had started watching Arsenal in 1957 when I only went to a few League games, I feel that I can only comment on some of the outstanding highlights such as the Man Utd goalie, Fabien Barthez, passing to Thierry Henry in Arsenal's 3-1 victory at Highbury, Dennis Bergkamp's wonder "goal of the season" at Newcastle in March when he flicked the ball one side of the defender and then went around the other side of him before passing it into the net, and Robert Pires almost beating Aston Villa on his own at Villa Park.

I also cannot forget Lauren's winning penalty against the Team from the Lane at Highbury in April and, obviously, the highlight of the high-lights, Sylvain Wiltord's League title and 3rd Double-winning goal for Arsenal against Man Utd on May 8th, exactly thirty-one years after they won the first title of my time following Arsenal, which I watched in a pub with my old mate George Hammond just like when the pair of us listened to the radio together in the "Gunners" pub all those years ago in 1971. To cap it all, I actually managed to get a ticket for the last game of the season to see Arsenal parade both of the trophies after beating Everton 4-3 at Highbury on May 11th. My old mate, Hoyboy, even man-aged to get in for this match with his son after putting on his best scouse accent and blagging two spare tickets among the Everton fans in the Clock End.

The only downside was Lee Dixon and Captain Fantastic, Tony Adams, retiring after the game, but just in case any of you need reminding, although I doubt it, Arsenal have won the League at Old Trafford, Anfield, The Lane and, in the1930's, Stamford Bridge.

CHAMPIONS LEAGUE

In the 1st Group Stage, Arsenal lost 1-0 against Mallorca in Spain, with Ashley Cole sent off, then beat Schalke 3-2 at Highbury before losing 1-0 against Panathinaikos in Greece and then in the return fixtures, Arsenal beat Panathinaikos 2-1 and Mallorca 3-1 at Highbury to ensure progress, before losing to Schalke 3-1 in Germany.

In the 2nd Group Stage, Arsenal lost 2-0 against Deportivo La Coruna in Spain before beating Juventus 3-1 at Highbury and only drawing 1-1 with Bayer Leverkusen in Germany after being in the lead until injury time. In the return fixtures, Arsenal beat Bayer Leverkusen 4-1 at Highbury and then crashed out of the competition after surprisingly losing at home

2-0 to Deportivo La Coruna and then unsurprisingly, losing 1-0 against Juventus in Italy.

LEAGUE CUP

Sylvain Wiltord scored a hat trick as Arsenal thrashed Man Utd 4-0 in the 3rd Round at Highbury, then Arsenal beat Grimsby Town 2-0 in the 4th Round, also at Highbury, before losing 4-0 to the eventual winners Blackburn Rovers, at Ewood Park, in the 5th Round.

FA CUP

Arsenal beat Watford 4-2 at Vicarage Road in the 3rd Round and then Liverpool 1-0 in the 4th Round at Highbury, where Dennis Bergkamp, Martin Keown and, in a moment of madness for throwing coins back into the crowd, Jamie Carragher of Liverpool, were all sent off.

In the 5th Round, Arsenal beat Gillingham 5-2 at Highbury before drawing 1-1 with Newcastle at St James' Park and then winning the replay 3-0 at Highbury with Robert Pires suffering an injury that unfortunately, caused him to miss the remainder of the season.

At Old Trafford, an own goal by Festa gave Arsenal a 1-0 semi-final victory against Middlesbrough.

CARDIFF – 2002

Due to an Administration error at the Arsenal Box Office, I received a ticket for the final against Chelsea in Cardiff on May 4th. Someone obviously thought that I still had my Bond, as it never happened again. Hoyboy and his son stayed at my house again and we drove to Cardiff on the morning of the match, where we again met up with many of the

"Usual Suspects" in Henry's bar, including Putney and his son Jordan, Roger Taylor, Tony Adelizzi, Bob "Jonah" Jones, Henry Jones, Spandau and his sons, Ben and Jordan Moss, Young Johnny Collins, Danny Killington and Tony Gallagher.

ARSENAL WIN FA CUP FINAL VS CHELSEA – 2002

I must mention how well organised these Cup finals were because we hardly saw any Chelsea fans until we were in the stadium, although, after taking a wrong turn, I did manage to find myself near the Chelsea fans queuing to get on their coaches after the game. Luckily, none of my old mates from the "Cages" were there to spot me.

The Romford Pele, Ray "it's only" Parlour and "We love you Freddie, because you've got red hair" Ljungberg scored the goals as Arsenal won 2-0 for the first part of the third Double.

Arsenal finished as Premier League Champions in front of Liverpool.

Arsenal won the FA Cup after beating Chelsea 2-0.

Blackburn Rovers won the League Cup after beating the Team from the Lane 2-1. Don't laugh!

Real Madrid won the European Champions League after beating Bayer Leverkusen 1-0.

SEASON 2002-03

Patrick Vieira replaced Tony Adams as captain and Alex Manninger and Richard Wright were transferred with Pascal Cygan, Gilberto Silva, Rami Shabaan and Kolo Toure being bought before in January 2003, Matthew Upson and Steve Sidwell were both sold.

Before the season began, Arsenal won the Community Shield 1-0, with a goal from new signing Gilberto Silva, against the previous season's League Runners – Up Liverpool, in Cardiff.

PREMIER LEAGUE

On August 27th 2002, I took, my 8-year-old grandson, Guy, to see his first game at Highbury, sitting in the third row of the North Bank Lower, when Arsenal played West Bromwich Albion, who by a strange coincidence, had also been the opposition when I attended my first game back in 1957.

By a not so strange coincidence, after seeing Arsenal win 5-2, Guy was hooked, just like I had been in 1957, and he would also soon be hooked on Subbuteo as well, until he got a PlayStation.

RAY PARLOUR &
TRINGY – 2017

In September, with a draw at Elland Road against Leeds, Arsenal beat Forest's record of 22 away League games unbeaten, and also set a new record of scoring in 47 consecutive League games, and then in October, Wayne Rooney scored a late winner for Everton to inflict Arsenal's first defeat of the season. In November, Arsenal beat the Team from the Lane 3-0 at Highbury to go top of the League, with Thierry Henry scoring "the goal of the season" after running diagonally through most of their hapless defence before scoring at the North Bank End.

After a 5-1 victory at Maine Road at the beginning of March, Arsenal were five points clear, but by the end of the month, they were only on top through goal difference, until, with a disappointing draw at Bolton, despite leading 2-0 with only ten minutes to go, Arsenal effectively sent the title to Old Trafford, before a 3-2 defeat at relegation-threatened Leeds confirmed Man Utd as the Champions.

In their last two games of the season, Jermaine Pennant scored a hat trick in Arsenal's 6-1 victory against Southampton at Highbury, and, as I had already bought my ticket in anticipation of Arsenal winning the League up there, well, you can only dream, can't you? I went to Sunderland's "Stadium of Light" for the last game of the season with Hoyboy and his son, to see Freddie Ljungberg score a hat trick in Arsenal's meaningless, 4-0 victory. So, despite being top of the table in March, Arsenal had disappointingly finished as runners-up.

CHAMPIONS LEAGUE

In the 1st Group Stage, Arsenal beat Borussia Dortmund 2-0 at Highbury before travelling to Eindhoven to win 4-0 against PSV, with Gilberto setting a new record when scoring after only 20 seconds and Arsenal then beat Auxerre in France 1-0 but lost the return fixture 2-1 at Highbury before losing 2-1 against Borussia Dortmund in Germany and drawing 0-0 with PSV at Highbury to progress.

In the 2nd Group Stage, Thierry Henry scored a hat trick in Arsenal's 3-1 win against Roma in Italy, before Arsenal then drew the next four games, 0-0 with Valencia, which I went to, and 1-1 versus Ajax at Highbury and in Amsterdam, 0-0 with Ajax again and 1-1 with Roma back at Highbury.

After John Carew scored both goals in Valencia's 2-1 victory in Spain, Arsenal were eliminated.

LEAGUE CUP

After leading 2-0, Arsenal surprisingly conceded three goals in the second half against Sunderland at Highbury to exit the competition in the 3rd Round.

FA CUP

Dennis Bergkamp scored his 100th Arsenal goal in the 2-0 win against Oxford in the 3rd Round match at Highbury and, in the 4th Round, Arsenal beat non-league Farnborough Town 5-1, also at Highbury after the game was switched due to their ground being deemed unsafe to host the game.

Then Ryan Giggs missed an open goal in the 5th Round before Edu and Sylvain Wiltord scored to beat Man Utd 2-0 at Old Trafford before, in the 6th Round, Chelsea forced a draw with a late equaliser at Highbury but an own goal from John Terry and goals from Sylvain Wiltord and Lauren gave Arsenal a 3-1 win in the replay at Stamford Bridge despite Pascal Cygan getting sent off.

I managed to get tickets to take Guy to Old Trafford for the semi-final against Sheffield United, where we sat with Hoyboy and his son, a few rows behind Spandau and his banner.

Freddie Ljungberg scored the only goal of the game and David "Safe Hands" Seaman made a wonder save, in his 1,000th Arsenal appearance, to prevent United from equalising in the second half, thereby sending Arsenal to their third consecutive FA Cup final in Cardiff.

Although I managed to get a ticket for the final, I never went as Guy couldn't go with me and so I gave my ticket to Rikki Hammond as he hadn't been to a final in Cardiff.

Robert Pires scored the only goal in the 1-0 victory against Southampton and Arsenal became the first team to retain the trophy since the Team from the Lane in 1982.

Arsenal finished 2nd in the Premier League behind Champions Man Utd.

Arsenal won the FA Cup after beating Southampton 1-0.

Liverpool won the League Cup after beating Man Utd 2-0.

Milan won the Champions League, beating Juventus 3-2 on penalties after a 0-0 draw.

One day in the summer of 2003, Guy was looking through my collection of Arsenal shirts, when he came across one of ex-goalkeeper John Lukic's and he asked me if he could have it I replied "Only if it fits you", so he pulled it over his head and with the neck halfway down his chest, the sleeves hanging down to his ankles and the rest of the shirt crumpled up on the floor around his feet, he proudly exclaimed, "It fits!" We still laugh about it to this day.

Due to the deaths of Teddy Taylor and JC, Granty, Harnetty and Spook now preferring to play golf and George and Rikki Hammond not going to games so often after moving further away from London, the buzz had gone from the match days in the "Crusoe" and, in season 2002-03, I had only attended one home Premier League match, one away Premier League match, one Champions League home match and the FA Cup semi-final at Old Trafford. This set a precedent for the future, where I would mainly only go to Champions League matches, or if I was taking Guy with me.

In June 2003, Roman Abramovich bought Chelsea FC, and English football changed forever.

Apparently, when Roman offered to buy the club, Ken Bates had to get all the members of the Chelsea Board to agree to the sale and they all agreed except for one member who couldn't be contacted at his home in Florida, until he was finally located on a golf course and was informed that he had to ring Ken Bates urgently. After this Board member had also agreed with the others, Chelsea was sold. You might be asking by now, what's this got to do with my story? Well, the golf-playing Board member was none other than Stuart Thompson, one of my old Chelsea-supporting mates from the "Cages" in the council flats in Westminster back in the '60s.

"THE INVINCIBLES" – SEASON 2003-04

During the summer, David Seaman surprisingly joined Man City and Jens Lehmann replaced him and Phillipe "Ponderous" Senderos, Gael Clichy, David Bentley and Cesc Fabregas were promoted into the first-team squad and Jose Antonio Reyes also joined from Seville in January 2004, while Jermaine Pennant went out on loan to Leeds United.

INVINCIBLES CELEBRATE WITH FANS – HIGHBURY 2004

Arsenal lost the Community Shield match against Man Utd on 4-3 on penalties after a 1-1 draw.

LEAGUE CUP

Cesc Fabregas became the youngest ever Arsenal player when he started against Rotherham in the 3rd Round game at Highbury, which Arsenal won 9-8 on penalties after a 1-1 draw, and then

Arsenal beat Wolves 5-1 in the 4th Round at Highbury before winning 2-0 at West Bromwich Albion in the 6th Round.

In the semi-final 1st Leg at Highbury, Juninho scored the only goal in Middlesbrough's 1-0 win and with Martin Keown getting sent off, Arsenal also lost the 2nd Leg 2-1 due to a Reyes' own goal.

FA CUP

Arsenal beat Leeds at Elland Road 4-1 in the 3rd Round, then Middlesbrough 4-1 at Highbury in the 4th Round, Chelsea 2-1 in the 5th Round, also at Highbury and then, with such an outstanding performance that it even had the home fans applauding, 5-1 away at Portsmouth.

Alex Ferguson was so worried about the forthcoming semi-final at Villa Park, that he demanded all "proper Man Utd blokes" should make the effort to go to the game, and to their credit, the United fans responded and there was hardly a woman, child or tourist visible in the thousands that turned up to see Arsenal lose 1-0 to a Paul Scholes' goal.

CHAMPIONS LEAGUE

In the Group Stage in September, Arsenal played Inter Milan at Highbury and I went to this game where I bought a large framed picture of Thierry Henry, his favourite player, for Guy, from the "Gooner" stall before the game. I gave it to Vic Wright to store for me in the Supporters Club until after the match, but when Arsenal were trailing 3-0 half time, I was so fed up that I wanted to go home but couldn't as I had to wait to get the picture back.

THIERRY HENRY & VIC WRIGHT 2004

Arsenal then drew the next game 0-0 against Lokomotiv Moscow in Russia before losing 2-1 to Dynamo Kiev in the Ukraine and, in the return fixtures, Arsenal beat Dynamo Kiev 1-0 at Highbury before Thierry Henry inspired them to an incredible 5-1 victory in the San Siro stadium against Inter Milan. Arsenal eventually finished top of their group with a 2-0 win against Lokomotiv Moscow at Highbury. I offered to take Guy to the match in the San Siro, but someone had told him stories about English fans getting stabbed at football matches in Italy, and he declined my offer.

Arsenal beat Celta Vigo 3-2 in Spain in the 1st Leg of the knock-out stage before a 2-0 victory at Highbury put them up against Chelsea in the quarter-finals, where, after the 1st Leg at Stamford Bridge ended in a 1-1 draw, and after taking a 1-0 lead in the first half of the 2nd Leg at Highbury, Arsenal conceded two goals, including a late winner from Wayne Bridge, and were eliminated.

This was one of the worst nights of my life following Arsenal, as I honestly believed that, up to that time, this was probably the best chance of winning the one trophy Arsenal fans have never seen.

PREMIER LEAGUE

Arsenal won 26 and drew 12 of their 38 League games to win the title undefeated, and, as this was a truly remarkable achievement, this team has been remembered as "The Invincibles" ever since.

For once, Arsenal began the season instead of finishing it, with a 2-1 victory against Everton at Highbury, despite having Sol Campbell sent off, and were three points clear of Man Utd by the end of August. Then, in September, Arsenal came from behind to draw at home with Portsmouth after Robert Pires allegedly dived to win a penalty, before travelling to Old Trafford where Patrick Vieira was sent off after trying to kick Ruud Van Nistelrooy and in the last minute. With the score 0-0, United were awarded a penalty, but Van Nistelrooy smashed his shot against the bar, and moments later, the referee blew for time, which was the cue for several angry Arsenal players to surround Van Nistelrooy, with Martin Keown being the main culprit. Six Arsenal players were later charged with improper conduct and Lauren, Ray Parlour and Patrick Vieira received bans; strangely, Martin Keown didn't. At the start of October, Arsenal won 2-1 at Anfield despite being a goal down after ten minutes and finished the month one point ahead of Chelsea.

Arsenal were then held to a 0-0 draw by Fulham at Highbury to finish November in 2nd place, a position they still held at the end of 2003, but by the end of January, they were first again, two points clear of Man Utd, and they continued to win every game in February to finally finish the month nine points clear of Man Utd and Chelsea.

After drawing 1-1 with Man Utd at Highbury in March, Arsenal set a new record of 30 matches unbeaten since the start of the season, still seven points clear of Chelsea at the end of the month. Then on Good Friday, Arsenal beat Liverpool 4-2 with a Thierry Henry hat trick at Highbury and a week later Thierry Henry scored four goals in the 5-0 win against Leeds, also at Highbury, which left Arsenal only needing a draw away against the Team from the Lane to become Premier League Champions again. On April 25th, after leading 2-0 at half time, Arsenal somehow only managed a 2-2 draw, but nobody from the red half of North London cared, as, for the second time in my generation's lifetime, Arsenal won the League at the Lane.

I got a ticket for the 0-0 draw with Birmingham at Highbury the follow-ing week, as my old mate Hoyboy was also going to the game. After the match, we were having a drink in the "White House" pub in Highbury Quadrant with John Landers, Sim and one of the "4 wheels boys" Craig, when, for some unknown reason, an altercation started between Craig and a couple of other blokes. Things got a bit lively, especially when the doors burst open and a coachload of "Daventry Gooners" charged in, trying to get at Craig. It later transpired that they thought we were all fans of the Team from the Lane and after someone hit Craig with a bottle and he fell down unconscious behind us, we stood, protectively, in front of him and a Mexican stand-off ensued. Imagine; Arsenal fans wanting to have a row with three old North Bank boys, Hoyboy, John Landers and myself – how ironic is that? Anyway, we explained that we were also

"Gooners" and they returned to their coach but to make a crazy situation even stranger, for some odd reason, the manager then barred us from his pub but not the blokes from the coach. Money talks, methinks?

Apparently, while all this was going on, somebody had rung my mate, Vic Wright, at the Arsenal Supporters Club to inform him that Hoyboy, John Landers and myself were about to have a row with a coachload of blokes and might need a bit of help. Vic's response? "They'll be alright".

Keep the Faith, Vic.

I managed to get two tickets in the North Bank Upper Tier for the last game of the season against Leicester at Highbury, so a 10-year-old Guy and myself saw the Champions Arsenal win 2-1 to become the unbeaten "Invincibles.", before parading the two trophies.

Man Utd won the FA Cup after beating Millwall 3-0.

Middlesbrough won the League Cup after beating Bolton Wanderers 2-1.

Porto won the Champions League after beating Monaco 3-0.

Sadly, my all-time favourite "Gunner", Joe Baker, died in October 2003, 11 years after I met him.

SEASON 2004-05

During the summer of 2004, I took my grandkids, Guy and Hollie, to their one and only tour of Highbury Stadium. They loved posing for photos in the dressing room, Director's seats etc., also seeing inside the Marble Halls for the first time were Manuel Almunia, Matthieu Flamini, Emmanuel Eboué, Seb Larsson, Arturo Lupoli and Robin Van Persie.

Justin Hoyte and Jonathan Djourou were promoted from the Youth team and Martin Keown, Ray "Romford Pele" Parlour and Sylvain Wiltord were all transferred.

PREMIER LEAGUE

Cesc Fabregas became Arsenal's youngest ever Premier League player on the opening day of the season, when Arsenal beat Everton 4-1 at Goodison Park. In my opinion, Cesc is the best player Arsenal have had since Dennis Bergkamp, Patrick Vieira and Thierry Henry retired.

Guy and I went to the next home game, where, after seeing Middlesbrough leading 3-1 with only about thirty minutes remaining, Arsenal came back to win 5-3. Arsenal then extended their unbeaten run to a record 49 games before travelling to Old Trafford, where a dubious penalty decision allowed Ruud Van Nistelrooy to help win the game 2-0 for Man Utd and prevent Arsenal from reaching the magic number of 50 games unbeaten. After the game, tempers boiled over in the dressing rooms with a slice of pizza being thrown at the United manager, Sir Alex Ferguson.

In November, Arsenal won at the Lane 5-4, the highest ever score between the two clubs, and then in December, Arsenal drew 2-2 with Chelsea at Highbury, which left Chelsea five points clear at the top of the table. In February, Arsenal lost 4-2 against Man Utd at Highbury and dropped to 3rd position, where, in the tunnel before the game, Patrick Vieira and Roy Keane had almost come to blows after heated words were exchanged between them.

Also in February, Arsenal fielded a team without an English player for the first time in their history in the 5-1 victory against Crystal Palace at Highbury.

In May, Arsenal beat Everton 7-0 in the last home game of the season at Highbury to finish as runners-up to the "Russian Billionaire"-backed Chelsea, who won their first title for 50 years, confirming what I had said previously; "The times they are a-changing".

CHAMPIONS LEAGUE

Arsenal finished top in the Group Stage after beating PSV 1-0 at Highbury before drawing both away games 1-1 versus Rosenborg in Norway and 2-2 against Panathinaikos in Greece and then in the return fixtures, 1-1 draws with Panathinaikos and PSV before a 5-1 win against Rosenborg.

In the first knock-out phase, Arsenal lost the 1st Leg 3-1 to Bayern Munich in Germany, where, due to the heavy snow, the Bayern and Arsenal fans, including Gary Davies and Hoyboy, indulged in a good-humoured drunken snowball fight inside the stadium.

Despite winning the 2nd Leg 1-0 at Highbury, Arsenal were eliminated.

LEAGUE CUP

A young Arsenal team won 2-1 away at Man City in the 3rd Round before the same youngsters beat Everton 3-1 in the 4th Round at Highbury and, in the 5th Round, Arsenal lost 1-0 at Old Trafford.

Arsenal finished 2nd in the Premier League behind Champions Chelsea.

Arsenal won the FA Cup, beating Man Utd 5-4 on penalties after a 0-0 draw.

Chelsea won the League Cup after beating Liverpool 3-2.

Liverpool won the Champions League, beating Milan 3-2 on penalties after a 3-3 draw.

The 5-3 win against Middlesbrough in August 2004 was my last ever Arsenal Home League game.

FA CUP 2004-05

In the 3rd Round, Arsenal beat Stoke City 3-1, and in the 4th Round, Wolves 2-0, before drawing 1-1 against Sheffield United in the 5th Round, with all these games being played at Highbury.

Arsenal then won the replay at Bramall Lane on penalties after a goalless draw and, in the 6th Round, Arsenal won 1-0 at Bolton Wanderers to reach the semi-final in Cardiff against Blackburn Rovers, which Arsenal won 3-0.

I managed to get tickets for the final for Guy and myself, and after meeting some of my mates in what was almost becoming our regular pub, "Henry's" bar, including John, Michael and Billy Sanger and Putney and his son Jordan, we took our seats in the stadium where we found ourselves sitting in front of JC's son, Johnny and his son, Stanley.

Although Man Utd had dominated most of the game, thanks to an inspired performance from Christiano Ronaldo, they had to settle for a penalty shoot-out. When Paul Scholes walked up to take his penalty, Guy said to me, "He always misses penalties". I replied, "I bet he scores this one".

Amazingly, the ever-reliable Paul Scholes promptly hit it straight at Jens Lehmann. Guy, who was now standing on his seat, just said, "I told you". Bloody kids get all their information from PlayStations nowadays. Captain, Patrick Vieira, scored with his last-ever kick for Arsenal to win the FA Cup and then Wayne Rooney was announced as "Man of the Match" on the tannoy, which left all the Arsenal fans laughing even more, because Ronaldo had terrorised the Arsenal defence throughout the game.

So, Guy had seen Arsenal lift the FA Cup a year after seeing them get the Premier League trophy and he didn't have to wait 18 years, unlike my generation.

SEASON 2005-06

ALL ROADS LEAD TO PARIS

Apart from watching Arsenal playing in different stadiums in Britain and Europe, I've also managed to get a photo of the ground of the local team when I've been on European City visits with my wife. Due to these trips, I've seen the stadiums of Sparta Prague, Real Sociedad, Napoli, Atletico Madrid, Fiorentina, Real Betis, Sevilla, Valencia, Bordeaux, Maritimo and Hertha Berlin.

BEAUTIFUL BARCELONA

As I had already taken Guy to visit my mates, Charlie, Alan and Tommo in Spain, where we took a tour of the Nou Camp stadium before seeing Barcelona, with Ronaldinho in the team, play Atletico Bilbao, it was only natural that when Arsenal qualified for the European Champions League, I would take him to a match at another famous stadium if possible.

MARVELLOUS MADRID

Arsenal finished top in the Group Stage after beating Thun 2-1 at Highbury and Ajax 2-1 in Holland and Sparta Prague 2-0 in Czechoslovakia before beating Sparta Prague 3-0 at Highbury and Thun 1-0 in Switzerland then drawing 0-0 with Ajax at Highbury in the return fixtures to progress.

In February 2006, in the 1st Round of the knockout phase, Arsenal were drawn against the "Galacticos" of Real Madrid. Well, you don't get much more famous

WITH GUY – REAL MADRID 2006

284

than them, so Guy and I went to Spain for the 1st Leg with Dodger and Tony Adelizzi.

We arrived the day before the game and, after a tour of the stadium and museum, we bumped into Spandau, who'd just bought a match ticket in the Arsenal section from a Spanish bloke outside the ground. As Dodger and Tony were looking for tickets, they also bought one each from the same fella, although they became a bit concerned as they were printed on very flimsy paper and could possibly be counterfeit. But desperate times, etc.

Never judge a book by its cover, though, as the tickets turned out to be legit, or maybe the turnstile man had dodgy eyesight, and the three of them got into the stadium for the match the next night.

We then went off for a quick look at the stadium of Atletico Madrid and some of the other sights of the city, before meeting up with our mates, Lenny Togwell and Knottsy, for a few drinks, where Guy was enthralled listening to some of the stories about the old days on the North Bank. So much so, that on the day after the game when we were sitting on the plane waiting to take off, he loudly said to me, "Grandad, you were a bit of a nutter when you were young, weren't you?" Most of the people sitting in the seats near us on the plane immediately turned to see who this nutter was.

As the song says, "Nowhere to run, nowhere to hide"!

MATCH DAY

On the day of the match, we met up with my mates, Mick Callis and Paul Walsh in Plaza Mayor for a few beers before heading to the stadium. They had come on a one-day trip with the Arsenal Travel Club. As it was a bitterly cold evening, Guy and myself had about four layers of clothing on but after a while sitting in the stadium, we were strangely feeling very warm, and then Guy noticed that there were giant heaters hanging down from the stadium roof above our heads; maybe English clubs should take note?

ARSENAL & REAL MADRID TEAMS
LINED UP – MADRID 2006

Spandau and his banner were just to our right, and the stage was set for history to be made, and history *was* made, as Arsenal turned in a very professional performance with Thierry Henry scoring a marvellous solo goal to beat Zinedine Zidane, Sergio Ramos, David Beckham, Roberto Carlos, Raul, Ronaldo and Robinho etc., 1-0, and become the first-ever English team to beat Real Madrid in the Bernabeu stadium in this competition. The travelling "Gooners" celebrated in style as the songs of "1-0 to the Arsenal" and "Jose Antonio, Jose Antonio" reverberated around the fast-emptying stadium.

As we were leaving the stadium by walking down a circular passageway, every few yards there were riot police standing by watching the Arsenal fans and next to them, dressed all in black, wearing balaclavas and menacingly wielding large batons, were what looked like vigilantes itching for a fight. Nervously, Guy tugged my arm and whispered to me, "The Spanish police look very fierce, Grandad" and as I didn't want to frighten him, I replied, "That's because they're scared of us", whereupon his back immediately straightened up and he marched out of the stadium with his head held high. Ooh to be a Gooner!

After the game, we found a bar for us to celebrate in and the barmen happened to be Atletico Madrid fans and so they kept giving us tapas as a reward for beating their arch-rivals. When that bar closed, we found another open one near our hotel and stayed there until the early hours and then, when I told Guy that we were leaving, he replied, "What bar are we going to now?" He was 11 years old and seemed upset when I told him, "No more bars, it's way past your bedtime".

This was one of the best days ever in both of our times following Arsenal, as we never thought we'd ever see them win in the Bernabeu.

I managed to get a ticket in the North Bank Lower for the 2nd Leg 0-0 draw which eliminated "Los Galacticos". I also got a ticket for the Ist Leg of the Quarter-final at a very noisy Highbury, where Cesc Fabregas inspired Arsenal to a 2-0 win against ex-Arsenal legend Patrick Vieira's Juventus, before drawing the 2nd Leg 0-0 in Turin, to progress to the semi-final of the competition for the first time.

VILLAREAL

On April 19th 2006, I had managed to get a ticket in the East Stand Upper for the semi-final 1st Leg at Highbury against Villareal, where Kolo Toure scored the goal in Arsenal's 1-0 victory.

This would be my last match in the great old stadium that I have so many happy memories of, as, much to the surprise of most of my family and friends, I never attended the "Final Salute" game against Wigan a few days later, because I deliberately wanted a European Cup/ Champions League semi-final to be my "Arsenal Stadium" finale as, in my opinion, there couldn't be a better end to my lifetime at Highbury than seeing "The Arsenal" chasing my "Ultimate Dream".

In the 2nd Leg in Spain, only a few hundred Arsenal fans travelling with the Official Travel Club had tickets for the game, because Glasgow Rangers fans had caused mayhem in a previous match, although Hoyboy and his son managed to get two tickets from a friend of Denton in the Corporate section. Jens Lehmann saved a late Villareal penalty, as Arsenal drew 0-0 and would now be playing against Barcelona in the final in Paris and my "Ultimate Dream" was getting closer.

PARIS – MAY 17TH 2006

EUROPEAN CHAMPIONS LEAGUE FINAL

Most estimates reckon that between 80,000-100,000 Gooners descended on Paris for this match; a few more than went to Anderlecht with me and my mates in 1970 then?

I knew many fans who made the journey on the day without match tickets, and as it was such a scramble to get a ticket, a few of my mates had even gone over there a couple of days earlier to see if the touts had any available.

Although, I dare say that if dear old JC had still been around, I'd have been sitting with him in the Barcelona fans end.

I struck lucky eventually, though, as my workmate, Popple, who's a Chelsea fan, had a contact who worked in the media, and he offered me a deal whereby if Chelsea got to the final then he would have the two tickets but if Arsenal got there instead, they were mine. What a touch!

So, the day before the match, Putney drove Jordan, Guy and myself to Dover, where we met John Sanger, "Young Radford" Adrian and his son Paul, Jimmy Brown and his mates before getting on the ferry and then proceeding to Paris.

During the journey from Calais, we stopped at a lay-by to use the toilet and Guy couldn't believe it when, for the first time in his life, he saw the imprint for two feet and a hole in the concrete floor instead of the usual ceramic toilet, and his instinctive reaction brought a shocked, "Cor Blimey" and we all burst out laughing, before continuing our journey to the French capital, where, on arriving, we drove to the stadium for a few photos and then checked in at our hotel.

On the morning of the match, we took in the major sights and then found a nice quiet restaurant near the Arc de Triomphe for some lunch. Well, it was quiet until Craig Simpson turned up with a set of klaxon horns, which he gave to Guy; imagine giving an 11-year-old kid one of those things?

We then made our way to the streets near the Gare du Nord station for the afternoon, where all the bars were packed with Gooners, and met some more of our mates including Dodger, Knottsy, Peter, Mark and Robert Landers, Roger Taylor, Tony Adelizzi, Mick Callis and Paul Walsh.

After a few beers, we all made our way to the stadium, where, on the way from the station to the stadium, to the amusement of all of us, we persuaded Craig to have a photo taken next to the coach of the "Daventry Gooners", his 'mates' from the "White House" pub who'd wanted to kill him in 2004.

WITH GUY ARSENAL VS BARCELONA –
PARIS 2006

Inside the stadium, Guy and myself had probably the best seats that I've ever had at a football match and the only annoying thing was that we were surrounded by corporate people in suits, some even with their wives, who weren't really interested in the football and this upset me as I knew that there were thousands of proper Arsenal fans, including some of my old North Bank mates, who'd been going to games for years and couldn't get in for the biggest game in the club's history, including Hoyboy. Although, unsurprisingly, he did manage to nick a ticket from a tout outside the stadium for his son.

About fifteen minutes after kick-off, a bloke finally arrived to sit in the empty seat next to me, and, as you would expect, I verbally assaulted him for being late, to which he replied, "I had trouble getting in because there was such a big crowd". I almost exploded and said to him, "Do you know what the occasion is? We're not exactly playing West Bromwich Albion, are we? Of course there's a lot of people trying to get in!" I think only the fact that my grandson was with me stopped me from clumping this idiot.

Guy was so surprised at my anger that he asked me if I knew the fella. "No, I don't, and I don't want to", was my reply.

As you will all know, Jens Lehmann got sent off early in the game and Manuel Almunia came on as his replacement, with Robert Pires having to be the fall guy and, despite Sol Campbell giving Arsenal the lead, Barcelona won 2-1, and Guy had seen Arsenal lose a game for the first time when he'd been in the stadium; what a match to lose his unbeaten record! It was the worst I've ever felt after seeing Arsenal lose a game, in all my years of supporting them, especially as I firmly believed that Arsenal were destined to win the trophy that night and fulfil my "Ultimate Dream".

After getting lost on the Metro, we didn't get back to our hotel until 2 am the next day, and when Guy asked me what time would we have got back if Arsenal had won, I simply replied, "Friday."

FAREWELL TO THE FAMOUS HIGHBURY

SEASON 2005-06

Alexander Hleb joined in the summer of 2005 and Patrick Vieira joined Juventus before Abou Diaby, Emmanuel Adebayor and Theo Walcott also joined in the winter transfer window and as part of the "Final Salute to Highbury", Arsenal wore the 1913-style redcurrant-coloured kit.

COMMUNITY SHIELD

Cesc Fabregas scored but Arsenal lost 2-1 to two Didier Drogba goals against Chelsea at Cardiff.

LEAGUE CUP

In the 3rd Round, Arsenal beat Sunderland away 3-0 and then in the 4th Round, Reading 3-0 at Highbury before requiring penalties to defeat Doncaster Rovers away 3-1 after a 2-2 draw in the 5th Round, and then Arsenal lost at Wigan1-0 in the1st Leg of the semi-final before drawing 2-1 in the 2nd Leg at Highbury and therefore being eliminated on the away goals rule.

FA CUP

Arsenal beat Cardiff City 2-0 in the 3rd Round at Highbury and then lost 1-0 away against Bolton Wanderers in the 4th Round.

PREMIER LEAGUE

Didier Drogba also scored the goal at Stamford Bridge when Chelsea beat Arsenal for the first time in ten years and would become a constant thorn in the side of future Arsenal defences until he left the club in 2012. In October 2005, during the 1-0 victory against Man City at Highbury, Robert Pires and Thierry Henry received a lot of criticism for their arrogance, after cocking up a penalty kick between them, when trying to be too clever, resulting in City receiving a free-kick instead.

In January 2006, Thierry Henry scored a hat trick in a 7-0 thrashing of Middlesbrough at Highbury and then in February, Sol Campbell went missing for five days after requesting to be substituted during the 3-2 home defeat against West Ham. On April 15th, Dennis Bergkamp scored his final goal for Arsenal after 11 years, in a 3-1 win versus West Bromwich Albion at Highbury, before Arsenal drew with the Team from the Lane 1-1, which meant the last Champions League place was still in doubt.

After winning the next two games at Sunderland and Man City, Arsenal needed to win their last-ever game at Highbury against Wigan Athletic to pip the Team from the Lane for 4th position.

On a historic day, in front of a crowd of 38,359, of which the vast majority were very emotional Arsenal supporters, including many legendary ex-players, Arsenal came from being 2-1 down to eventually win the last-ever game, after 93 years at the "Famous Highbury Stadium", 4-2, thanks to a Thierry, (who else?) Henry hat trick, and bring down the curtain on a major part of Arsenal's history before they made the short journey to their new, state-of-the-art stadium, although, sadly, the European Cup/Champions League trophy, wouldn't be going with them.

The Team from the Lane later complained that their pre-match lasagne had given them food poisoning before their defeat at West Ham on the same day. All I can say is, considering how many defeats they've had over the years, they must have eaten tons of the stuff by now?!

Arsenal finished 4th in the Premier League behind Champions Chelsea.

Liverpool won the FA Cup, beating West Ham 3-1 on penalties after a 3-3 draw.

Man Utd won the League Cup after beating Wigan Athletic 4-0.

Barcelona won the Champions League after beating Arsenal 2-1.

2006 – ENTERING THE EMIRATES

On July 22nd 2006, the Emirates stadium was officially opened with a Testimonial match against Ajax for one of the greatest ever Arsenal players, Dennis "the non-flying Dutchman" Bergkamp.

The first game that Guy and myself, along with my mate, Billy Abery and his son, attended at the new 60,000 capacity stadium was Arsenal's 2nd Leg 2-1 victory in the Champions League 3rd Qualifying Round against Dinamo Zagreb on August 23rd 2006. Therefore, my last match at Highbury was in the Champions League and my first match at the

Emirates was also in the Champions League. Our first impression of Arsenal's new home was that it was like being at a European away game, architecturally magnificent and spacious, but with one difference – it was Arsenal's and although it was fantastic for the future generations of "Gooners", in my opinion, Highbury will always be in the hearts of my generation of Arsenal supporters.

SOME EMIRATES FACTS

- The first League goal scored – 19/8/06 – Olaf Mellberg for Aston Villa.
- The first Arsenal League goal scored – 19/8/06 – Gilberto Silva against Aston Villa.
- The first Arsenal League penalty scored – 9/9/06 – Thierry Henry against Middlesbrough.
- The first Arsenal hat trick scored – 22/9/07 – Emmanuel Adebayor against Derby County.
- The first own goal scored – 23/9/06 – Phil Jagielka of Sheffield United.
- The first Arsenal League own goal scored – 3/3/07 – Cesc Fabregas against Reading.
- Arsenal's first League victory – 23/9/06 – 3-0 against Sheffield United.
- Arsenal's first League draw – 19/8/06 – 1-1 against Aston Villa.
- Arsenal's first League defeat – 7/4/07 – 1-0 against West Ham.
- First player sent off – 2/1/07 – Osei Sankofa of Charlton Athletic.
- First Arsenal player sent off – 2/9/07 – Phillipe Senderos against Portsmouth.

GUY'S NEW TEACHER

When Guy returned to school in September 2006, a new teacher had arrived and, in an attempt to bond with the boys in the class, the teacher asked them if they liked football. When they nearly all replied, "Yes," he then asked which teams they supported and got the usual answers; Arsenal, Chelsea, Man Utd and Liverpool. The teacher then said that he was an Arsenal fan and asked which boys supported Arsenal. Obviously, Guy put his hand up and the teacher asked him, if he'd ever been to the Emirates or any other stadiums. When Guy stated that not only had he been to the Emirates but also Highbury, Wembley, Old Trafford, Millennium Cardiff, Stade de France, Nou Camp, and the Bernabeu, the teacher asked if he was the classroom liar, whereupon all the other boys shouted, "No, his grandad took him". I think I can be proud of that as my epitaph.

So far, up until the end of season 2019/20, I have never been to a Premier League match and only one FA Cup and one League Cup match at the Emirates, although I did take my grandchildren to the Emirates Cup games in the summers of 2007, 2008 and 2009.

Chris and I even went with Mick Callis and his wife, Mel, to see Bruce Springsteen and The E Street Band there in August 2008.

Apart from those matches, I have limited myself to European Champions League matches against the more famous clubs, plus the Europa League semi-final versus Atletico Madrid in 2018.

SEASON 2006-07

Also entering the Emirates for the first time were Alex Song, Tomas Rosicky, Julio Baptista, William Gallas and Denilson, while those that left the club before playing there for Arsenal were Sol Campbell, Robert Pires, Seb Larsson, Arturo Lupoli, Jose Antonio Reyes, Lauren, Pascal Cygan and, in highly controversial circumstances, Ashley Cole.

Although Arsenal only lost one Premier League game at their new home, against West Ham, and did the double against the future

Champions Man Utd, too many drawn games cost them valuable points and in the FA Cup, after beating Liverpool 3-1 at Anfield in the 3rd Round and also Bolton 3-1 in a replay at the Reebok Stadium after a 1-1 draw, in the 4th Round, Arsenal were eliminated 1-0 in the 5th Round at Blackburn Rovers, after a 0-0 draw at the Emirates.

In the League Cup, an Arsenal team comprising of mostly youngsters, as usual, reached the final after beating West Bromwich Albion at the Hawthorns 2-0 in the 3rd Round, then Everton 1-0 at Goodison Park in the 4th Round, before incredibly, winning 6-3 against Liverpool at Anfield in the 5th Round, and then finally, in the semi-finals, Arsenal came from being 2-0 down to draw 2-2 at the Lane before finishing the job by winning 3-1, with myself in attendance, at a very noisy Emirates.

After Theo Walcott had given the young Arsenal team the lead in the final, two goals from Arsenal's bogeyman, Didier Drogba, won the trophy for a very experienced Chelsea side, while some of Arsenal's star players sat on the bench, to the frustration of many Gooners.

After beating Dinamo Zagreb in the Champions League Qualifying Round, Arsenal beat Hamburg 2-1 in Germany, Porto 2-0 at the Emirates and then lost to CSKA Moscow 1-0 in Russia before progressing to the knockout stage after drawing 0-0 with CSKA Moscow and beating Hamburg 3-1 at the Emirates and finally drawing 0-0 with Porto in Portugal in the return fixtures.

In the 1st Leg of the knock-out stage, Arsenal lost 1-0 against PSV Eindhoven in Holland before being eliminated after only managing to draw 1-1 in the 2nd Leg at the Emirates, a game that I had gone to with Tony Adelizzi.

Arsenal finished 4th in the Premier League behind Champions Man Utd.

Chelsea won the FA Cup after beating Man Utd 1-0.

Chelsea won the League Cup after beating Arsenal 2-1.

Milan won the Champions League after beating Liverpool 2-1.

ARSÈNE'S MISSED DOUBLES?

Without wishing to be too critical of his magnificent achievements in winning two Doubles in 1997-98 and 2001-02, Arsène Wenger almost won another five Doubles in his first ten years.

In season 1998-99, only a late goal from Jimmy Floyd Hasselbaink at Leeds denied Arsenal the Premier League title as they finished 1 point behind Man Utd and a missed penalty by Dennis Bergkamp followed by a wonder goal from Ryan Giggs in the semi-final stopped Arsenal from reaching the FA Cup final against Newcastle, who they'd beaten the year before.

In 2000-01, Arsenal finished 2nd in the Premier League, 10 points behind Man Utd and narrowly lost the FA Cup final to Liverpool.

In 2002-03, Arsenal finished 2nd in the Premier League, 5 points behind Man Utd, after losing at Leeds to a late Mark Viduka goal but won the FA Cup against Southampton.

In 2003-04, Arsenal's Invincibles won the Premier League but lost 1-0 to Man Utd in the FA Cup semi-final, after resting Thierry Henry for the match.

In 2004-05, Arsenal finished 2nd in the Premier League, although, they were a massive 12 points behind Chelsea and won the FA Cup on penalties against Man Utd.

So, in hindsight, with a little bit of luck, Arsène Wenger's Arsenal career could have been even more impressive.

However, in my opinion, I still think he should have won the Champions League at least once, considering the many world-class players he bought over the years.

I previously stated that I don't go to Premier League matches anymore, therefore, I can only relate the details and stories of the other games that I've attended since Arsenal moved to the Emirates.

2007 – 2008 – 2009

I went to the Champions League home games against Sevilla in 2007 and Milan in 2008 and then, along with my mates, Mickey English, Franco and Tony Adelizzi, to the 1st Leg of the knock-out stage game against Roma in February 2009, where, as we reached our seats in the Upper Tier, I noticed that we were sitting directly in front of all the Roma fans and Mickey loudly asked me, "Why are we sitting with the Raddies?" Supposedly, to avoid an international incident, a steward standing nearby promptly offered him a seat in another part of the stadium.

Then Franco, whose parents came from the Calabria region of Italy, started chatting to the Roma fans in fluent Italian. When he told them that he was going to the 2nd Leg in Rome, he asked if he would be safe in the stadium but he was totally shocked when they replied, "No, you have the wrong accent". What chance would I have had then?

NEW WEMBLEY

I managed to get tickets for the FA Cup semi-final against Chelsea in April 2009, where Didier Drogba scored the winner to maintain his stranglehold on Arsenal defenders after Guy and myself had viewed the "New Wembley". Our opinion? It was just a bigger version of the Emirates.

CHAMPIONS LEAGUE

I also got a ticket for another semi-final defeat, this time against Man Utd in the 2nd Leg of the Champions League at the Emirates in May 2009, when, after I witnessed what is probably the best pre-match atmosphere at the Emirates since it opened, Christiano Ronaldo scored 2

EMIRATES – ARSENAL VS MAN UTD
CHAMPIONS LEAGUE 2009

goals including a long-range free-kick, to kill my "Ultimate Dream" yet again, as United won 3-1.

MY 60TH BIRTHDAY

I celebrated my 60th birthday on the last day of season 2008-09 in a pub near Highbury, where, during the course of the day, about fifty old and not so old mates and their kids plus Andy Leach, the Gooner son of my cousin, Johnny, called in to have a drink with me. Hardly anybody left the pub to go to the game and as a nice surprise, Vic, Hazel and Kelly Wright presented me with a signed birthday greeting from Arsène Wenger and also brought Charlie George and Sammy Nelson along, where they would see their old mates, Hoyboy and Putney again. After the obligatory photos and a few beers, Charlie and myself were trying to name all the barely remembered players that we'd both seen at Arsenal when we were kids, such as Gerry Ward, Derek Tapscott, Dave Bacuzzi, Len Wills, Johnny Petts, Len Julians, Mike Tiddy, Ray Swallow, John Snedden, Gordon Ferry, Con Sullivan, Peter Goy and the aptly named Gordon Nutt. To cap a perfect day, Hoyboy even conned Charlie into buying a round of drinks, a magical funny moment! Since this day, most of us have continued to have a reunion drink at least twice a year. My mate, Tommo, in Spain even sent me a signed photo from his pal, Alan Simonsen, the ex-European Footballer of the Year, wishing me a happy birthday.

60TH BIRTHDAY GREETINGS FROM ALAN SIMONSEN [DENMARK] & TOMMO

GLASGOW CELTIC

As a present for my 60th birthday, my old mate, Granty, paid for me to go with him to Glasgow to meet up with our Scottish pals, Tommo, his

MATCH TICKETS – 2000'S

son Dan and Alan Frame, who had come over from Spain for a week to visit their families, where another old mate from our times in Spain, Jimmy McAllister, also turned up for a few? beers.

Luckily, this trip coincided with Arsenal playing Celtic in the Champions League Qualifying Round at Celtic Park and I managed to get tickets for us in the Arsenal section, although Granty refused to go as he's a die-hard Rangers fan. Like I've said before, in my opinion, sport – politics – religion; they don't mix. However, in hindsight, I'm glad that Tony Adelizzi had his ticket instead, because as I sadly didn't realise it at the time, this 2-0 victory for Arsenal would be the last time that I saw Tony before he tragically died of a heart attack in February 2010 aged 50, a few days before I was due to go with him to the Porto Champions League game in Portugal.

We would all sing the "4 Wheels on My Wagon" song at Tony's funeral in Clerkenwell. He was a proper "Gooner" and although most of us had only known him for about 14 years, he is still sadly missed.

OPORTO 2010

Like I said previously, I was supposed to be going with Tony Adelizzi and Vic Wright on the one-day trip to Oporto with the Arsenal Travel Club to meet up with our mates, Mick Callis and Henry Taylor, but obviously only 4 of us met out there, although I did bump into Tringy, who hardly ever misses a game. While the

PORTO VS ARSENAL – 2010

others settled for a few beers in a riverside bar, I spent a very enjoyable afternoon visiting the various Port Lodges on the hills opposite. So much so, that I even fell asleep in the stadium during Arsenal's 2-1 defeat.

After beating Porto 5-0 in the 2nd Leg at the Emirates, I then went to the Quarterfinals 1st Leg 2-2 draw with Barcelona, before travelling to Spain with Putney, Vic Connell, Dodger and Sanger so that we could spend a few days with our old mates, Charlie MacCready, Tommo and Alan Frame before meeting Mick Callis and Vic Wright at the Nou Camp for the 2nd Leg. After the game started, our hopes rose briefly when Nicholas Bendtner scored after 18 minutes to put Arsenal 1-0 ahead, before a certain Argentinian genius named Lionel Messi equalised 3 minutes later and then proceeded to score another 3 goals to shatter my "Ultimate Dream" for another year, with a performance that even had most of the Arsenal fans applauding him off at the end of the game.

BUENOS AIRES

A year later in February 2011, I achieved another of my boyhood dreams when Chris and myself went to Buenos Aires in Argentina for a holiday and saw a match at the famous "La Bonbonera" stadium, home of Boca Juniors, Maradona, Batistuta, Tevez and many others. This was on the day after taking a tour of the stadium where I even managed to get a photo of myself holding the "Copa de Libertadores", the South American equivalent of the European Champions League, on the pitch.

Before the match, we couldn't fail to notice a restaurant where they had a massive charcoal-fired grill, covered with tasty-looking steaks and sausages that they sold in large bread rolls.

I remarked to my wife that, "They should open one of these up in Drayton

WITH COPA DE LIBERTADORES IN "LA BONBONERA' – 2011

Park". Unfortunately, we never got the chance to sample them as we'd already eaten earlier that day.

Inside the stadium, the atmosphere was as incredible as I'd imagined it would be, with the ground full twenty minutes before kick-off, except for a large area on the blue and yellow painted terraces behind one of the goals. Suddenly, we

BOCA JUNIORS FANS – "LA BONBONERA STADIUM" – 2011

could hear hundreds of Boca fans singing and chanting as they marched down the street outside before entering the ground together and filling up the gap.

These fans never stopped singing throughout the game and for about twenty minutes afterwards, and most of the time, they were bouncing up and down as well. Maybe they were on the old "Colombian Marching Powder"; who knows? Either way, it was the best support I've ever seen but disappointingly, the game ended in a 0-0 draw, so I can only imagine what it would have been like if Boca had scored.

The next day, we toured the "Estadio Monumental" stadium and museum, home of River Plate and where Argentina won the World Cup in 1978, before going to another match to see Independiente at home against River Plate. We decided to skip dinner as we fancied one of the steak rolls that we had seen the previous night at the " La Bonbonera", so imagine our disappointment when there wasn't anywhere selling cooked food and we had to make do with a couple of packets of crisps and a can of coke, although at least we saw a goal when River Plate scored in the last minute.

If anyone ever gets the chance to go to a game in South America, I thoroughly recommend it, as it's a wonderful, once in a lifetime experience!

A few days later, we flew to Santiago in Chile and visited the "Estadio Nacional" and "Estadio Monumental", home of the famous Colo Colo club.

Arsenal lost 1-0 to Birmingham City in the League Cup Final whilst we were in Argentina.

ARSENAL PLAYERS REUNION DINNER

In 2011, Spook, Putney, Jordan, John and Billy Sanger, Vic Connell, Adrian and Paul Morizzi, Mickey Pearce, Bobby King and Tringy went to a players' reunion dinner, organised by Charlie George and Sammy Nelson. We all had a good time meeting Pat Rice, Pat Jennings, Don Howe, Peter Marinello, Willie Young, Peter Storey, Jon Sammels, David Price, Alan Skirton, Eddie Kelly and Bobby Gould, amongst others, but the highlight for Spook and myself was talking to Graham Rix and Liam Brady, like old mates, for about 30 minutes outside the stadium afterwards.

You couldn't put a price on moments like that.

GERMANY CALLING

BERLIN - 2013

In August 2013, Chris and I took our granddaughter, Hollie, to Berlin for a few days, where, after the obligatory shopping and sightseeing, we managed to get to visit the Olympic stadium that was built in the 1930s, and which is now the home of Hertha Berlin FC.

BORUSSIA - 2013

In November of the same year, I went by car with Mick Callis, Henry Taylor and Terry Jones to my first Arsenal match in a German stadium, at Borussia Dortmund. Although Mick and Henry go to many games nowadays, the reason Terry, who hadn't been to an Arsenal game in Europe

TERRY [DORTMUNDER] JONES –
BORUSSIA DORTMUND VS ARSENAL
2013

"YELLOW WALL" – BORUSSIA
DORTMUND VS ARSENAL 2013

since Ajax in 1971, and I went, was to see the famous "Yellow Wall" of Dortmund fans.

Henry had made all the travel arrangements and we stayed in a hotel directly opposite the stadium and on the morning of the game, we visited the "Dortmund Museum" and saw the usual memorabilia on display, including "my elusive Champions League trophy" that they won in 1997.

In the evening, after a few beers and a Bratwurst sausage roll, without sauerkraut this time, (remember the bubble in Torino?), we literally just crossed the road to enter the stadium, where the police were doing the mandatory pat-down of Arsenal fans, checking for any weapons, flares etc., but not the local Dortmund fans. Now, for many years, Terry has always argued that my head is bigger than his, but when I stepped up to be searched, the officer checked my pockets, patted me down as normal and then let me pass, but when Terry approached him and put his arms up to be frisked, the copper just said, "Dortmunder?" and let him through the police cordon. As you can imagine, I was now in hysterics and told Terry, "The copper thought you was a German, because of the size of your head". What a result! Terry can't argue about our head sizes anymore, as I just call him "Dortmunder". Inside the stadium, we bumped into my old mate, Tony "Spandau" Moss, the man with the famous banner, and unbeknown to me at the time, this was the last Arsenal game that I would ever see him at, although I did visit and often call him, before he died in January 2017, after suffering, with great bravery and humour, from a lengthy illness.

After a couple of beers in the hotel bar afterwards, Terry and I decide to go to our room, and on the way, we shared the lift with two very tall, unhappy-looking Dortmund fans. After a few moments of uncomfortable silence, Terry started singing, "Always look on the bright side of life", at which the two Germans then burst out laughing and shook our hands. At the return game, Guy brought his mate, Tom, from Devon, to his see his first match and when he seemed surprised that I had never met a trawler-man before, I replied, "You don't get too many trawlers around Highbury".

BAYERN – 2017

As I was only rarely going to any foot-ball matches by now, when Mick Callis offered me a seat on a minibus with his mates, John Hernden, Paul Jacobs, Dave Blackborow, Keith Henshaw, Gary Williams and his teenage son George, to go and watch Arsenal play in the 1st Leg of the Champions League at Bayern Munich in February, I gladly accepted.

MICKEY CALLIS & MATES -BAYERN MUNICH 2017

After driving across France, we eventually arrived in Munich at midday on the day of the match, where, after checking in to our hotel, we made our way to the historic "Hofbauhaus Bierkeller" for some food and a few large glasses of very nice draught beer, before later, along with a few thousand other Gooners, we merrily made our way to the impressive stadium, only to see Arsenal get slaughtered 5-1. Funny that, because I don't recall see-ing the Arsenal team in the Bierkeller with us before the game, although most of them played as though they had been. As a measure of how poor Arsenal played that night, the stadium announcer mockingly asked over the tannoy, "Can we play you every week?" and after the game, we

BAYERN MUNICH VS ARSENAL –
ALLIANZ ARENA 2017

returned to our hotel for a few nightcaps, and then the next morning, I managed to do a bit of sightseeing, while the others had a lie-in, prior to us all visiting the Bayern Museum at the stadium, before making our long way home. In the early hours of the next day, we arrived at an almost deserted Calais Customs Control point, where the solitary officer on duty asked Johnny, "Where have you been?" Johnny replied, "Munich," and when the officer asked him, "And what did you do there?" with one voice, eight tired and hungry blokes shouted, "Got fucking beat!" A truly funny, marvellous, magical moment. Bayern Munich also won the 2nd Leg 5-1 at the Emirates, and the writing was now on the wall for Arsène Wenger.

WEMBLEY WONDERS

ALAN CONNELL

Alan, who had a decent career as a professional footballer, is the son of Vic Connell, another old Original North Bank mate of mine, and I can remember back in the 1990s, I used to work with Terry Akanbar, who was the Assistant Youth Development Officer for the Team from the Lane. One day at work, when I mentioned to Terry that my mate's son was "training two nights a week at the Lane", he asked me, "What's the kid's name?" When I replied, "Alan Connell",

ALAN & VIC CONNELL
– 1997

Terry said, "That's the little bastard that turns up in his Arsenal kit!" As I was laughing so much, I could barely reply, "Yep, sounds about right". Incidentally, as a result of Alan wearing his Arsenal kit, the Team from the Lane supplied all the kids with club-branded training gear in the future.

One of the highlights of Alan's playing career was when he scored the goal that won promotion for Bournemouth from the 2nd Division in 2010 and another was when Putney, Jordan, Sanger and myself saw him play for Swindon against Chesterfield in the Johnstone's Cup Final at Wembley in March 2012. He also scored for Bradford City in their famous 3-2 penalty shoot-out victory against his beloved Arsenal, in the League Cup in December 2012, a goal which he refused to celebrate at the time, before he also won promotion from the 2nd Division with Bradford in the Wembley Play-Off Final in 2013.

Upon retiring, Alan became a member of the coaching staff at Bournemouth with Eddie Howe.

Arsenal were routinely playing at Wembley between 2014 and 2018 and I managed to obtain tickets for the following games;

2014 – FA CUP SEMI-FINAL VS WIGAN

Guy and myself met Hoyboy and his son before the game and we saw Arsenal eventually win 4-2 on penalties, after a 1-1 draw where a last-minute equaliser from Per Mertesacker saved the day but during this game, the first major rumblings of discontent with Arsène Wenger were now emerging.

2014 – FA CUP FINAL VS HULL CITY

After meeting Mick Callis and Brian Thompson before this match, I sat with Hoyboy and watched Arsenal go 2-0 down, before Kieran Gibbs headed a certain third goal for Hull off the line, which I didn't think Arsenal would have recovered from before Arsenal came back to win 3-2 but despite winning the FA Cup, the rumblings about Arsène Wenger were getting even louder.

JIM MAXWELL SHAKES HANDS WITH ARSENE WENGER FA CUP FINAL – 2014

2017 – FA CUP FINAL VS CHELSEA

Along with Guy, I met up with my old mates, Putney, Hoyboy and his son in a pub at Highbury Corner before the game for a few beers. After leaving the pub, we were travelling by tube to Wembley when we encountered some similarly aged Chelsea fans in our packed carriage. Typical of the new generation of Chelsea fans, they were singing about how "Arsenal had never won the Champions League", which is a sore point to most Gooners of our age, although strangely, they soon shut up when Young Hoyboy started singing "we've never won the Full Members Cup",

ARSENAL CELEBRATE WITH FANS –
FA CUP FINAL 2017

unlike the old Chelsea, who were only too happy to win that meaningless trophy back in 1986. However, I think the irony was lost on them, as they probably never knew that part of Chelsea's history, long before the Russians took over. Things got a bit heated but nothing happened as there were so many police on duty that day, but when we got off the tube, my Grandson, laughingly, said to me, "You lot were going to have it with them, weren't you? But you're all old-age pensioners now". I just replied, "Old habits die hard". Inside the ground, I sat with Tringy, Vic and Kelly Wright and we all enjoyed seeing Arsenal's well-deserved, but surprising win.

2018 – LEAGUE CUP SEMI-FINAL VS MAN CITY

On February 25th 2018, I went to Wembley with Guy for probably my last time and saw Arsenal lose 3-0 to Man City, in a very one-sided match that further enraged many Arsenal fans and the grumblings about Arsène Wenger had now reached such a crescendo that it was no surprise when he announced that he would be leaving the club at the end of the season. However, he did leave Arsenal with a wonderful farewell present when he signed Pierre-Emerick Aubameyang.

MY LAST MATCH AT THE EMIRATES?

On April 26th 2018, Guy and I went to the Europa League semi-final 1st Leg game against Atletico Madrid, which ended in a 1-1 draw and Arsenal were then eliminated when they lost the 2nd Leg 1-0 in Spain. I have not been back since.

TRIBUTE TO ARSÈNE WENGER

Like many Arsenal fans, I believed that Arsène should have left Arsenal a few years prior to 2018, but I can only thank him for all the trophies that were won with the wonderful football that his teams played, including some of the greatest, truly world-class players who have ever worn the famous red and white shirts in the history of "The Arsenal". In future years, when people ask what Arsène Wenger did achieve, I can only think of the words of Sir Christopher Wren, the architect of St Paul's Cathedral, who once quoted, "If you seek my epitaph, then look around you", as, in my opinion, without Arsène Wenger, Arsenal would not be the massive club it is today, playing in a marvellous stadium and with a multitude of fans all over the world. Merci beaucoup, Monsieur.

MY 70TH BIRTHDAY

In July 2019, I celebrated my 70th birthday with my cousin Albie and his Arsenal-loving children, Lesley, Ian and Barry and their families at Albie's home in France, where we reminisced about our days at Highbury in the '50s and '60s, with a few bottles of wine, of course.

WITH MY COUSIN ALBIE WARD
& HIS SON BARRY – JULY 2019

BOB STANLEY – DIED 2014

BARRY BAKER – KENNY HALL –
PETER MAYNARD – 2017

KENNY BANHAM [DIED 2019] &
MANNY BUTTIGIEG [DIED 2020]

SOME ORIGINAL NORTH BANK
[OLD] BOYS – 2018

FINAL WORDS

I hope you've enjoyed reading the stories of my fantastic lifetime following "The Arsenal" and I would like to thank all of my family and friends for their support and encouragement in its creation, especially my old mates, who have travelled most of the way with me on this journey, since we all met up as teenagers on the Arsenal Supporters Club coaches and the North Bank back in the '60s plus Hazel, Kelly and Vic Wright. Sadly, two more of my mates, Lenny Togwell and Manny Buttigieg, both died in June 2020 before I finished writing this book, but their memory, like that of the others who have passed, will live on.

Back in 1971, Lenny Togwell gave us this song;
[To the tune of The British Grenadier].

> *Some talk of Ronnie Greenwood and some of Don Revie,*
> *Of Catterick and Shankly and Tommy Docherty,*
> *Of Bowen and Ramsey, you will all agree,*
> *There's none so fair as can compare,*
> *With good old Bertie Mee.*

My only regrets are that I never saw Pelé and Maradona play live and that Arsenal have not won the European Cup/Champions League yet.

This book will, hopefully, have either brought back many wonderful, funny memories or been a history lesson for "Old Gunners and Gooners" of all ages.

I would like to dedicate this book to my dear brother, George, who died in June 2014 aged 80, because without him taking me to Highbury back in 1957, none of this would have happened.

My cousin Albie Ward and I bought George a "Memorial Brick" at the Emirates stadium.
    It was the least I could do!

"KEEP THE FAITH."

Eddie Symes – September 2020.

Oldgunnersandgooners@gmail.com

GEORGE & MYSELF – PARIS 1995

Lightning Source UK Ltd.
Milton Keynes UK
UKHW020703111121
393745UK00007B/249